With best wishes
Julia C MacDonald

The Faithful, the Fallen and the Forgotten

Sons of the Rhins in the Great War 1914-1918

Julia C MacDonald

ISBN: 978-0-9569331-0-2

Published by: Clayhole Publishing

15 Lochryan Street

Stranraer, DG9 7HP

Printed by Stranraer and Wigtown Free Press, Stranraer.

CONTENTS

Nameless his grave on a battlefield gory,
Only a cross o'er a mound of brown earth;
Died in the pride of his youth and his glory;
Far from his friends and the land of his birth.

Anon.

Introduction

As small children my sister and I spent many happy holidays at my Aunt and Uncle's house. Their home stood just before the fork in the road at Sandhead which goes through the village or up to the school. Their front window had a square on view of Stoneykirk War Memorial which sits just outside Sandhead at Motte Hill. My sister and I would climb the steps and sit beside the memorial watching the world go by, and watching for our father who would occasionally take us round his run in the back of the post-van amongst the mail. Though we read the names on the memorial and counted them we had no idea of who the men were.

As an adult I have an interest in local and family history. After a number of years away from Stranraer, one of the first things I did on my return was to visit Stoneykirk War Memorial and tell my own children tales from my childhood. When they were reading the names on the memorial I realised one of the names on the memorial was J. McClelland, spelt exactly the same way as my mother's maiden name. In my quest to determine if this man was a relative I realised that while a few of us attend the annual remembrance ceremonies, an ever declining number of us actually remember the men who gave their lives whilst serving our country in the First World War.

This book attempts to describe a little about each of the men whose names are on memorials in the villages of the Rhins and Stranraer. Moreover, whilst researching each memorial I have found men from almost all areas who are not on their local memorial. Whatever the reason for their omission, some were no doubt an error; I feel these men still had local connections and deserve to be remembered here. I have named them at the end of each of the sections.

Inevitably with the passing of time many details have been lost and all that remains is the name of a man whose life we may never know about. Some of the details may be incorrect – I may have listed a different man with a local connection, and I apologise wholeheartedly for any mistakes I may have made. I have relied very heavily on the details of a man's life from the local newspaper archives of the 'Galloway Advertiser and Wigtown Free Press' and those details may not have been accurate at the time of printing. My hope is that I have got the majority of the details correct and that all these years later we should not forget the thousands of man who fought and died in the most horrendous circumstances of the First World War.

With the passing in 2009 of the last men who saw active service in the war, I believe we have forgotten many of the men who served their country. It is far easier to trace those who served and were killed than the thousands more who were injured, and more still who saw their friends die.

Where only initials and surnames were recorded on the memorials, in a number of cases there were a few possibilities. Where possible I have recorded these possibilities if there is a clear local connection.

Almost every local cemetery contains family headstones which have transcriptions referring to a family member killed in the First World War. Where possible I have visited these cemeteries and surprisingly found further names not on local war memorials. I have researched these men and depending on the village cemetery where they are named, I have added them in at the end of those chapters.

The memorials included in this book are not the only memorials in the area. Many churches contain memorials which name those who served as well as those who gave their lives. To name a few, Ardwell Church, New Luce Church, St. Joseph's Chapel and the Town Kirk in Stranraer all have these types of memorials. Other villages have a memorial hall with a plaque inside displaying the names of those who served. I have chosen to try to only cover the memorials which are outdoors and accessible to everyone. One day I hope someone will take the time to cover other these other memorials.

While some of the photographs are from family of those who gave their lives, the majority of photographs of soldiers are from the Galloway Advertiser and Wigtownshire Free Press. During war newspapers were heavily recycled and of poor quality and this shows in the photographs that have been included.

To honour the memory of the men whose lives and deaths I had researched, I made the moving trip to France and Belgium to see the landscape that was once the Western Front. On the Menin Gate, Thiepval, Tyne Cot, and Beaumont Hamel amongst others, I was able to pick out the names of those men I had come to know a little about and who have no known grave. Where the names were within reach, I traced my fingers over the engraving with the words 'Their name liveth for evermore,' going round in my head. Their loved ones may never have got to see these names engraved on these grand and solemn memorials amongst the thousands of other lost men. The memorials and thousands of graves at the front and home, serve to remind us of the consequences of war. The names of the men who gave their lives only record part of the story. There was no room to add details on any of these memorials such as 'beloved son', 'ploughman', 'loving father', let alone details of where the man had once lived. This book attempts to remember a little more about the men behind those names.

I have no doubt that when this book is published more people will come forward with photographs, information and corrections and I will happily collate this information for changes should a further print run be necessary.

Finally I was never able to determine if the J. McClelland on Stoneykirk Memorial, whose name sparked my curiosity, was a relative.

CAIRNRYAN WAR MEMORIAL

Cairnryan War Memorial was unveiled by the oldest member of its congregation, Mrs Turriff, on Sunday 21st September 1919. The service, to a large congregation of parishioners, had been conducted by the Rev. A. Murray Macgregor. The tablet, made of best white Creetown granite, and featuring a bronze laurel wreath, was sculpted by Messrs Dodds and Sons, Dumfries and fixed into position in a window recess outside the front of the church the by James Dorman of the Oyster Tanks, Cairnryan.

Cairnryan Church, the War Memorial standing in the archway of the porch.

The War Memorial tablet was removed before the church was demolished around the 1980s and it now stands in the cemetery opposite Lochryan House. It is set against an arched stone dyke with a small granite cross above the tablet, it reads:

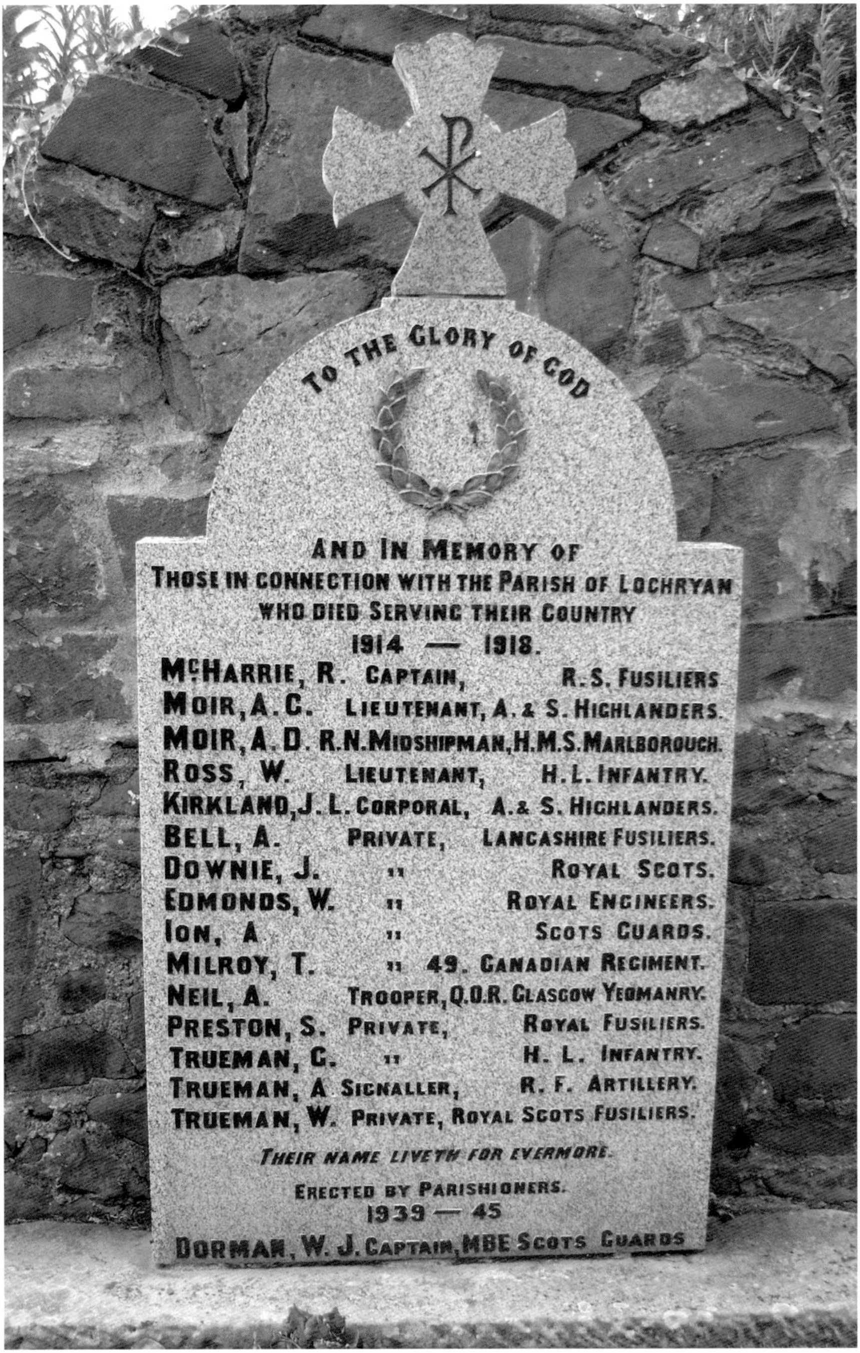
TO THE GLORY OF GOD
AND IN MEMORY OF
THOSE IN CONNECTION WITH THE PARISH OF LOCHRYAN
WHO DIED SERVING THEIR COUNTRY
1914 — 1918.
McHARRIE, R. CAPTAIN, R.S. FUSILIERS
MOIR, A.C. LIEUTENANT, A. & S. HIGHLANDERS.
MOIR, A.D. R.N. MIDSHIPMAN, H.M.S. MARLBOROUGH.
ROSS, W. LIEUTENANT, H.L. INFANTRY.
KIRKLAND, J.L. CORPORAL, A.& S. HIGHLANDERS.
BELL, A. PRIVATE, LANCASHIRE FUSILIERS.
DOWNIE, J. " ROYAL SCOTS.
EDMONDS, W. " ROYAL ENGINEERS.
ION, A. " SCOTS GUARDS.
MILROY, T. " 49. CANADIAN REGIMENT.
NEIL, A. TROOPER, Q.O.R. GLASGOW YEOMANRY.
PRESTON, S. PRIVATE, ROYAL FUSILIERS.
TRUEMAN, G. " H. L. INFANTRY.
TRUEMAN, A. SIGNALLER, R. F. ARTILLERY.
TRUEMAN, W. PRIVATE, ROYAL SCOTS FUSILIERS.
THEIR NAME LIVETH FOR EVERMORE.
ERECTED BY PARISHIONERS.
1939 — 45
DORMAN, W. J. CAPTAIN, MBE SCOTS GUARDS

TO THE GLORY OF GOD AND IN MEMORY OF THOSE IN CONNECTION WITH THE PARISH OF LOCHRYAN WHO DIED SERVING THEIR COUNTRY 1914-1918.

McHarrie, R. Captain, ...	R.S.Fusiliers
Moir, A.G. Lieutenant, ...	A. & S. Highlanders
Moir, A.D. R.N. Midshipman, ...	H.M.S. Marlborough
Ross,W. Lieutenant, ...	H.L .Infantry
Kirkland, J. L.Corporal, ...	A. & S. Highlanders
Bell, A. Private, ...	Lancashire Fusiliers
Downie, J. "	Royal Scots
Edmonds, W. "	Royal Engineers
Ion, A. "	Scots Guards
Milroy, T. "	49 Canadian Regiment
Neil, A. Trooper, ...	Q.O.R. Glasgow Yeomanry
Preston, S. Private, ...	Royal Fusiliers
Trueman, G. "	H.L Infantry
Trueman, A. Signaller, ...	R.F. Artillery
Trueman, W. Private, ...	Royal Scots Fusiliers

THEIR NAME LIVETH FOR EVERMORE

The memorial lists the men in rank order, then alphabetically. There are fifteen names from the 1914-1918 conflict on the memorial.

There were in fact two Great War memorials at Cairnryan Church. The second memorial listed sixty names of all those who served from Cairnryan including those who died. A small cross was added beside the names of those who were killed. This memorial is also rare in that it has on it the names of three local women from who saw service.

A number of years ago, when the old library and council yard were being cleared, one of the workmen approached the then curator of the museum. "There's a war memorial in the county yard. Do you want it? Otherwise it's going in the skip". Needless to say the memorial was saved but so far has been in storage.

This second memorial has on it the names of two men, marked with a cross, who died in the war and whose names are not featured on the memorial which now stands in the cemetery. Had it not been for the council workman, the museum curator and John Cameron, these two men who gave their lives for this country, would have been forgotten along with the names of those who served, were injured, and fought, and saw many of their friends fall.

The memorial which remains in storage and gives the names of those who served and were from Cairnryan.

Capt. Robert McHarrie, 1st/5th Battalion Royal Scots Fusiliers. Killed in action 9th June 1918.

Robert McHarrie was the youngest son of James McHarrie, Ann House, Stranraer. His father was, amongst other trades an ironmonger. Aged 17, Robert joined the Territorials of the Royal Scots Fusiliers and received his commission as second Lieutenant in 1912. When war broke out he immediately volunteered for active service abroad. His company received a send off from the local people, the Town Council, Magistrates and Provost Fox at the Drill Hall, across the road from his home.

The Company was stationed at Cambusbarron and Robert developed pneumonia there and was invalided to hospital. This prevented him from Foreign Service for quite a while, although on recovery, he certainly seems to have made an impression as in September 1914 he was promoted to Captain and held the position of Adjutant to his battalion.

He was ordered to the front three weeks before his death. Robert was 22 when he was killed by shell fire. He was given a funeral a few miles behind the firing line with full military honours. Amongst those in attendance at his funeral was Pte. James Connor, Royal Scots Fusiliers who was from Stranraer. Robert is buried at Sandpits British Cemetery, Fouquereuil grave reference II.D.12.

Lieut. Archibald Gifford Moir, 7th Battalion Argyll and Sutherland Highlanders. 25th April 1915.

The parish of Cairnryan was horrified when they were notified of the first death in from the village. Archibald was well known locally and the reality of the consequences war was already reaching thousands of doorsteps. Archibald was born around 1890 in Alloa. The Rev A. Murray Macgregor spoke at the beginning of May with emotion at his service on hearing of the death of Archibald:

"The first death of our brave defenders connected with Cairnryan was announced last week, to the regret of all in this district. 'Lieutenant Gifford Moir of the 7th Argyll and Sutherland Highlanders, killed in action.' This was the startling message which came to us with such cruel suddenness from the battlefield. Snatched away from us in the prime of his young and generous manhood, torn for ever from his devoted parents almost before they had time

to realise the sacrifice they had made in parting from their eldest and dearly loved son, our young friend has yielded his life cheerfully, bravely, in defence of home and country. We shall miss him sadly, not merely because of his own and his family's connection with this village, but also because of his bright, kindly, unselfish disposition, and of the promise which seemed opening out of a long happy, and useful life, now, alas, brought to a violent and untimely end."

The minister's speech continues at length, mentioning the unspeakable horror of the recent sinking of a ship off the coast of Ireland with the loss of 1200 lives. Though he did not mention the name of the ship, it was the Lusitania.

Archibald had already had a citation for bravery having been Mentioned in Despatches. His father was Mr A. P. Moir of Marshill, Alloa, a solicitor and banker. By the 1911 census, Archibald was a law student, but the family are all still living in Alloa. Whatever the connection the entire family must have lived in the Cairnryan area during the war. It is likely Archibald was a relative of the below named Archibald Douglas Moir due to the Cairnryan and Alloa Connections. There were two other men with the name Moir on the second memorial, who served in the war and survived. Captain Robert Gifford Moir, D.S.O., M.C. is very likely to have been related, as is the below named Archibald Douglas Moir.

Archibald Gifford Moir is buried at Bedford House Cemetery, Ieper, enclosure 4, XII.J.5.

Midshipman Archibald Douglas Moir. HMS Marlborough. Killed in action 17th October 1917.

CWGC lists Archibald as having been killed on the above date on HMS Mary Rose and his death notice in the local paper confirms that he was normally on HMS Marlborough but had temporarily been posted aboard HMS Mary Rose. The Mary Rose was present at the Battle of Jutland which saw heavy British losses.

On the morning of 17th October 1917 HMS Mary Rose and HMS Strongbow were escorting a convoy to Scandanavia. The convoy was spotted by two German cruisers and the British ships sailed towards them to engage. Strongbow was disabled and sank slowly. Mary Rose was sunk quickly by gunfire. The German cruisers then destroyed almost all of the merchant convoy.

Archibald, who was only 17, is commemorated on Chatham Naval Memorial. He was the son of Mr and Mrs James W. Moir, Dunmar, Alloa. His father was a banker and a solicitor. It is likely he was related to the above Archibald Gifford Moir due to the Cairnryan and Alloa connections.

There were two other men with the name Moir on the second memorial, who served in the war and survived. One of those men Lieutenant James W. Moir, was Archibald's brother.

2nd Lieut. William Ross, 9th Battalion Highland Light Infantry. Killed in action 12th April 1918.

I could find out very little additional information on William Ross who was named in the local newspaper as the son of John and Jessie Ross. The 1911 census did not yield any more personal information. He died aged 20 and is commemorated on panel 9 of Ploegsteert Memorial, Belgium.

Lance Corp. John Kirkland, 201661. 1st/5th Battalion Argyll and Sutherland Highlanders. Killed in action 1st August 1918.

Only two men with the name J. Kirkland are recorded as having been killed whilst serving in the Great War with the Argyll and Sutherland Highlanders, however both have their rank recorded as Pte.

With the very near local connections of Barr and Girvan the man named above is very likely to be the man on the Cairnryan Memorial, though his rank is recorded in CWGC and SNWM as Private. There is the possibility however that the man on the memorial transferred regiments and is not the man whose details are given above.

There is another possibility as at the time there was a Mr John Kirkland from Gillespie Farm, Glenluce reported as having his son missing in action, however the newspaper reported the first name of his son as William, and he would have been of age to be serving in the war.

The above named John Kirkland is buried in Oulchy-le-Chateau Churchyard Extension, Aisne, grave reference I.B.5.

Pte. Alexander Bell, 241980.
1st/6th Battalion Lancashire Fusiliers.
Killed in action 10th August 1917.

On the 1901 census Alexander is listed as living with his parents at 50 Lochryan Street, Stranraer. He was the second youngest of the seven sons and daughters of John and Maggie Bell His parents were later listed as living at 3, Firwood St., Middleton Junction, Manchester. By 1911 the census would suggest the same man is still in Wigtownshire working as a carter to the McConchie family at Crouse Farm, Kirkinner. Before the war he had perhaps moved his employment to Cairnryan.

The family must have had some connections with the Manchester area before the war since Alexander had enlisted into the Lancashire Fusiliers. Alexander was 23 when he was killed. With no known grave he is commemorated on Thiepval Memorial pier and face 3C and 3D.

Pte. John Downic, 202758.
13th Battalion Royal Scots.
Killed in action 1st August 1918.

John Downie had lived in Cairnryan and had grown up there. His parents were William and Grace Downie of Midton Road in Ayr and they had moved there from Cairnryan at some stage after John was killed.

John joined the army in 1916 and had been on active service for around a year. He had worked on the railways with Glasgow South Western Railway Co. Ayr.

Of over 600 casualties who are buried at Raperie British Cemetery there are special memorials to men from the Hereford Regiment and one man from the Royal Scots. Aged 21 when he was killed, John is the single casualty of the Royal Scots buried at Raperie British Cemetery, Villemontoire, grave reference IX.A.1.

Pte. William Edmunds, Royal Engineers. Unknown date of death.

CWGC records show there were three possibilities for a man with this name and regiment. Research is made more difficult as his name is spelt two different ways on the two Cairnryan War memorials. One possibility is that he was the man who was married to Jane Gilmour. Her father had been a light-keeper and was probably the light-keeper at Cairnryan. This particular William was stationed for a time at Lloyds Signal Station, Cornwall, and his wife Jane died. His father-in-law had by that time moved to live at 18 Lochryan Street, Stranraer.

Another possibility is that he was one of five adult children living with their parents, James and Maggie, at West Freugh Farmhouse at the time of the 1911 census. Perhaps before the war this William worked in the Cairnryan area. All of this is speculation however and unless a relative comes forward or new evidence emerges, his identity and connection to Cairnryan may never be known.

Pte. Adam Ion, 10529. 2nd Battalion Scots Guards. Killed in action 9th October 1917.

Adam was the son of Thomas and Jessie Ion from Stronord. His father was the gamekeeper there. Adam had previously been in the army before joining the Wigtownshire Constabulary. In 1911 Adam married a young widow Agnes (McKie (nee Hume). As a constable he was stationed at Cairnryan where he lived at the police station with his wife who was known as Annie and family.

After his death a few friends erected a headstone in Cairnryan Cemetery in his memory. The headstone also commemorates the death of his stepson William McKie, who died one month after him in Cairnryan, the headstone is very close to the war memorial.

His wife and family inserted the following poem in the local newspaper:

He has gone from my gaze like a beautiful dream,
I scarce can believe it, so strange does it seem,
I would give all I have, though it caused me great pain,
To gaze on the face of my loved one again.

I know he has gone to that beautiful home,
And, Father, I bow to Thy will;
But, Oh! For the touch of a vanished hand
And the sound of his dear voice that's stilled.

Adam is buried in Artillery Wood Cemetery, Belgium, grave reference V.D.19. His brother John Ion was also killed and both men are named on the war memorial in Minnigaff.

Pte. Thomas Milroy, 252132.
49th Battalion Canadian Infantry.
Died 30th October 1917.

Born on 7th August 1886 in Stranraer the third son of Mr Thomas and Mary Milroy (nee Murray) of High Mark, New Luce. Thomas was almost 30 years old when he enlisted in Canada in 1916. He had a dark complexion, dark hair and blue eyes. He was 5 feet 8 inches tall and had a long scar on his left hand.

He is buried in Poelcapelle British Cemetery, Belgium, grave reference XIX.B.8. Thomas is also on the war memorial at New Luce and the one at Inch as well as being named on the family headstone in New Luce Kirkyard.

Trooper Andrew McWilliam Neil, 2425.
Queen's Own Regiment Glasgow Yeomanry.
Killed in action 17th November 1915.

Andrew was the son of Andrew and Clementina Neil formerly of Drummucklock, Cairnryan. His father employed a number of men at Drummucklock. After the war the family later moved to West Dhuloch

Andrew had a sister, Alexandra who died aged five from diphtheria. In what must have been a very sad time indeed for his parents, another sister, Jean died a month after Andrew on Christmas day. Another sister, Elizabeth was a nurse and sadly she too died in spring 1920.

Andrew was killed whilst on service with the Mediterranean Expeditionary Force in Turkey. Andrew would likely have known all three of the Trueman brothers listed below as they also were from Drummucklock.

Aged 19, Andrew is buried in Pink Farm Cemetery, Helles, grave reference III.B 14. He is named on the family headstone in Leswalt Old Kirkyard.

Pte. Samuel Preston, SP/2186.
24th Battalion Royal Fusiliers.
Killed in action 13th November 1916.

Samuel had been a gamekeeper in Dumbartonshire. He had been a popular member of the community in Cairnryan where he had lived with his parents, William and Margaret Preston (nee McCracken), and his sister Agnes, before becoming a moving away for employment. Samuel had joined the Sportsman's Battalion of the Royal Fusiliers when he enlisted.

He was first reported missing before his parents were given the news that he was now presumed killed on that date. Samuel is commemorated on the Thiepval Memorial, pier and face 8C, 9A and 16A. He is also named on the family headstone in Cairnryan cemetery.

Pte. George Trueman, 29068.
14th Battalion Highland Light Infantry.
Killed in action 14th June 1916.

Cairnryan War Memorial contains 15 names from the Great War. It is very sad that three of those named on this memorial were all brothers and the only sons of Mrs Thorburn of Kildrochet, Lochans. George was the brother of Archie and William who are both listed below.

Before the war he had worked for Mr Neil at Drummucklock, and he and his brothers would have known his employer Andrew Neil senior's son, also Andrew, very well. Andrew is listed above.

George was 22 when he was killed. The eldest son of Annie Thorburn, he was married to Elizabeth Wright. He is buried at Vermelles British Cemetery, grave reference III.C 22.

Driver Archie Trueman, 831773. 306th Bde. Royal Field Artillery. Died from wounds 27th August 1918.

Born in the parish of Kirkmaiden, Archie was the brother of George and William listed above and below. In a tragic blow for their mother both Archie and William died on the same day. Before the war Archie had worked at Burnbrae, Symington.

His mother received the following message through Cairnryan's minister:

> *"Please express to his mother the sympathy of the officers, NCOs and men of this battery with her in her great loss. Trueman was a real good fellow, an excellent signaller, and one of the stoutest hearted men we had, and exceedingly keen on his job."*

A further letter was sent expressing similar sentiment.

> *"Gunner Trueman was a man in whom trust could be placed, and all the time I knew him he always carried out his difficult, and often dangerous duties with great steadiness. He is a very great loss to his section and to the battery and will be sadly missed by all ranks."*

Archie is buried in Aire Communal Cemetery, Pas de Calais, grave reference IV. C 14. His sister served in the war and is named on the second memorial alongside another two Cairnryan women.

Pte. William Trueman, M/331969.
1st Base Mechanical Transport Dept. Army Service Corps.
Died from wounds 27th August 1918.

William was the first of the three Trueman brothers to be posted abroad. Before the war he was a dairyman for Mr Hannay at the Challoch. William was 19 when he died from tetanus after being wounded in action. He is buried in St Sever Cemetery Extension, Rouen, grave reference Q.V.H 16. William is also on Leswalt War Memorial since he worked at the Challoch.

It would have been a devastating blow to Mrs Thorburn to have three of her sons killed in the war. Her daughter, Annie Trueman is listed on the second Cairnryan Memorial of those who served their country. Annie had enlisted in the W.R.A.F. on 1st October 1918 and was stationed at R.N.A.S. Luce Bay. When she enlisted, she would have known that all three of her brothers had already been killed in the war.

The Stranraer to Larne ferry, Princess Maud, passes Cairnryan lighthouse around 1910. Princess Maud continued to sail throughout the war, whilst her sister ships Princess Victoria and Princess May were commissioned by the Admiralty.

Sons of Cairnryan Remembered

The below named men were on the second memorial in the inside of the church at Cairnryan, rescued from a skip but now in storage. These two men died in the war as their names had a small cross beside them. They were brothers who were born in Cairnryan but had moved away before the war, nonetheless they are sons of the village and their names should not be forgotten. I was unable to trace their names on any Ayrshire war memorial as the next most likely place where they should have been remembered. They died within five days of each other.

Pte. James Ralph, 29863.
6th/7th Battalion Royal Scots Fusiliers.
Died of wounds 12th April 1917.

Killed within days of each other, James and John were the sons of James and Jeannie Ralph of Claddy East Farm (where the ferry terminal now is). They had several siblings who all grew up in the farm including Bertie, Agnes, Mary, and Jeannie. Their grandparents came from High Barnultoch. James had worked as a conductor on the Ayr Corporation Tramways before the war.

Though both of the sons were raised in Cairnryan, a short time before the outbreak of war, the family moved to Prestwick. Their connections were not severed though, as it was obvious from the marking of the small cross beside each of the brother's names that the minister had kept in contact. However both brothers names do look like they have been added late – since the other names are rank and alphabetical order.

James was injured and taken to a casualty clearing station where he died from his wounds. He is buried at Duisans British Cemetery, grave reference III.G 20. His brother is named below.

Pte. John Ralph, 331956.
6th Battalion Highland Light Infantry.
Accidentally killed 17th April 1917.

Nineteen year old younger brother of the above named James, John also worked on the tramcars as a conductor. John was accidentally killed when a dug-out collapsed on top of him and he could not be recovered in time to survive. Of the thousands of casualties listed with the CWGC it is almost comforting to know that James and John are listed beside one another.

John is buried in St Leger British Cemetery, grave reference D 13. Again it seems very sad that both of these men's names are missing from the war memorial standing in the cemetery. If it were not for a council workman offering to give the second memorial to the museum instead of going into the skip, these men would be almost certainly forgotten.

A third brother, Gilbert was twice suffering from shell-shock and had been in hospital at the time of his brother's deaths.

Their parents had moved to 11 Pleasantfield Road, Prestwick. Both of the men were born in Cairnryan.

DRUMMORE (KIRKMAIDEN) WAR MEMORIAL

The most southerly War memorial in Scotland was unveiled in bright weather on Sunday 31st May 1920 in the Parish of Kirkmaiden. It stood high on a mound and was made from red Aberdeen granite; the pedestal base supported a 16 feet high Celtic cross.

After a service in Kirkmaiden Kirk led by Rev. A. Muir, which was attended by many men in uniform and a large congregation, all made their way in a procession to the hill where the War Memorial stood draped in a Union Jack. A few words were said by Mr K. McDouall of Logan, who unveiled the monument as the sound of the last post was played. The unveiling revealed the names of the fallen on four polished panels around the base. Those who had returned from war saluted the memorial. Rev. MacMorland performed the dedication, before the National Anthem 'God Save the King' was sung.

Kirkmaiden around 1910

The memorial was moved in the 1970s to the grounds of the church within Drummore village. The inscriptions on the memorial are neither in order of rank or in alphabetical order. Rank and regiment are given with each name. Some of the lead lettering is now missing from the memorial. The inscription reads:

Front panel:

AUT VINCERE AUT MORI (translated – Either conquer or die).

LANCE CORPL.	CHARLES PEEBLES	R.S.F.
PTE.	DAVID PEEBLES	"
	JAMES W. WILSON	"
	JOHN MONTGOMERY	"
	JAMES ECCLES	"
"	JAMES MURRAY	"
"	MATTHEW N. McCLUMPHA	"
"	EDWARD MORLAND	"
"	WILLIAM McGAW	M.C.C.
"	JOHN CUNNINGHAM	S.G.
	JAMES BRAID	R.N.

ERECTED BY THE INHABITANTS TO THE MEMORY OF THE BRAVE MEN OF THIS PARISH WHO FELL IN THE GREAT WAR 1914 – 1918.

Second panel:

PTE.	ALEXANDER McMEEKIN	E.K.R.
"	ALEXANDER BALLANTYNE	A.I.F.
LANCE CORPL.	WILLIAM CHALMERS	C.E.F.
CORPL.	MATTHEW McC COBBLEDICK	
SAPPER	JOHN C HARVEY	
	WILLIAM CHALMERS	R.E.
DRIVER	DAVID McDOWALL	A.S.C.
LANCE CORPL.	ALEXANDER CHAMBERS	5TH D.C.
SUB LIEUT	JAMES McCULLOCH	R.N.V.R.

Third panel:

PTE.	WILLIAM LECKIE	R.H.
"	JAMES ECCLES	S.H.
"	DAVID BLACKWELL	C.H.
	THOMAS STEVENSON	
SERGt.	JAMES JOHNSTON	H.L.I.
PTE.	SAMUEL S. McKEAND	
	JOSEPH J. PAXTON	
	JOHN LITTLE	
	WILLIAM A. McKIE	M.R.

Lance Corporal Charles Masterson Peebles, 20757.
1st Battalion Royal Scots Fusiliers.
Killed in action 14th July 1916.

Charles Masterson Peebles had served his apprenticeship as a draper with Mr J. Findlay of Stranraer. He had worked in the drapers for eight years before the outbreak of the war. A keen footballer he played with the Stoneykirk Club and the Railway Swifts. Although his normal position was full back he was said to be flexible enough to play in any position. He had a reputation for being a 'clean' player throughout the district, though apparently gave as good as he was given when it came to hard knocks.

Charles' parents were Mr and Mrs William Peebles of Creechan Park, Drummore. They had two other sons serving in the army. Private William (Bill) Peebles was in the Scots Guards, and brother Private David Peebles was reported missing shortly after Charles death, and is named below. Bill was injured on at least one occasion and had a letter sent to his mother to say he had been injured on the head and left hand during a bomb attack on German trenches, at that time he was in hospital in France. Bill's wounds were serious as he lost most of his lower jaw.

Charles is buried in Flatiron Copse Cemetery, Mametz Somme, France grave reference IV.A 10.

Private David Peebles, 20807.
2nd Battalion Royal Scots Fusiliers.
Killed in action 30th July 1916.

Brother to the above Charles Peebles, David was born in 1895. David had lived with his parents and siblings at Creechan Park, Drummore. July 1916 was a very sad time for their parents and family as both brothers had been killed in the Battle of the Somme.

The family gave up the farm and moved to Drummore village. After the war one of the brothers who remained, Robert, died tragically in a shooting accident in 1930. John had the shop at Stoneykirk for many years, William had been seriously wounded but returned and married in 1922 and he lived at Kenmuir, Ardwell. James was a grocer and lived in Firpark Terrace, Glasgow. Their two sisters both married and lived locally, Helen (Nell) became Nell Gorman, and Jeanie became Jeanie Bell.

Like thousands of others, David's body was never recovered. He is commemorated on Thiepval Memorial, Somme, pier and face 3C. His is one name amongst the 72,000 on the memorial with no known grave.

His brother William (Bill) is referred to in a number of letters published in the local newspaper from James McCormack, and Samuel McCandlish, and since the letters name a few local men, I have included them in the Stranraer section.

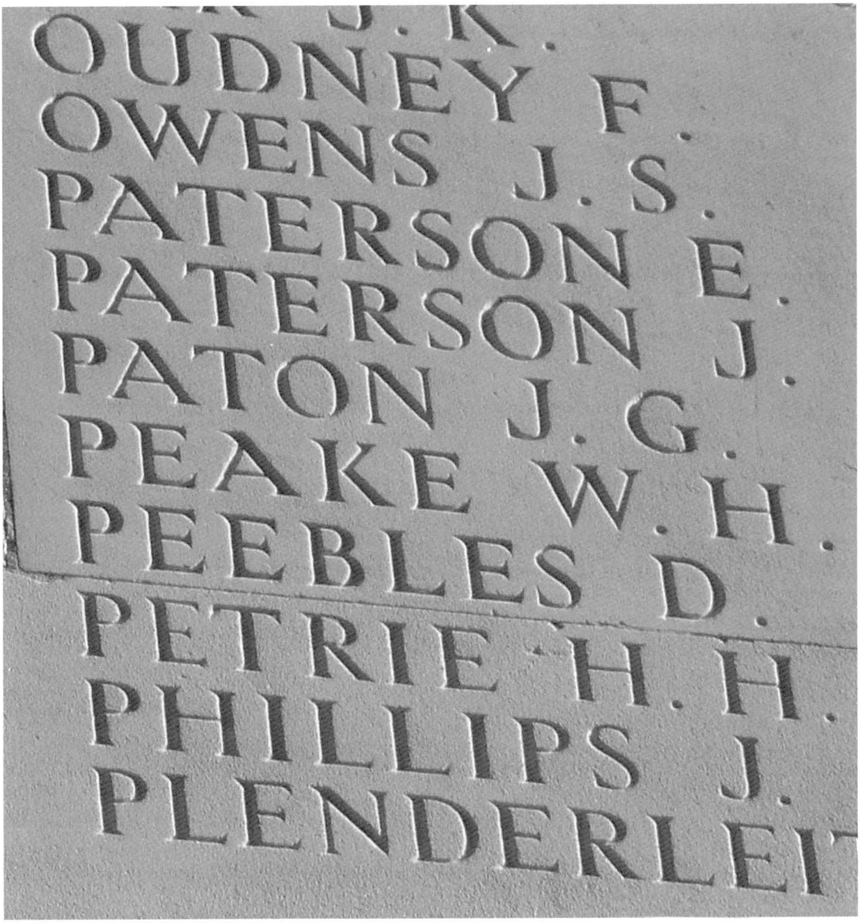

David Peebles is one of the 72,000 names on the memorial to the missing at Thiepval.

Lance Corporal James Watson Wilson, 295403.
12th Battalion Royal Scots Fusiliers.
Killed in action 30th September 1918.

James lived with his wife and two young sons at Craig Street Drummore. He was killed in action at Flanders aged just 27.

James had been part of a push which successfully recovered the village of Wulverghem from German occupation early in the month he died. He is buried in the nearby Kandahar Farm Cemetery, Belgium, grave reference I.A.6.

Private John Peat Montgomery, 15327.
6th/7th Battalion Royal Scots Fusiliers.
Died 12th August 1916.

John Peat Montgomery was the son of Hugh and Elizabeth Montgomery, Main Street, Drummore. John had a sister, Mrs Marion Ramsay who lived in Glasgow. His father, Hugh, was attached in the war to the Royal Naval Volunteer Reserve serving on board H.M.T. Penguin.

John had been on active service for about fourteen months before his death and was attached to the machine gun section of the Royal Scots Fusiliers, a job where he would have been a main target of the enemy.

He is buried at London Cemetery and extension, Longueval, grave reference I.A 26.

Private James Eccles, 14292.
1st Battalion Royal Scots Fusiliers.
Killed in action 12th March 1915.

James was an uncle to the below named James Eccles. Both men belonged to the extended Eccles family, five of whom were serving at the same time. James was born in Kirkmaiden in 1872 and enlisted at Drummore. He was one of three brothers all serving at the same time.

James had served eight years in the army and had fought in the Boer War. His record and experience meant was called up as a reservist on the outbreak of war, with an immediate posting to France. His early calling to the war meant he served in some of the most severe battles. He was killed at Neuve Chapelle aged 42, and is commemorated on the Ypres (Menin Gate) Memorial, Belgium, panel 19 and 33.

A third man with the name James Eccles, more than likely a relative, is on Portpatrick War Memorial.

Private James Murray, 10901.
1st Battalion Royal Scots Fusiliers.
Died of wounds 1st October 1914.

James Murray's parents lived in Portlogan. He was born and was brought up in the parish of Kirkmaiden.

Though there were few other details on James' life, he is buried in Vailly British Cemetery, Aisne, France, grave reference II.E.9.

Private Matthew Nelson McClumpha, 8112.
1st/5th Battalion Royal Scots Fusiliers.
Killed in action 30th December 1915.

Matthew was the son of Mr and Mrs William McClumpha of Auchabrick, Portlogan, they had previously lived at Killumpha and are likely to have known the below named Edward Morland very well. By the time of his death they lived Glebe Cottage, Stoneykirk. He married Isabella Fleming in 1914 and their baby daughter was born in 1915 in Stranraer. His wife and daughter lived at 12 Millhill Street, Stranraer.

Matthew was killed in action at the Dardanelles on 30th December 1915 having taken part in very heavy fighting in Helles. He is buried at Twelve Tree Cops Cemetery, Turkey, grave reference II.A 1. Matthew is also named on the Stranraer War Memorial.

Private Edward Morland, 16239.
7th Battalion Royal Scots Fusiliers.
Killed in action 25th September 1915.

Edward Morland worked with his father as a dairyman at Killumpha, Portlogan and he is likely to have known the above named Matthew McClumpha very well.

He was the son of John and Ellen Morland and they lived at the dairy-house on the farm. He had previously been reported as wounded and missing before official confirmation was received by his father that he had been killed. He was 21 at the time of his death and he is commemorated on Loos Memorial, Pas-de-Calais, France, panel 46 to 49.

Private William McGaw, 97880.
49th Company Machine Gun Corps.
Killed in action 16th August 1917.

Youngest son of Robert and Jeannie McGaw (nee McKerrow) of Drummore, William and his brothers James and Kerrow were all on active service. Robert McGaw had a grocers business in Drummore and William had worked there prior to enlisting.

In an old autograph album from 1914 which is signed by a number of Drummore residents, including the McGaw and McKerrow families, Williams' brother James quotes a Robert Burns poem:

And man, whose heaven-erected face
The smiles of love adorn
Man's inhumanity to man
Makes countless thousands mourn.

The family received a letter from Second Lieutenant Halliwell stating that William had been killed during an offensive near Ypres and offering his sympathy. William was 21 and is commemorated on Tyne Cot Memorial, Belgium, panel 154 to 159 and 163A. He is also named on the family headstone in Kirkmaiden Old Churchyard.

Guardsman John Cunningham, 11512.
1st Battalion Scots Guards. Killed in action 10th June 1915.

John Cunningham was born and enlisted in Stranraer. He was the son of Joseph and Sarah Cunningham (nee Paul) of Port O'Spittal, Lochans. John married Grace Heron on the 3rd April 1914 at Kirkmaiden. He worked as a ploughman at Droughduil, Dunragit and lived at Cowans, Portlogan.

Captain Cuthbert who commanded John's company sent the following letter:

> *"It is with deepest regret that I have to inform you that your husband, who was in my Company, was last night, about 7.30, struck by a bomb from a trench mortar, which hit him in several places, so that he died, but very bravely, without a grumble. He was one of the best men in my Company, and I am extremely sorry to lose him. He will be buried with all due respect in this village, about half a mile behind the trenches. I am truly sorry to give you such sad news."*

A further letter from Sergeant Savage stated:

> *"Private Cunningham was wounded at 7pm, he died about an hour afterwards...he was one of the best in the section, always merry and smiling."*

John is buried in Vieille-Chapelle New Military Cemetery, Lacouture, France grave reference II.A 3. He is also named on Stoneykirk War Memorial at Sandhead. A photograph of him was printed in the local newspaper at the time of his death, but it was of too poor a quality to be reproduced here.

Deck Hand James Braid, H.M. Yacht Adventuress, Mercantile Marine Reserve. Died 24th September 1918.

James Braid was the son of a lighthouse keeper. At the time of his death his father was the principal keeper of the Mull of Galloway lighthouse. His parents were Charles Hunter Braid and the late Ellinor Braid, who had died at Mull of Galloway in 1915. His father was later the keeper at Rona Lighthouse, Raasay, Kyle of Lochalsh. It is recorded with the CWGC that James died from illness on board the yacht. His body was returned to Kirkmaiden churchyard for burial.

The Scottish National War Museum lists James' death as on board HM Yacht Yarta though his death in the local newspaper at the time also lists on board HM Adventuress. It is possible James was normally on board one of the yachts and had been temporarily serving on board the other. James was only twenty years old when he died.

The inscription on the bottom of his military headstone reads:

"Sleep thy last sleep, free from care and sorrow."

Private Alexander McMeekan, G.13260.
7th Battalion The Buffs East Kent Regiment.
Killed in action 11th October 1917.

Spelt as above on the CWGC. Alexander was the son of William and Elizabeth McMeekan, Cairngarroch, Drummore. He had three brothers all serving in the army at the same time. William was 36 at the time of his death. He had served eight years in the Royal Irish Lancers, four more years in the Reserves and his time had expired before the war broke out. He enlisted in Glasgow immediately on the outbreak of war.

Alexander served under the name John White. He is commemorated on Tyne Cot Memorial, Belgium.

Private Alexander Ballantyne, 4278.
21st Battalion Australian Infantry.
Killed in action 26th August 1918.

Alexander Ballantyne was born in the parish of Kirkmaiden. He was the son of Alexander and Jessie Ballantyne (nee Muir) of Main Street, Drummore. Alexander was one of a number of brothers and sisters including, Robert, Christina, Jane, and William who are all on the 1901 census as living at Shore Street Drummore. Alexander attended Portlogan Public school before he decided on a trade as a seaman. He served on ships that were used as troop carriers. By the age of nineteen he had emigrated to Australia. In Melbourne he enlisted in the Australian Expeditionary force and later boarded the troop transport ship Wiltshire with his regiment, to go to the war on 7th March 1916.

The 21st Battalion were vital in their push to halt the German advance of 1918 and the battalion had so many losses that there was an attempt to disband them. Alexander was killed on 26th August 1918 aged 25. On his Australian forces record of his death it is written that contact could be made with another seaman in Melbourne, David Torrance. The name Torrance has definite sea connections (and farming) in Wigtownshire. It is possible both men had travelled together to Melbourne.

Alexander is commemorated on his family headstone in Kirkmaiden parish churchyard, and on the Villers-Bretonneux Memorial, Somme, France, and the Australian War Memorial on panel 93.

Lance Corporal William Chalmers, 432220. 49th Battalion, Canadian Infantry (Alberta Regiment). Killed in action 16th September 1916.

Born on the 25th February 1883 in Glasgow, William was the son of Mary and William Chalmers. He was brought up by his grandparents in Drummore. Many Scots at the turn of the century were leaving for Canada or Australia to seek a better life and good employment. Whilst his only brother James went to Australia, William went to Canada. It was there William enlisted on 5th January 1915. He had spent two months training with the 101st Edinburgh Fusiliers.

The Canadian military archives are detailed and easy to access; it is even possible to see the enlistment form and handwriting of the person being researched. William's occupation was listed as a fireman, although the local newspaper recalls that he had been an electrical engineer. He was 5 Feet 8 ½ inches tall, with a dark complexion, grey eyes and black hair.

William died in one of the most notorious and bloody battles in the war, the Battle of the Somme. In previous fighting he had already been twice wounded and gassed once, although he recovered from those injuries. By the end of the battle there were around one and a half million casualties, with around twenty thousand British soldiers having been killed on the first day. During the battle that started in July 1916, William had already been wounded twice and gassed once.

His uncle was Captain David Chalmers of Drummore and he was a cousin of the below named William McMillan Chalmers. Brothers James and William listed each other as next of kin when they enlisted, suggesting both parents had either died or were no longer in contact. When notification was received of his death by his Aunt and Uncle, they were too upset to write to his brother James in Australia. They asked their friend Jeannie C. McGaw to write:

> *Dear Pte. Chalmers,*
>
> *Your Uncle has just been in and he has asked me to write you a little note, and I am very sorry it must convey sad news. Your Uncle received notice yesterday morning from the War Office that your dear brother Willie has been killed in action on 15th or 16th September. He meant to have written to you ere this, but waited on, not having heard from Willie for about three weeks.*
>
> *I feel exceedingly sorry that I should be the bearer of such sad news, and will you please accept my most sincere sympathy. I know it is a hard blow and can only direct you to Him, - the God of consolation.*
>
> *The toll of this war has been heavy, and oh may the warning appeal to multitudes, so that though the death roll be sad and its victims many, they may be far exceeded by those written in glory – the Roll of Life.*
>
> *Your Uncle and Aunt were too much upset to be able to write themselves but otherwise they keep fairly well.*
>
> *Again assuring you of my heartfelt sympathy, I remain, yours very sincerely*
>
> *Jeannie C. McGaw.*

James, who was serving in the Australian Imperial Forces, also received a letter of sympathy from General Sir Sam Hughes which read:

> *"Will you kindly accept my sincere sympathy and condolence in the deceased of that worthy citizen and heroic soldier, your brother, Lance-Corporal William Chalmers. While one cannot too deeply mourn the loss of such a brave comrade, there is a consolation in knowing that he did his duty fearlessly and well, and gave his life for the cause of liberty and the upbuilding of the Empire."*

William is buried in Courcelette British Cemetery, Somme, France. VIII.E.24

Corporal Matthew McColm Cobbledick, 187312.
8th Battalion Canadian Infantry.
Killed in action 9th August 1918.

Matthew was the son of Janet McColm and his stepfather Thomas Cobbledick of Lucas House, Drummore. He was born on 11th November 1883. He enlisted in Canada on 4th January 1916 and listed his second cousin Tom McColm also living in Canada as his next of kin. At the time of enlisting his trade was listed as teamster – which at that time usually meant truck driver. According to his enlistment papers he was 5 feet 8 inches tall, had a 41 inch girth, a dark complexion, grey eyes and dark brown hair.

Le Quesnel, a small village, had been taken by the Germans in spring 1918. On the day Matthew died, there was a successful push by the Canadian Infantry to take the village back. He is buried at Le Quesnel Communal Cemetery Extension, Somme, France, grave reference A 37.

Sapper John Clunie Harvey, 2691460.
6th Field Company Canadian Engineers.
Died 30th October 1918.

Youngest son of Mr and Mrs Harvey of Fineview, Drummore, John was born on 20th August 1891 in Drummore. He was married to Nettie Campbell whose address was given as 19th Avenue, Yakima, USA. Before the war he had been a blacksmith and did vehicle repairs. Having served in the US Armed Forces he enlisted on the 3rd May 1918. Small in stature he was 5 feet 5 ¼ inches tall, with a ruddy complexion, reddish hair and blue eyes.

In the spring of 1918 an outbreak of pneumonia spread killing millions. Known as 'Spanish Flu', soldiers from the USA brought the disease with them and with close contact on troopships the disease quickly spread. John died from pneumonia at Bramshott Camp, Canadian Hospital. He is buried in Bramshott Churchyard, Hampshire grave reference III.A 6.

Sapper William McMillan Chalmers, 44001.
73rd Field Company, Royal Engineers.
Killed in action 25th September 1915

William was born on the 2nd October 1888 in Drummore, the fourth son of Captain David and Sarah Chalmers (nee McCracken), his father was a Master Mariner. By the 1901 census he was listed as a scholar, living with his parents in Stair Street, Drummore along with his brother Thomas and sister Mary. His father's business grew as he was part owner of the harbour at Drummore, along with the Marshall family. By the time of the war, local newspapers listed their home as Gladstone Villa, Drummore. William was a cousin of the above named Lance Corporal William Chalmers.

Before he enlisted at Clydebank he lived in Stranraer. He was married to Harriett Chalmers who was living at 15 Leopold Avenue, West Didsbury, Manchester, after the war.

The British Red Cross wrote to his mother:

> *"I regret to say that the only news we have succeeded in obtaining about the above is extremely sad. Sapper Mason, now in a hospital abroad, states that Sapper Chalmers went over the parapet just in front of where he himself was waiting in reserve, at the very beginning of the advance on 25th September, Sapper Chalmers was following Lieut. English, who was instantly shot through the breast. I regret to say that Sapper Mason adds that Sapper Chalmers was also killed in the attack and that he saw his body. Sapper Mason was under the impression that a burial party had gone out three days later and buried Sapper Chalmers where Lieut. English is buried, at a place called 'Quality Street' – this is the main road leading to the trenches."*

The Battle of Loos was fought in September 1915 and the day William was killed was the date Douglas Haig commanded the army to attack the German machine gun position with poison chlorine gas. By the end of the battle around fifty thousand British troops were lost.

William is commemorated on Loos Memorial, Pas de Calais, France, panel 4 and 5. He is named on the family headstone in Kirkmaiden Old Churchyard.

William's cousin, Corpl. Enest Victor Ince was awarded a Military Medal for Gallantry in the Field.

Private David McDowall, M2/148976. 618th Motor Transport Company, A.S.C. Died 1st April 1917.

David McDowall was the youngest son of Mr and Mrs Samuel McDowall of Drummore. He lived in Stranraer and enlisted at Ayr. He had been employed as a driver prior to enlisting. He was sent out to East Africa in January 1915 where he became ill.

On April 1st at Dar-es-Salaam aged just 30 he died from Blackwater Fever, a complication of Malaria. David is buried in Morogoro Cemetery, Tanzania, grave reference III.B 4, and he is named on the family headstone in Kirkmaiden Old Churchyard. The headstone is beside those for the sailors from the Rio Verde, a ship sunk by torpedo from a German U-boat off the Mull of Galloway during the war.

Lance Corporal Alexander Chambers, GS/11735. 5th Dragoon Guards. Killed in action 26th November 1917.

Alexander Chambers was called after his father, and was born in Kirkmaiden parish. The youngest member of the family, they lived at Auchneight. When he was old enough, Alexander lived in Kirkcowan, and travelled to Galashiels to enlist.

Alexander was killed during the Battle of Cambrai and he is buried in Orival Wood Cemetery, Flesquieres, grave reference I.A.18. He is also named on the family headstone in Kirkmaiden Old Churchyard. The family headstone lists his date of death as 22nd November 1917.

Sub-Lieutenant James McCulloch, H.M. Yacht Kethailes, Royal Naval Reserve. Died 11th October 1917.

The yacht Kethailes served as a patrol vessel in the Irish Sea. It was involved in a collision with another vessel close to the Blackwater Light Vessel off Wexford. James body was never recovered and it was never made clear which ship the yacht had been in collision with.

James was the son of James and Mary McCulloch (nee Mason) of Drummore and husband of Helen McKee of Falkirk. Prior to enlisting he had been a third officer with the Anchor Line, sailing on their New York to Liverpool and Glasgow service.

James is commemorated on Portsmouth Naval Memorial reference 27, and is named on the family headstone in Kirkmaiden Old Churchyard.

Private William Leckie, 292652. 1st/7th Battalion Black Watch. Killed in action 23rd April 1917.

William Leckie was born at Gartmore, Stirlingshire and enlisted at Dunblane. His parents, John and Susan Leckie were the local connection as they were from Auchness, and later Longrigg. Ardwell. William was 23 at the time of his death.

In April 1917 here had been heavy fighting in Roeux where Scottish forces were attempting to liberate it from the Germans. The village was won and lost on a number of occasions as it was situated on a series of caves making warfare very difficult.

William had been a ploughman in Perthshire before enlisting in the Scottish Horse. He later transferred to the Black Watch. William had two brothers who both served in the navy during the war. He is buried in Brown's Copse Cemetery, Roeux, grave reference II.B.9.

Private James Eccles, 1399.
1st Battalion Seaforth Highlanders. Died 31st May 1916.

Private James Eccles (jnr) and other Eccles family members who saw service. David, William and Robert.

The Eccles family of Drummore had three sons and two grandsons all serving in the war at the same time. James was one of the grandsons, born in Portpatrick and aged only 19 when he died. He was the nephew of the above named James Eccles. His mother was Mrs Alexander, sister to the above named James Eccles, she lived at Bridge House, Drummore.

James became ill with enteritis whilst serving in the Persian Gulf. He did not recover and is buried in Amara War Cemetery, Iraq, grave reference XX11.H7.

Private David Blackwell, S/23423.
5th Battalion Cameron Highlanders.
Killed in action 16th April 1918.

David Blackwell was born on 29th November 1886 at Logan to Mary Blackwell, Glen Street Stranraer, a domestic servant and James Purdie a builders foreman living at Little Lochans. It was David's sister Mrs Mary McClintick of Balgown, Kirkmaiden who received official confirmation of his death.

David had moved to Lockerbie for work and before the war was employed by the Mr H. Wallace of Scalehill, Lockerbie and it was there he enlisted.

Twice wounded prior to his death and aged only 32, David died with many others as a result of the German spring offensive of 1918. He is commemorated on Tyne Cot Memorial, Belgium alongside the names of 35,000 other men with no known grave. The memorial reference is 136 to 138.

Private Thomas Stevenson, 25803. 2nd Battalion Queen's Own Cameron Highlanders. Died 25th August 1917.

Thomas Stevenson was a grocer who had served his apprenticeship with Mr A McGaw of Drummore. When his apprenticeship was completed he became a travelling salesman in Glasgow. He was a grandson of the late Captain William Stevenson and a nephew to Thomas and Agnes Milligan of Shore Street, Drummore.

Thomas enlisted in the Lovat's Scouts in 1914 on the outbreak of war. Sometime later his regiment was attached to the Cameron Highlanders for transport work and he went out with them to Salonica. There he took ill and was a patient in No.18 Stationary Hospital, where he died of dysentery. He is buried in Lahana military cemetery, grave reference III.C.8.

Sergeant James Johnston, 2699. 12th Battalion Highland Light Infantry. Killed in action 29th September 1918.

James was the son of Elizabeth Johnston and the late Robert Johnston of Portlogan. He had a sister named Margaret. Prior to the war he had been employed as a gamekeeper at Dunblane. When war broke out, James travelled to Glasgow to enlist. When he died he was only twenty nine years old.

The village of Zantevoorde had fallen to the German side in 1914 and remained under their control for the following four years. On 28th September the village was taken back. Although CWGC lists James' date of death as 29th September, the family headstone in Kirkmaiden Old Churchyard reads that he 'fell in action on 28th September 1918'. He may have died a day after he was wounded.

He is buried in Zantvoorde British Cemetery, Belgium, grave reference I.G.21. Of the 1583 graves there, only 449 names are identified in the cemetery.

Private Samuel McKeand, 13742. 15th Battalion Highland Light Infantry. Died of wounds 24th July 1916.

Samuel McKeand was born and lived in Kirkmaiden. He was a well known local and had been a farm worker. Before the war he had left farm work and gained employment on the trams in Glasgow with the Glasgow Corporation. On the outbreak of war he joined the tramway division of the Highland Light Infantry.

His father, Mr McKeand from High Currochtrie received word that his son Samuel had been wounded and was in the 23rd General Hospital. Further word came that the injury was a serious gunshot wound to the head, then shortly afterwards a telegram was sent to confirm he had died.

Only 21 when he died, he held a silver medal for being the best marksman in his Company. He is buried in Etaples Military Cemetery, Pas De Calais, France, grave reference XIV.E.10A.

Private Joseph James Paxton, 4268. 3rd/9th Battalion Highland Light Infantry. Died 18th March 1916.

Joseph was the youngest son of Mr William Paxton of Drummore. He had worked as a grocer in Ardwell, Stranraer and Glasgow. Joseph was married to Elizabeth Pickering and had two young children. Joseph was keen to volunteer himself for foreign service after training in Glasgow. He then spent further time training with the battalion in Ripon. He was not selected for the first draft abroad and became seriously unwell with peritonitis. He died after being operated on in Ripon Military Hospital.

Joseph's body was carried on a gun carriage to Ripon Station and given full military honours. On arrival at Drummore, his coffin was transported with military escort to the Kirkmaiden church. He had a large attendance at his funeral and interment in Kirkmaiden churchyard. He is named on the family headstone there. Joseph left a young widow, Elizabeth (nee Lochhead) and two small children. He was 29.

Private John Little, 281348.
1st/7th Battalion Highland Light Infantry.
Killed in action 20th April 1917.

John Little was born and enlisted in Glasgow. He was the only son of Mr and Mrs Little, Barncorkerie, Drummore. John's parents received word earlier in the war that he had been slightly wounded and admitted to the 3rd General Hospital in France. He recovered from those wounds then sometime later his regiment made their way to Egypt, where he was killed. He is buried in Gaza War Cemetery Israel, grave reference XXXI.F.3.

Corporal William Alexander McKie, 12143.
19th Battalion Manchester Regiment.
Killed in action 23rd July 1916.

William Alexander McKie was born in Tunstall, Staffordshire and lived at Pulinkum, Drummore. He enlisted in Manchester. He was the son of Agnes McKie, Main Street Drummore and the late Daniel McKie. William was 22 when he was killed and he is commemorated on the Thiepval Memorial, Somme, pier and face 13A and 14C. The memorial contains the names of over 72,000 men with no known grave.

William died having left no will, though he must have had an estate to leave. An advertisement in the Galloway Advertiser and Wigtownshire Free Press of May 1918 invited interested parties to make contact.

Sons of Kirkmaiden Remembered

For whatever reason long forgotten the following men had connections to the parish, but are not on the war memorial. For some the connection is that Kirkmaiden has provided them with their final resting place and that the people of the parish raised a memorial to them and their lost comrades.

Pte. John Dempster Burns, 3055.
28th Battalion Australian Infantry Forces.
Killed in action 29th July 1916.

John was born in the parish of Kirkmaiden and went to school at Sandhead. He became a farmer, and was a member of the Ayr and Galloway Volunteers and was one of the buglers.

He emigrated to Australia and it was there he enlisted. After a period of training he embarked on Medic in January 1916. He was sent to the Western front.

John is commemorated on Villers-Bretonneux Memorial and on the Australian War Memorial. He is not on any memorial locally.

Rifleman John Caven, 12987.
2nd Battalion New Zealand Rifle Brigade.
Killed in action 15th June 1917

John was the son of John and Maggie Caven of 9 Lyle Street, Greenock. The couple and their son had at one stage been living in the parish of Kirkmaiden and placed the notice of their son's death in the local newspaper.

John had emigrated to Hastings, New Zealand where he enlisted. On 6th May 1916 he set sail for Suez, but just over a year later he was at the front in France. It was there he was killed and he is buried at Longuenesse Souvenir Cemetery, Pas de Calais, grave reference IV.C.30.

Gunner John Forbes, 47828. 19th Brigade Royal Field Artillery. Killed in action 3rd May 1915.

Born in 1868 in and raised in the parishes of Stoneykirk, and Kirkmaiden, John's sister was Maggie Murray who lived in Portlogan. Perhaps because he had been a professional soldier for twenty eight years, John Forbes service to his country was viewed differently, or it was simply omission that he was not named on either memorial at Kirkmaiden or Stoneykirk . He had served at the Indian Frontier and in the South African Campaign with the 14th Hussars and held two medals and five bars for his services.

He had been sent to the front on the outbreak of war and it was there he was killed. With no known grave, John is commemorated on Le Touret Memorial, Pas des Calais.

Pte. Carr Simpson, 26169. 10th Battalion Scottish Rifles (Cameronians). Died 3rd December 1919.

Carr was the third son of Robert and Elizabeth Simpson (nee Graham) of Damnaglaur. Born on 6th June 1897 at High Drummore, he was one of eight children that included three sets of twins. There were five boys and three girls but sadly two of his sisters died in their infancy. Carr had been a ploughman before the war and had a close friend in Agnes-Grace McGaw and had given her a gold signet ring as a sign of their friendship.

He enlisted on 20th January 1916 to the 10th Battalion of the Scottish Rifles (Cameronians). Carr was seriously injured and lost his arm in the war and he was honourably discharged from service on 10th October 1917. The wound would not heal and had become infected. At the site of the wound a malignant tumour developed and within seven months of this diagnosis he died at home at Damnaglaur. Two weeks before he died, he managed to come down the stairs to see the family wedding of his sister Jenny to James Cochrane.

Aged just 22 when he died, he is named on the family headstone in Kirkmaiden Old Churchyard. His brother, Morland Simpson remained friendly with Agnes-Grace and her sister Ina, and he knew that each year Agnes-Grace visited his grave on 11th November to lay poppies. She never married, and it was on 11th November 1972 that Agnes died aged 75. When Agnes-Grace died, her sister Ina passed the signet ring down to Carr's great niece, Kathryn Simpson. It is poignant that Agnes-Grace died on Remembrance Day.

The week after Carr's death, Rev. David Williamson wrote a poem which was published in the local newspaper:

EPITAPH TO A SOLDIER
(to the memory of Carr Simpson, Kirkmaiden)
Why do the radiant and the free
Die first in this dark world of ours;
Melt like a wave upon the sea
Or fade like fragile flowers?

No Nobler spirit e'er was laid
In reverence 'neath the hewn grass;
What nature so divinely made,
From memory cannot pass.

Rapt from the glory of our gaze,
The light still burns where he has been;
No sunset crowns our Autumn days
With beauty more serene!

It seems particularly sad that Carr is not included on the war memorial as he fought for his country and there is little doubt that he died as a result of his injuries. Whilst the minister was moved to write a poem to him, again one wonders what the criteria was for having his name placed on the Parish Memorial, it is likely the death would have to be within a certain time from armistice, although other parishes include those men who died as a result of injury. Although he is not on any local war memorial, or the SNWM, Carr is listed on the CWGC.

The village they left behind

The war was once again brought to the doorstep of those in the parish of Kirkmaiden on the 9th October 1917. A defensively armed steamship hoped to settle overnight in Luce Bay. It was close to the R.N.A.S. station where submarine scouting airships were patrolling the waters, and perhaps the crew of the vessel felt the area would be safe As darkness fell she was around one and a quarter miles East from Drummore. Lights of another vessel were seen approaching. Submarine UC-75 under the command of Johannes Lohs opened gunfire on the unprepared Main. The ship quickly sank with the loss of twelve lives. As daylight came local people did what they could to rescue survivors and recover the bodies. The Captain of the ship was found alive, though his own son was amongst those who died.

Being so close to the shore the vessel could be seen as a daily reminder to those living close by of the dangers of the war. When the ship was successfully salvaged, locals paid to see the damage that had been done. The money collected went towards a memorial which stands in Kirkmaiden Churchyard. The memorial also remembers those who were killed on the Rio Verde which was sunk around four months after the Main.

The Rio Verde was torpedoed by U-86 without any warning as she passed Crammag Head. A few of the men from the ship managed to reach Clanyard Bay. Twenty men lost their lives and five of those men are buried in Kirkmaiden Old Churchyard. A further grave, with no dates, is to an unknown sailor of the First World War.

There is very little information available on the men from the Merchant Navy, who served in the war. Perhaps because so many merchant vessels were being sunk and so many seamen killed, in some cases their details were scant or not recorded at all before the vessel set sail.

The inscription on the memorial reads:-

In memory of our gallant Merchant Seamen of the Steamers "Main" and "Rio Verde" who lost their lieves by enemy action in Luce Bay and at Crummag Head 1917. Erected by subscription from visitors boarding the salved steamer "Main" while at Drummore August 1920.

The cost of the burials of the five men who had been killed on the Rio Verde met with disapproval from the council. In a meeting shortly afterwards, the council agreed that the gravedigger and the undertaker had both charged the Admiralty excessively for the cost of burying the men. £6 10s had been charged for the digging of one grave for the five bodies, and £103 had been charged by the undertaker. This charge had included coffins for nine and the removal of four bodies to Stranraer. It was suggested to the council that 75 shillings for grave digging would have been sufficient, and they were informed that the undertaker, when requested had reduced their account by £17. In the end the council refused to pay the full amount to the gravedigger stating that 72s 6d was sufficient for the work done.

The names of the men who were buried there are:

Donkeyman. G Wallace.
Merchant Navy, SS Rio Verde.
Killed in action 21st February 1918.

Assist. Cook W. Arlow,
Merchant Navy, SS Rio Verde.
Killed in action 21st February 1918.

Seaman Walter Marsh,
Newfoundland R.N.R., SS Rio Verde.
Killed in action 21st February 1918.

Walter was in Newfoundland Royal Naval Reserve and was a gunner aboard the Rio Verde. He was the son of Arthur and Sarah Marsh, Dunfield, Trinity, Newfoundland.

Third Engineer W. Richardson,
Merchant Navy, SS Rio Verde,
Killed in action 21st February 1918.

Second Mate J.T. Buchanan,
Merchant Navy, SS Rio Verde,
Killed in action 21st February 1918.

A Sailor of the Great War. Known Unto God.

GLENLUCE WAR MEMORIAL (OLD LUCE)

The original site of Glenluce War Memorial

A plaque inside Glenluce Public Hall lists the names of those who served in the war, and for such a small village there are over 270 names. Those who died have their names marked with an 'X', however there are considerably fewer names marked with an 'X' than those on the large memorial in the centre of the village.

On the sunny Sunday afternoon of 8th May 1921, in a ceremony that began at 3.30pm, Glenluce War Memorial was unveiled by the Earl of Stair to a large crowd. The cenotaph style design was by James Miller of Glasgow. The 16 feet high Creetown Granite was sculpted by Mr W.R.MacKenzie from Newton Stewart, and featured a bronze laurel wreath near the top. Glenluce builder Mr Clive constructed it.

After a committee had discussed appropriate sites, the Earl of Stair was approached and he gifted the chosen spot, facing the Bay of Luce, on the South of the village, high on a grassy mound on the Stairhaven Road.

The ceremony was held at the memorial and conducted by Rev. A.T. Hill and R.Ingles. and after a fitting speech by the Earl of Stair, Col. Brown read out the full names, ranks and regiments of the fallen men.

The memorial now sits centrally in the village in Lady Stair Park. The inscriptions are on four panels around the base. The names are inscribed as last name and initial only. No ranks or regiments are listed. It reads:

First panel:

ERECTED TO THE MEMORY OF THE MEN CONNECTED WITH THE PARISH OF OLD LUCE WHO FELL IN THE GREAT WAR 1914- 1919.

Second panel:	Third panel:	Fourth panel:
J. ALEXANDER	B.M. HUNTER. M.B. CH.B.	T. McCRACKEN
A. AIRD	J. HERON	D. McCULLOCH
J. ADAIR	J. JARDINE	W. McCULLOCH
J. BELL	A. KENNEDY	D. McCULLOCH
E .BLUNN	T. KERR	H. McGARVA
S.CAMPBELL	D. LAIDLAW	W. McGARVA
J. CAMPBELL	J. LAVERIE	T. McGILL
R. CLANACHAN	J. LYNCH	A. McHARRIE
A. CLANACHAN	J. LYON	A. McLELLAN
W. CLIVE	J. MACKIE	A. PARKER
R. CROSBIE	A. MILROY	J. PARKER
W.DORANS	W.R. MILROY	J. RALSTON
H. DOUGAN	G. MURRAY	J. REID
R. FLEMING	A. McCAIG	W. TEMPLETON
J. FULTON	P. McCLYMONT	W. WATSON
A. GRAHAM	G. McCREADIE	R.F. WILSON
W. GRAHAM	J. McCREADIE	J.F. WILSON
R.J. HARVEY	J. McCRORIE	

Pte. James Alexander, 36918. 9th Battalion Cameronians (Scottish Rifles). Killed in action 30th September 1918.

James was the eldest son Mr and Mrs William Alexander of Airyhemming. His parents William and Jemima were later to move to South Boreland, Dunragit. His brother Thomas had died in infancy and his sister Jeanie had died aged 12.

Before the war James had worked for some time at United Creameries in Dunragit. James enlisted on 8th August 1917 and was posted to France on 8th April 1918.

James is commemorated along with 35,000 other names of men with no known grave on the Tyne Cot Memorial, Belgium. He is also named on the family headstone in Glenluce Cemetery.

Pte. Andrew Aird, 5836. 1st Battalion Cameron Highlanders. Killed in action 24th October 1914.

Andrew Aird was first reported as missing on 24th October 1914. He was a familiar face with all in Glenluce as he was the local postman there. He lived in the village with his wife Sarah and three children. Andrew's parents were John and Grace Aird who lived in Sorbie.

Andrew was 35 when he was killed and is commemorated on the Ypres (Menin Gate) Memorial to the missing, Ieper, Belgium.

Pte. John Adair, 111051. Royal Army Medical Corps. Died 27th October 1917.

A son of Mrs Mary Lawrie, John lived in Church Street Glenluce. He died at the Military Isolation Hospital, Aldershot.

John's body was returned to Glenluce for burial and the funeral took place on Thursday 1st November 1917 at Glenluce Cemetery where he is buried. John is also named on the plaque inside Glenluce Public Hall.

Pte. James A. Bell, 16811.
7th Battalion Royal Scots Fusiliers.
Killed in action 26th September 1915.

James Bell had been in the employ of the Earl of Stair as a gardener at Lochinch Gardens for some years. Later he moved a promoted post as foreman gardener with Colonel Buchanan, Drumpelier, Coatbridge.

His brother John Bell of Dunragit received notice that James had been injured then missing at the Battle of Loos. His family inserted the following poem with his death notice in the local newspaper. With no known grave, he is commemorated on Loos Memorial.

Resting from all sin and sorrow,
Resting from fatigue and pain,
Faithfully he fought his battle,
Death to such is endless gain.
Anchored by love, death cannot sever;
Sadly we miss him, and will for ever;
Some day, some time, we shall see,
The dear face we now hold in memory.

Gunner Edwin Blunn, 200069.
1st Battalion Tank Corps.
Died from wounds 29th September 1918.

Edwin was married to Peggy Saunders and they lived in Main Street, Glenluce. His mother lived in Manchester.

During the war the village of Tincourt became the centre for a casualty clearing station. It was to Tincourt Edwin was taken with wounds from battle. He did not recover and is buried in the cemetery at Tincourt, Somme, grave reference V.J.35.

Pte. Sam Campbell, 285379.
1st/5th Battalion Royal Scots Fusiliers.
Died from wounds 12th January 1916.

Sam was one of three sons of Mr and Mrs James Campbell of Main Street, Glenluce all serving in the armed forces. He had been a coachman at Patna in Ayrshire before he enlisted in December 1914.

Sam was 22 years old and had been in heavy fighting in July 1915 in the Dardanelles and fought alongside one of his brothers as they had both become bomb throwers. He was wounded on the 30th December at Gallipoli and died in Malta of the wounds he received. He is buried at Pieta Military Cemetery, Malta. Sam is named on the memorial inside Glenluce Hall.

Sam's brother John was also reported as having died from his wounds on the 9th May 1917, by which time his parents had moved to Kilbirnie. Before the war John, like many other locals, had moved to work for the Glasgow Corporation on the Tramways. He had been a conductor there.

John had been seriously wounded in five places the previous summer and had been invalided home. On his recovery he had been sent once more to the Western front. However at that time John was reported to be serving in the Royal Scots, it is unlikely therefore, that Samuel's brother is the man named on the war memorial. It is possible that there was a mistake in reporting John's death as he is not listed with the CWGC or SNWM as having died on the date given.

Pte. John Campbell, S/2934.
8th Battalion Seaforth Highlanders.
Killed in action 25th April 1917.

John was born in Glenluce, the son of John and Mary Campbell. His parents later moved to Stirling. He was 25 and was married to Dorothy Campbell when he was killed.

John is buried at Guemappe British Cemetery, Wancourt, grave reference I.D.23. He is also named on the memorial inside Glenluce Hall.

Corp. Robert Clanachan, M2/205104.
880th Military Transport Coy., Army Service Corps.
Died 19th October 1918.

Robert was the youngest son of Alexander Clanachan of Church Street, Glenluce. He had two sisters Jeanie and Maggie as well as his brother Alexander, named below. He had been on active service for three years.

The influenza virus of 1918 took many lives. Robert died of pneumonia at the Salonika front, Serbia. The majority of those in Skopje Military Cemetery did not die in battle but from the influenza virus and Robert is buried there. His brother mentioned below was killed in action. Both brothers are also named on the family headstone in Glenluce Cemetery.

Pte. Alexander Clanachan, 123128.
58th Battalion Canadian Infantry.
Killed in action 17th September 1916.

Brother to the above Robert Clanachan, Alexander was born in Church Street, Glenluce on 24th May 1886. Alexander emigrated to Canada and it was there he enlisted on 8th September 1915. He had dark hair, hazel eyes and a dark complexion and was 5 feet 6 inches tall.

Alexander is commemorated on the Vimy Memorial which stands in grounds containing restored trenches and tunnels. He is also named on the family headstone in Glenluce Cemetery.

Pte. William Clive, 193548.
13th Battalion Canadian Force.
Died from wounds 10th October 1916.

William was the youngest son of the late Mr and Mrs David Clive of Kilfillan, Glenluce. His sister was Mrs Turley, Knockeen, Barr. William had a number of sisters and brothers, nephews and nieces who all died very young. He had emigrated to Canada around 1907.

William joined the Quebec regiment on 3rd March 1916. He had a dark complexion, dark hair and grey eyes. He was five feet seven and a half inches tall.

Contay British Cemetery was chosen as a burial ground for casualties from the 49th Casualty Clearing Station and it is there William, who was 36, is buried. He is also named on the family headstone in Glenluce Cemetery.

Pte Robert H. Crosbie, 295424.
12th Battalion Royal Scots Fusiliers.
Died 26th November 1917.

Prior to the war Robert worked at United Creameries Dunragit and would have known James Alexander listed above very well. Robert's mother lived in Main Street Glenluce.

The General Hospital Cairo was where sick and injured men were sent for treatment from Egypt and Gallipoli. Aged 22, Robert became ill and died there from dysentery. He is buried in Cairo War Memorial Cemetery, grave reference O.30. Robert is named on the memorial inside Glenluce Hall.

Corp William Dorans, 6954.
1st Battalion Royal Scots Fusiliers.
Killed in action 13th November 1914.

William Dorans was a reservist who was called up immediately on the outbreak of war. He had worked for Mr Fraser of Craigenholly and lived there with his wife and two children. William was the eldest son of Mr and Mrs Dorans of Larbrax. When his father died, his mother married Mr Hugh Fraser on 1st January 1915.

William had two brothers, Kenneth and Samuel and they were both serving in the army at the same time. Kenneth was in the 1st/5th K.O.S.B., and had been a ploughman at Balgreggan before the war. Samuel was in the Ayrshire Yeomanry and had been working on Cairngarroch Farm before the war – where his future stepfather was the farmer at the time.

William is commemorated on the Menin Gate Memorial to the missing, panel 19 and 33. His name is also on Leswalt Memorial.

Lance Corp Henry Dougan, 9070. 2nd Battalion King's Own Scottish Borderers. Killed in action 30th June 1915.

Henry (Harry) joined the local regiment of the army in 1905 and on the outbreak of war was sent to India. He was given leave in January 1915 but returned to France in April. He was a tailor who had learned his trade with Mr Straiton of Glenluce. He was known as Harry.

On his death the following letter was received from Belgium by Mrs Freeman of 81 Sheuchan Street, Stranraer.

> *"I am requested to convey the sincere sympathy of Lance Corporal Dougan's comrades in C Company in your recent sad bereavement. A sniper in the German trenches was proving himself a nuisance, and, in attempting to dislodge him, Lance Corporal Dougan was hit from an unexpected quarter. He was rendered unconscious immediately and never recovered, his death occurring ten minutes later. He is buried beside others of his own Corps, who have died performing the same duty. Every Briton knows what that is without my attempting to enlarge upon it. – A. Murray Coy. Serg.-Major, C Coy., KOSB."*

Although the above letter refers to Henry being buried amongst comrades, the CWGC does not list a known grave for Henry. He is commemorated on the Menin Gate Memorial, and he is also named on the plaque inside Glenluce Public Hall.

Pte. Robert Fleming, 40814. 1st Battalion Royal Scots Fusiliers. Killed in action 13th November 1916.

Robert worked alongside James Alexander and Robert Crosbie named above at United Creameries at Dunragit. He lived with his mother at Creamery Cottages, Dunragit, his father James had died some time previously. Mrs Fleming received notice that Robert was missing .

Robert had joined the army early in 1916. He was 26 when he was killed in action at Beaumont Hamel. He is commemorated on the Thiepval Memorial and the memorial inside Glenluce Public Hall. Robert is named on the family headstone in Glenluce cemetery where his date of death is recorded as 15th November 1916.

A number of local men who were killed in the war had worked at United Creameries, Dunragit.

Pte. John Fulton, 128.
12th Battalion Argyll and Sutherland Highlanders.
Killed in action 19th September 1918.

John was the son of John and Fanny Fulton of Low Airyolland, New Luce. He died in Greece and was buried in Karasouli Military Cemetery near the town of Polikastro.

James Fulton from East Boreland may have been a relative of the above John, possibly a brother, or cousin, he was injured in 1916 and sent to Perth Royal Infirmary to recover, on his return to the front he was taken prisoner of war in 1918.

Pte. Alexander Graham,
1st/5th Royal Scots Fusiliers.
Killed in action 1st October 1918.

Before the war Alexander had worked for more than five years at Barnsallie, Glenluce for Mr John Fisher. His father Mr William Graham lived at Cairnhandy, Ardwell. Alexander's eldest brother John had emigrated to Australia and he enlisted there, he had not been heard from since the first Australian landings at Gallipoli and was feared killed or drowned.

Alexander had enlisted in July 1915 and spent over two years in Egypt. He had been allowed a brief leave home before being sent to France. His father received news his 24 year old son was missing before it was officially confirmed that he had been killed. Alexander is commemorated on the Vis-En-Artois Memorial, France. He is also named on Stoneykirk Memorial, Sandhead, and the family headstone in Stoneykirk Churchyard.

Pte. William Graham, 240873.
1st/5th Battalion Royal Scots Fusiliers.
Died of 30th June 1918.

William was born in Glenluce and had lived there all his life until he enlisted at Stranraer.

William most likely died at one of the hospitals near to where he is buried. It is not known if he died from wounds or of illness. He is buried in Terlincthun British Cemetery, Pas de Calais, grave reference I.C.20.

R. J. Harvey, unknown service or date of death.

It is always possible that this man was known by his middle name, and I would speculate that with the possibility this name was James, he could be the man buried in the Glebe Cemetery, Stranraer. That particular James Harvey has a military headstone, and is not named on any other local memorial.

There were not that many men with the name Harvey and the initial 'R' killed in the war, but none of their remaining records give a clear link to Glenluce. There were a number of local men born in the parish of Leswalt,

Inch and Stranraer all with the same first initial, who would have been of age to serve in the war, and this man is almost certainly one of those men.

Interestingly this man's name was missed out from the unveiling ceremony record, and whether that meant that the local newspaper missed it out, or if it was missed from being read out at the ceremony we may never know. More information may be discovered about him once the 1911 census is published.

Capt. Bentley Moore Hunter, Royal Army Medical Corps, attd. to 1st Battalion Cambridgeshire Regiment. Killed in action 31st July 1917.

Born in Glenluce to Charles and Susan Hunter on 28th April 1888. Bentley attended Stranraer High School then went on to Glasgow University to study medicine. He apparently passed all his exams very easily and won prizes in Opthamology and Clinical Medicine. He gained his degree in medicine and a Master's degree in surgery, graduating in 1909.

After gaining a commission in 1915 he was sent to the Greek Islands, Egypt, France and then Belgium. His commanding officer sent the following message to his family:

"Your son was killed trying to save the lives of others, as he has done so many times before. I, fortunately, had the satisfaction of telling him some few days before that I had recommended him for some sort of award."

His Chaplain also sent the following message:

"His staff say they will never have another like him. He was so generous-minded and willing to help others. I shall never forget the way he carried on down south when the other medical officer was killed. He was simply splendid."

With no known grave he is commemorated on the Menin Gate.

Company Quartermaster Serg. John Heron, 43rd Battalion Canadian Infantry. Killed in action 8th October 1916.

Born in Glenluce on 11th July 1886, John was a carpenter before the war and had served his apprenticeship with Mr Sloss of Stranraer. He had also spent 3 years with the RGA before emigrating to Canada around 1911. It was there he joined up in December 1914 and was sent over to England in June 1915. He was married to Janet Parker and had two small children who were living in the Barracks at Glenluce, having come over from Canada.

John was 5 feet 11 inches tall with a fair complexion, blue eyes and grey hair. He was 28 when he enlisted. He was sent on to France in February 1916 and came through very heavy fighting at the front. He is commemorated on Vimy Memorial and is named on his wife's family headstone in Glenluce Cemetery.

Lance Corporal John Jardine, 372340. 8th Battalion London Regiment (Post Office Rifles). Killed in action 9th June 1917.

John was called after his father who farmed at Culquhasen. John had two sisters Lizzie and Mary. When his father died his uncle stayed on at the farm. His mother later moved to Sea View, Glenluce.

John was 35 when he was killed and he is buried at Mendinghem Military Cemetery which was formed at Proven where there was a casualty clearing station. John is also named on the family headstone in Glenluce Cemetery, as well as the memorial plaque in Glenluce Public Hall.

Pte. Kennedy Ambrose, PO/9978 (S). 1st Battalion Royal Marine Light Infantry. Killed in action 13th November 1916.

Kennedy was the son of Mary Gill (formerly Ambrose) and stepson of William Gill. He was born in Glenluce and lived there until he enlisted. It is more than likely in some records this man had his surname and forename turned around the opposite way in error.

Kennedy died aged 21. He is buried at Ancre British Cemetery, Beaumont Hamel, grave reference IV.E.37. His death and photograph were in the local newspaper, and his name was read out at the unveiling ceremony, as Kennedy Ambrose. The name is unlikely to be another man. His name is written as Kennedy Ambrose on the plaque inside Glenluce Memorial Hall.

Lance-Corp. Thomas Wingate Kerr, 6th/7th Battalion Royal Scots Fusiliers. Died from wounds 7th September 1917.

Grandson of Mr Wingate Parr of Balcarry, Glenluce, and brother of Nellie Kerr, Main Street, Glenluce, Thomas had been a railway porter at Glenluce Station prior to the outbreak of war. He would have worked alongside George Murray named below.

Known as Tom, he had a gunshot wound to the chest whilst fighting in France and he was removed to 7th Canadian General Hospital, Etaples. He developed tetanus as a result of the gunshot wound and died. He was 23 years old. His sister received word that he had died on the 3rd September, but CWGC records this as 7th September. He is buried in Etaples Military Cemetery, grave reference XXV.P.13, and named on the plaque inside Glenluce Public Hall.

Pte. Duncan Laidlaw, 202993.
7th Battalion Cameron Highlanders.
Killed in action 3rd August 1917.

Prior to the war Duncan worked as a painter in Ayr with Messrs Bennett & Co. He was the son of Alexander and Helen Laidlaw (nee Thompson), Church Street, Glenluce, later of Vicarhill. Duncan had a sister, Agnes.

Duncan had undergone eight months of training after he enlisted, then he was sent home for a brief furlough in June 1917 before being posted to France. His parents had received word that he had gone missing some time between 31st July and 3rd August on the Western Front. He had barely been in France for a month before being killed.

Duncan is commemorated on the Menin Gate Memorial. He is also named on the family headstone in Glenluce Cemetery, as well as the memorial inside Glenluce Public Hall.

Pte. John Laverie,59513.
25th Battalion Northumberland Fusiliers.
Died 26th April 1918.

John was born in Glenluce, he was the son of David and Margaret Laverie of Glenburnie Cottage, Glenluce. His father was a foreman quarryman, and his eldest brother James was also a quarryman. In the 1901 census he was listed as being the youngest of seven children who all grew up in Glenburnie Cottage. He Died aged 23.

It is likely that John was a cousin of John Lavery from Minnigaff who was also killed in the war, and is named on the war memorial there. Although the spelling is different with the CWGC, it is spelt Laverie on the census and other records, and there were only two families in Wigtownshire with that surname at the time.

John is commemorated on Tyne Cot Memorial panel 19 to 23 and 162.

Pte. James Lynch, 26686.
1st/7th Battalion Duke of Wellington's.
Died from wounds 11th April 1918.

Son of Robert and Elizabeth Lynch (nee McFadzean), of Chippermore, Portwilliam and later Glenluce. James was 28 years old when he was killed. His mother had died when he was just six years old. He had at least two sisters, Maggie and Jeanie, and a brother, William. Jeanie had died in 1910. Two more Lynch names are listed alongside his on the memorial plaque inside Glenluce Public Hall and it is possible they were other brothers.

James had initially been in the King's Own Scottish Borderers but had been transferred. His father inserted the following poem in the local paper on his death:

His warfare o'er, his battle fought,
His victory won, though dearly bought,
His heart was good, his spirit brave,
His resting place a soldiers grave.

James is buried in La Kreule Military Cemetery, Hazebrouck, grave reference I.A.35A. He is named on the family headstone in Glenluce Cemetery.

Pte. James Lyon, 51036.
13th Battalion Royal Scots.
Killed in action 28th March 1918.

James was the eldest son of John and Margaret Howat Lyon of Glenluce Schoolhouse. As was so often the case he was reported missing first to his parents before it was later confirmed that he had died on that date. James was 19 years old. He is commemorated on Arras Memorial, bay 1 and 2, and is named on the memorial plaque inside Glenluce Public Hall.

Lance Sergeant John Mackey, 1st/9th Battalion London Regiment. Killed in action 14th April 1917.

John was a son of James and Helen Mackey (nee Digney). His sisters were Elizabeth and Mary and he had a brother James who had died when he was four. The family lived in Church Street, Glenluce. John was 27 when he was killed. His family inserted the following poem into the local newspaper:

Nameless his grave on a battlefield gory,
Only a cross o'er a mound of brown earth;
Died in the pride of his youth and his glory,
Far from his friends and the land of his birth.
No loved one stood around him
To bid a last farewell:
No word of comfort could he leave
To those he loved so well.
We little thought his time so short
In this world to remain,
Or thought when from his home he went
He would ne'er return again.

John is named on the family headstone in Glenluce Cemetery and he is commemorated on Arras Memorial, bay 10. His name is spelt Mackey on the CWGC as well as the family headstone. This could mean the man on the memorial is a different man, but it would then also mean that this man was missed off the memorial, and that would be more unlikely as he lived his life in Glenluce before the war.

Lance Corp. Andrew Matthew Milroy, 66093.
5th Coy. Canadian Machine Gun Corps.
Killed in action 17th September 1916.

Andrew was a son of James and Jemima Milroy (nee Hamilton). He was born on 22nd April 1885 in Glenluce. He registered his trade as a travelling salesman. He had emigrated to Canada along with thousands of Scots not long after the turn of the century, hoping for a new life in Canada.

In 1915 he enlisted in Canada, recording his mothers address as Millisle Dairy, Garlieston. His father had died at Over Airies in 1911.

Andrew was a striking figure of 6 feet tall with a clear complexion, blue eyes and fair hair. He had a scar on the base of his left thumb.

He is commemorated on Vimy Memorial and is named on the family headstone in Glenluce Cemetery, as well as the memorial plaque inside Glenluce Public Hall.

Gunner William Robert Milroy, 109390.
119th Brigade Royal Field Artillery.
Killed in action 18th April 1918.

William was the adopted son of Mr and Mrs Costley of Fineview, Glenluce. His parents had also received word that his brother, A. Milroy who was serving with the Egyptian Expeditionary force was admitted to 24th Stationary Hospital, Kantara on 25th April 1917.

The 54th Casualty Clearing Station was based in the town of Aire, and it was there William died. He is buried in Aire Communal Cemetery, grave reference II.D.19

Pte. George Murray, 202557.
16th Battalion Royal Scots.
Killed in action 22nd October 1917.

George was the son of David and Jeanie Murray (nee McNally), Main Street Glenluce. Before the war he had worked with the Portpatrick and Wigtownshire Joint Railway as a porter at Glenluce Station. He would have worked alongside Thomas Wingate Kerr who is named above.

George had already lost two brothers who died in childhood. Another brother James, died as a result of an accident.20 years old when he was killed, George is commemorated on Tyne Cot Memorial and he is named on the family headstone in Glenluce.

Note: Although only one A.McCaig is named on the war memorial, there were two men with the same initial and last name whose names were read out at the unveiling ceremony, and two who are named as having died on the plaque in Glenluce Public Hall.

Sergeant Alexander McCaig, 17169.
15th Battalion Royal Scots.
Killed in action 9th April 1917.

Born in 1892 to Hugh and Robina McCaig (nee McLeod). Alexander had a sister, Jane, who died in infancy and two brothers William and James. Another brother, Robert died aged 21 in 1925. Alick was in his 24th year.

Alexander is buried in Bailleul Road West Cemetery, grave reference A.10. He is also named on the family headstone in Glenluce cemetery, and is named on the memorial plaque inside Glenluce Public Hall.

Pte. Andrew James McCaig,
44th Battalion Canadian Infantry.
Killed in action 4th September 1918.

Born in Glenluce in 1891, Andrew was the second son of Mr A McCaig, Inspector of the Poor House, Glenluce. Andrew had emigrated to Canada in the hope of a new life, and it was there he enlisted. He had been a clerk by trade.

Andrew listed his Aunt Helen Carson from Glenluce as his next of kin. The detailed Canadian records record that he was 5 feet 6 inches tall with a fair complexion, blue eyes, and was balding with brown hair.

At the unveiling ceremony the name of Private Carson McCaig of the Canadians was also read out, he is likely to have been a brother or a cousin of Andrew, however he is not listed on the Canadian archives, CWGC or SNWM under the name Carson and is not named on Glenluce Memorial.

Andrew is commemorated on Vimy Memorial, he is also named on the memorial plaque inside Glenluce Public Hall.

Pte. Peter McClymont, 31492.
15th Battalion Royal Scots.
Killed in action 28th April 1917.

Peter was one of five brothers all on active service during the war. His parents were from East Boreland, Glenluce.

Peter's brother William, was in the Royal Scots Fusiliers. He was wounded and hospitalised at No 24 Stationary Hospital, Kantara. Pte. A. Milroy from Glenluce, brother of William Milroy listed above would have been in the same hospital at the same time. The men were miles from home, and from a very small village, yet fate mean meant they met in hospital.

At around the same date of Peter's death, one of his other brothers, John, serving with the Highland Light Infantry was admitted to hospital with trench fever, a condition caused by the bites and excretions of body lice, and very common in the trenches.

Peter was married and lived with his wife at Balcraig Moor, Portwilliam. His wife first received word that he was missing before being notified in June that he had been killed on the date of being reported missing.

Peter is buried at Lievin Communal Cemetery Extension, grave reference V.B.2.

Pte. George McCreadie, 432611.
49th Battalion Canadian Infantry.
Killed in action 9th October 1916.

George was born on 13th May 1886 and was the son of Andrew Ross McCreadie and Jeanie McCreadie of High Main Street, Glenluce. He worked as a labourer when he emigrated to Canada. He enlisted in January 1915 and was described as 5 Feet 8 inches tall, with a fair complexion, brown hair and brown eyes.

George married Annie McGarva on his return from Canada on 21st July 1915 at Glenjorrie Cottage, Glenluce. The witnesses were Henry Milroy and Jean McGarva. Their honeymoon was short as George was sent to the front. He is buried at Courcelette British Cemetery, grave reference X.A.6.

Pte. James McCredie, 24657.
6th Battalion Kings Own Scottish Borderers.
Killed in action 3rd May 1917.

James was the son of John McCredie of 31 North Main Street, Wigtown. Before the war his painter and decorator business was doing very well. He was married to Catherine and they lived at Panmure Villa, Glenluce. James helped to run the Glenluce company of the Boys Brigade and sang in the church choir.

On the same date that James was killed his brother had been returned to Scotland for hospital treatment. James is commemorated on Arras memorial bay 6. James was 37. He is also named on the memorial plaque inside Glenluce Public Hall, where his name is spelt McCreadie.

The name is spelt McCredie on the CWGC and SNWM, and while this could mean the wrong man is listed here, James McCredie is not on the war memorial at Wigtown which is the likely alternative place. There was a John McCreadie of Portwilliam, who was killed in the war in 1917, though I was unable to find any connections he had with Glenluce - that John McCreadie is named on the war memorial in Garlieston.

Pte. James McCrorie, 271200.
16th Battalion Royal Scots.
Killed in action 16th April 1918.

James was born on 1st June 1889 in Auchentibbert in the parish of Stoneykirk to Robert and Margaret McCrorie. James married Mary McLelland on 27th February 1911 at Leswalt Manse. Peter McClymont and Bessie McCrorie were witnesses. Mary was a domestic servant at Mid Knockglass and James was a farm servant at Galdenoch Smithy, Leswalt. They were later to move to West Challoch, Dunragit. He joined the 16th Battalion Ayrshire Yeomanry before becoming a member of the Royal Scots.

Initially James was reported missing on the 9th April, then his family were informed he had been killed on that date, but the CWGC lists his date of death as 16th April 1918. He is commemorated on the Plogesteert Memorial in Belgium, panel 1, which contains the names of more than 11,000 men with no known grave.

Pte. Thomas McCracken, 100182.
10th Battalion Canadian Infantry.
Killed in action 11th November 1917.

Born on 22nd February 1887 in Portpatrick, Thomas was one of four sons of Mrs McCracken of Kilfillan, Glenluce, who were all serving in the armed forces at the same time. His father, John, had died at Lagganmore in 1908. His sister Margaret had been unwell with what was thought to be some sort of heart disease for a number of months and had died in 1905 aged 26. His brother Andrew also seems to have developed heart disease and died in 1911. It is likely that all the remaining brothers who enlisted thought they would be paid and fed well and have a better future than the bleak outlook of staying at home.

Thomas had emigrated to Canada and was an engineer by trade. When he enlisted there in July 1915 he had no other experience of serving in the armed forces. He was 5 feet 4 inches with a clear skin, light brown hair, and blue eyes. Under distinguishing marks it was recorded that he had a mole in the front of his right thigh.

His brothers were John, who had enlisted in the Royal Scots Fusiliers. John was a member of the old volunteer RGA and had received an efficiency medal for 16 years service. James had been on Government service since the beginning of the war and Charles, who had joined the Royal Naval Reserve.

Armistice was called a year to the day from Thomas' death. He is commemorated on the Menin Gate Memorial, panels 24-28-30. Thomas is named on the family headstone in Portpatrick Cemetery.

From the left: Thomas McCracken and his brothers who survived the war, Charles, James and John McCracken.

Chief Stoker William McCulloch, Royal Navy HMS Albacore. Killed in Action 9th March 1917.

Born on the 27th September 1874 in the parish of Stoneykirk. William was a son of James and Mary Heron McCulloch of Dunragit Home Farm and Stoneykirk. He was married to Annie Wallace, Enoch, Portpatrick. When William joined the navy he had brown hair, grey eyes, a fresh complexion, a burn scar on his head and another scar on his lower jaw. These scars would be frequent hazards of the job. He was 5 feet 7 inches tall. He served on a few different ships and during the war he was paid an additional gratuity. William was one of three brothers all on active service at the same time. The local newspaper later suggests a fourth son was also serving.

Though the CWGC lists his age as 33 when he was killed it also spells his name McCullock, it is spelt correctly on his naval records. William joined the Royal Navy aged 21 and had served at sea for 21 years until his death. He had served in the Battle of Jutland.

HMS Albacore suffered an explosion on the 9th March 1917 though the cause was not identified at the time, she may have hit a mine. William's wife received the following letter:

"I deeply regret to have to inform you that telegraphic information has reached this department to the effect that William McCulloch, chief stoker, belonging to HMS Albacore, was killed yesterday (9th March), when that vessel was damaged by explosion."

William is also on the Portpatrick War Memorial as well as the plaque inside Glenluce Public Hall. His brother David is named below.

Stoker, 1st Class David McCulloch, Royal Navy HMS Victory. Died 20th June 1916.

Brother of the above William McCulloch. David had also fought at the Battle of Jutland. HMS Victory has confusingly been used by the Royal

Navy as the name for their barracks in Portsmouth as well as for several ships including that of Lord Nelson. Nelson's ship was used as training and accommodation for naval ratings.

Spelt McCullock on Royal Navy records David was born on 25th September 1881 in Stranraer. He served on board a number of ships from including Victory, Dreadnought, Prince George, and Prince of Wales.

He had a period of illness in 1914, then little is mentioned again until he appears to have been taken to Chatham Hospital in February 1917. His notes simply say 'invalid' as reason for discharge. Whatever illness he had, he did not recover. He had been in the navy for 15years. His body was returned home and he is buried in Glenluce Cemetery. When his name was read out at the unveiling, the ship he was recorded as serving on was HMS Dreadnought. David is named on the plaque inside Glenluce Public Hall.

David McCulloch who died and his brother Robert who survived.
Robert was a dairyman in Ayrshire before the war

Pte. David McCulloch, 29393. Duke of Cornwall's Light Infantry. Killed in action 31st August 1918.

Born on the 17th March 1896 at Blackhill, Glenluce, David was the youngest son of William and Maggie McCulloch. David had been on active service since March 1916. He had another brother who was serving in the American Army. He originally enlisted in the Motor Transport Coy., but was later transferred to the Duke of Cornwall's Light Infantry.

Aged 22 when he was killed, David is commemorated on the Vis-En-Artois Memorial, panel 6. He is also named on the plaque inside Glenluce Public Hall.

Pte. Thomas Henry McGarva, 235128.
10th Battalion, Cameronians.
Killed in action 21st July 1917.

At the unveiling ceremony for Glenluce War Memorial Thomas Henry was referred to as Harry as this was the name his friends knew him by. His initial is also on the war memorial as 'H' and on the memorial plaque in Glenluce Public Hall.

Harry lied about his age, enlisting when he was barely 15 years old. The local newspaper reported his regiment as being the KOSB, but the CWGC records it as the Cameronians, and he perhaps was transferred. His parents were Robert and Catherine McGarva who were living at the British Consulate, Las Palmas. Harry spent five years of his short life growing up in Glenluce, and went to school at Glenluce Academy. His brother was 2 years older than him and the pair boarded with the McNally family at 1 Glenview, Glenluce. He was seen as a favourite by his schoolmates and teachers alike.

With no known grave, Harry is commemorated on Panel 22 of the Menin Gate Memorial.

Pte. William McGarva, S/17079.
6th Battalion Gordon Highlanders.
Killed in action 11th April 1918.

William was born in Glenluce, though by 1911 his name is not on the census and he is likely to have moved away, in the small village it is also more than likely that he was related to the above named Harry. William was the son of Robert McGarva of Tradunnock, Kilkerran, Maybole. He was 21 when he was killed and he has no known grave he is commemorated on Loos Memorial panel 115 to 119.

Pte. Tom McGill, 6544.
16th Battalion Australian Infantry.
Died of wounds 20th August 1917.

Tom was the second son of Mr and Mrs James McGill. One of three brothers all serving with the Australian Imperial Forces. They were grandsons of the late John Bell of Glenwhilly. The Bells of Glenwhilly also lost another grandson, George Bell who was killed at Gallipoli. The family had previously lived at the Changue, Portwilliam, but had emigrated to Perth in Western Australia, when Tom was around 20. He was a farmer to trade.

Tom enlisted in April 1916 and was sent to England aboard the troop transport ship Suffolk, in October that year. The battalion undertook more training before being sent to the front in February 1917. In April Tom was wounded in the arm by gunshot at Bullecourt and returned to England to recover. His younger brother had been discharged home to Australia due to ill health and his other brother had been wounded and was in hospital in France. Tom had barely returned to the front from his previous injury when he was wounded once again. Tom died of his wounds at 2nd Casualty Clearing Station and is buried at Trois-Abres Cemetery, Steenwerck, grave reference I.Z.31.

Gunner Alexander McHarrie, 16742.
115th Siege Battery Royal Garrison Artillery.
Killed in action 25th October 1917.

Alexander was the son of John and Susan McHarrie (nee McWilliam). His brothers and sisters were Isaac, John, Mary, Elizabeth, James, Jessie and Susan.

Like a number of his siblings he had been in Canada, but returned home immediately on the outbreak of war to enlist. His sister Mary was living in Church Street, Glenluce and she was listed as his next of kin. More than a few members of the family seem to have emigrated to Canada.

Alexander was 38 when he was killed. He is buried in Bard Cottage Cemetery, Belgium, grave reference VI.A.35. He is also named on the family headstone in Glenluce Cemetery as well as the memorial inside Glenluce Public Hall.

Pte. Andrew McLellan, 996.
2nd Battalion Argyll and Sutherland Highlanders.
Killed in action 21st October 1914.

Andrew was the son of John and Grace McLellan of North Street, Glenluce.

He was killed in the fighting at Les Maisnil on 21st October where the 2nd Battalion Argyll and Sutherland were fighting alongside the 1st Middlesex, but they were outnumbered and forced to retreat. German soldiers buried the British dead the following day.

The graves of those men included Andrew and they were brought into Le Trou Aid Post Cemetery, France, grave reference K.21.

Gunner Alexander Parker, 133831.
148th Brigade Royal Field Artillery.
Killed in action 7th October 1916.

Alexander was one of four sons of Alexander and Jane (Jeanie) Parker (nee Clanachan), Station Cottages, Dunragit on active service in the war. Another brother, George, had died in infancy, and there were also three sisters. Before the war Alexander had worked alongside his brother William at Dunragit Creamery.

Alexander died aged 23, from wounds received in battle. He is buried at Longueval Road Cemetery, Somme, grave reference A.11. He is also named on the family headstone in Glenluce Cemetery. He is likely to have been a cousin of the below named James Parker.

Above, brothers of Alexander Parker. Left to right: James served with the Royal Scots and had worked with Mr Jack Orchard. John served with the Highland Light infantry and had been a gardener at Dunragit Gardens, he was taken as a prisoner of war. William was a Lance-Corp with the Royal Scots and had worked with Alexander at Dunragit Creamery.

Pte. James Parker, 2614.
1st/5th Battalion Kings Own Scottish Borderers.
Killed in action 12th July 1915.

James' wife was told he had been missing since the date of the final charge at Achi Baba, which was unsuccessful and saw thousands of casualties. He enlisted in October 1914 and sent to the Dardanelles. James was in the same Corps as his brother, they had enlisted together. They both volunteered as bomb throwers on the day of the push. One took the right side of the river the other the left. Their father, Thomas Parker, who was a fisherman at Glenluce, received a letter from his other son, John, who had been injured and was in St. George's Military Hospital in Malta. He had not seen his brother since the 12th July. James is commemorated on Helles Memorial and he is named on the memorial inside Glenluce Public Hall. He is likely to have been a cousin of the above named Alexander Parker.

John Parker who was injured and his brother James who was killed.

Pte. James Ralston, 20577.
1st Battalion Royal Scots Fusiliers.
Killed in action 28th March 1918.

James was the eldest son of James and Sarah Ralston (nee Murray), of Mains of Park, Glenluce. Aged only 20 he was reported to his mother as being missing, It was June 1920 before she was told he was presumed to be dead and his intimation was placed in the local newspaper. With no known grave he is commemorated on Arras Memorial.

Gunner James Reid, 655297.
172nd Bde, Royal Field Artillery.
Killed in action 2nd June 1917.

Before the war James had worked at Rowallan Creamery in Kilmarnock. His parents lived at the Boreland, Glenluce. He enlisted on the outbreak of war.

Whilst serving in Belgium, he was killed. Letters from his Major and an NCO were sent to his family assuring them his death was instantaneous having been hit by a shell. They also expressed their sympathy. James is buried at Kemmel Chateau Military Cemetery, grave reference J.56., he is also named on the memorial plaque inside Glenluce Public Hall.

Lance Sergeant William Templeton, 432119.
49th Battalion Canadian Infantry.
Killed in action 5th June 1916.

William was the youngest son of John and Mary Templeton, Main Street, Glenluce. He was born there on 18th May 1889. William had emigrated and been living in Canada for around four years. There he worked in the telephone department as a linesman in Edmonton, and was said to have good prospects there.

He enlisted in Canada in January 1915. He was 5 feet eight and a half inches tall with a fair complexion, brown eyes and brown hair. He listed his mother as his next of kin.

Although he was posted as missing in June 1916 it wasn't until March the following year that his death was confirmed to his mother. He is commemorated on the Menin Gate Memorial.

Lance Corporal William Watson, 43031.
16th Battalion Royal Scots.
Killed in action 21st March 1918.

William and his two brothers had all enlisted on the outbreak of war. Their parents lived at Drumflower.

Before the war William had worked with his father as a rabbit trapper. Like so many others, he was first posted as missing before his death was confirmed. With no known grave, William is commemorated on Arras Memorial.

Lance Sergeant Robert Frederick Wilson, S/40940.
1st/6th Battalion Gordon Highlanders.
Killed in action 9th May 1918.

Known as Fred and brother to the below named Joseph Wilson, Robert was the second son of Joseph and Elizabeth Wilson of Over Airies, Whauphill.

Other local soldiers were serving in the 1st Battalion Gordon Highlanders and must have known Robert. One of those men was Pte. R.S. Sproule who wrote to his sister in Belfast that he had been at Hill 60 with the 1st Battalion and he would not say much about it as it would make the blood curdle.

Aged 28, when he was killed, Fred left behind a young widow. His brother had been killed just a few weeks before him. Fred is buried at Roclincourt Military Cemetery, and he is named on the family headstone at Inch. His name is on the plaque inside Glenluce Memorial Hall.

Pte. James Fleming Wilson, 203954.
Lovat Scouts - 6th Battalion Cameron Highlanders.
Killed in action 28th March 1918.

James was the third son of Joseph and Elizabeth Wilson (nee Jess), late of Mains Over Airies Whauphill. The couple had five children who died before the age of three. James had a sister Jeanie and a brother, Fred (Robert Frederick). James had for some years been in the service of the Earl of Stair before the war.

James is named on Arras Memorial, bay 9. He is also named on the family headstone in Inch as is his brother Fred who was killed in action 9th May 1918. His mother lived through the sorrow of having outlived seven of her children. James is also on Inch War Memorial. James' name was missing from the printed list of names read out at the unveiling ceremony.

Sons of Glenluce Remembered

For whatever reasons long forgotten, the following men are not on the war memorial, but were all sons in some way of the village of Glenluce or the surrounding area. For three sailors the connection is that Glenluce has looked after them and has given them their final resting place.

Some men with Glenluce connections are listed under other local war memorials as they are named on those, Samuel Cook who is named on the family headstone in the cemetery, is listed under Leswalt Memorial, John McGivern who worked at Airyhemming is named on Stranraer Memorial

Corp. William Campbell, 12808.
5th Battalion Canadian Infantry.
Killed in action 24th May 1915.

William was the third son of Jane and the late Walter Campbell, Main Street Glenluce. His parents had previously run the Caledonian Hotel in Stranraer.

In his death notification in the local paper he was listed as being in the 1st Canadian Western Cavalry when he was killed at Festubert. Aged 28 when he was killed he is commemorated on Vimy memorial. He may be the same man that is named on Stranraer Memorial.

Pte. David Fleming, 27190.
1st Battalion Royal Scots Fusiliers.
Killed in action 3rd May 1917.

The local newspaper records David as being married and living with his wife at West Challoch Farm, Dunragit, where he worked until the outbreak of war.

He was first reported as missing and later assumed killed. With no known grave, David is commemorated on bay 5 of Arras Memorial.

Serg. Alfred Ernest Gurney, 2nd Battalion Royal Scots. Killed in action 21st July 1916.

Alfred's father was living in Poonamallee, Madras. Alfred was married to Elizabeth Thompson and they had a son, Charles, born in 1916, his father Alfred may never have seen him.

Alfred is commemorated on the Thiepval Memorial and named on the family headstone in Glenluce cemetery. Sadly Alfred's son was killed whilst serving in the merchant navy in the Second World War.

Corp. Charles Hannah, 200932. C Company, 2nd Battalion Royal Scots Fusiliers. Killed in action 13th October 1918.

Charles was the son of Charles and Elizabeth Hannah of Balmesh, then later Church Street, Glenluce. He was married to Margaret Henderson from Crosshouse in Ayrshire and although he is a son of Glenluce his name is on the war memorial at Crosshouse.

Charles had previously won a Military Medal for bravery in the field and there was local pride in his heroism. When he died his parents inserted the following poem in the local newspaper:

When last we saw his smiling face

He looked so strong and brave

We little thought how soon he would

Be laid in a hero's grave.

Charles has no known grave and is commemorated on Tyne Cot memorial panel 60 to 61.

Pte. Henry McHarrie,
2nd Battalion Royal Scots Fusiliers.
Killed in action 18th May 1915.

Henry was the son of Hugh and Helen McHarrie (nee Little) of Glengorrie, Glenluce. He was reported as missing and then killed in action and is on the CWGC. He is not the same man as his namesake on Inch memorial but is likely to have been related. He was 22 when he was killed and he is commemorated on Le Touret Memorial as well as being named on the family headstone in Glenluce Cemetery.

At the unveiling ceremony of the war memorial, his name was read out alongside all the others as if it was meant to be on the memorial. It may have been an oversight, but it was never corrected. He is named on the plaque inside Glenluce Public Hall but it is sad that he seems to have been forgotten from the memorial that most people can access, particularly when it would seem that his name was intended to be on the memorial.

Pte. George McKie,
12th Battalion Royal Scots.
Killed in action 30th October 1915.

George was native to Culscadden, Garlieston. His grandparents were from Barnsallie and Glenhowl. George's aunt, Jeanie, lived at Low Glasnick. Although from Garlieston, George is not on the war memorial there, or on any Rhins memorial. He is buried at Larch Wood Cemetery, Belgium, grave reference I.G.3. He is included here as he named on his grandparent's headstone in Glenluce Old Kirkyard, and on the memorial inside Glenluce Public Hall.

Pte. Robert Morlan, 2nd Battalion Scots Guards. Died at home 7th January 1916.

Robert was employed as a policeman in the Partick division of Glasgow before enlisting on the outbreak of war. He was badly wounded at Festubert on 16th May 1915 and invalided home to Glasnick Crossing Cottage, Penninghame.

Although he went by the name Morlan or Morland, his parents were Robert McMorland and Margaret Flynn Stevenson from Challoch Dunragit. Robert was born on 21st August 1892 at Mains of Park, Old Luce. His father worked on the railway.

Robert did not recover from his injuries and died of tuberculosis at home aged 23. He is named on his parent's headstone at Glenluce cemetery. Robert is not listed with the CWGC or SNWM and does not have a military headstone and is not known to be named on any local war memorial.

A Sailor of the Great War. SS Main. 9th September 1917. Known unto God.

Shoulder to shoulder with two other sailors, his stone stands in Glenluce Cemetery. The Main was a defensively armed steamship that had hoped to settle in Luce Bay for the night. She was just over a mile outside Drummore when she was sunk by gunfire from uboat UC-75. In the early hours of daylight Drummore villagers helped rescue survivors, and recover bodies. Those whose bodies were found on the Glenluce side of the bay were buried in the churchyard at Glenluce.

A Sailor of the Great War. SS Main. 9th September 1917. Known unto God.

Comrade to the above unnamed sailor and shoulder to shoulder with two other sailors, his stone stands in Glenluce Cemetery.

A Sailor of the Great War. Known unto God.

A final resting place beside comrades in arms. There is no date on his stone and no name for the ship he came from. His family may always think his body was never recovered. Glenluce has provided his final resting place.

William McGarva. Died 13th January 1916.

When the names were read out at the unveiling ceremony, William McGarva was given no rank or regiment. Though it was obviously intended that the name was for the man who was killed in service, this William McGarva, a Glenluce Railway porter died on the day he registered his name to enlist. He would have worked alongside two other railway porters named on Glenluce war memorial - Thomas Wingate Kerr and George Murray, and he was to die at home during the war.

In January 1916 on a Wednesday morning William had made his way to Stranraer to take his Derby Armlet. It was that month because of high numbers of casualties, the voluntary "Derby Scheme" was altered to become conscription using the same criteria. Whilst it had previously been a voluntary scheme, for single men, married men could now be conscripted to serve abroad.

It was a wild day and William who had been drinking heavily took the evening train back to Kirkcowan. When they arrived there a small group of people hired a horse drawn coach to get back to their homes. The storm by this time was so wild that the horse could not go any further after just two miles. All the passengers had to get out and walk. Somewhere in the storm William became separated from the others. He was not found until the following Saturday, near to the Dergoals Cothouses on the low moor, after a search in which local schoolboys took part. He had died from exposure. Aged 35 William left a widow and four young children.

Another man from Glenluce - James McKenzie in 1914.

The men leaving from Glenluce Railway Station in 1914, where two of those named on the memorial had worked.

Glenluce men and their horses at the top of the street ready to leave for France. Many stories of devotion from horses, mules and donkeys emerged during the First World War. Whilst thousands of animals assisted those fighting the war, more than eight million horses were killed.

INCH WAR MEMORIAL (CASTLE KENNEDY)

On Sunday the 11th April 1920, after a very well attended service in Inch, led by Rev. Gilfillan and Rev. Hair, the congregation made their way out of the church and round to the old doorway that faced the gate to the main road towards Glenluce.

In the presence of the Earl and Countess of Stair, the Hon. Hew Dalrymple made a fitting speech before unveiling the memorial. After the sound of the "Last Post" and singing the National Anthem, floral tributes were laid. The Earl of Stair laid a heart-shaped wreath.

The plaque is cast in bronze. There is a rope at the side of the memorial which is attached to the church bell. It lists 32 names from the First World War only listed by surname, forenames and regiment. It gives no dates or ranks.

The inscription reads:

THIS MEMORIAL ERECTED BY PUBLIC SUBSCRIPTION IS GRATEFULLY DEDICATED TOTHE MEN BELONGING TO THIS PARISH WHO FELL IN THE SERVICE OF THEIR COUNTRY IN THE GREAT WAR 1914-1919

THOMAS BROWN	CAMERON HIGHLANDERS
JOHN FAGAN	ROYAL SCOTS
ALEXANDER FLEMING	ROYAL ARMY SERVICE CORPS
ANDREW F FORSTER	AUSTRALIAN INFANTRY
WILLIAM FORSTER	AUSTRALIAN INFANTRY
THOMAS J HAMILTON	ROYAL SCOTS FUSILIERS
WILLIAM HILL	ROYAL SCOTS FUSILIERS
JOHN JESS	SCOTTISH RIFLES
WILLIAM KENNEDY	ROYAL SCOTS FUSILIERS
CHARLES KERR	ROYAL SCOTS FUSILIERS
WILLIAM KILGALAN	ROYAL SCOTS FUSILIERS
JAMES R MARCHBANK	KINGS OWN SCOTTISH BORDERERS
JAMES MARTIN	SEAFORTH HIGHLANDERS
THOMAS MILROY	CANADIAN FORCES
ROBERT MITCHELL	ROYAL SCOTS
JOHN McCARLIE	KINGS OWN SCOTTISH BORDERERS
PETER McCLYMONT	ROYAL SCOTS FUSILIERS
WALTER McCRAE	ROYAL FIELD ARTILLERY
JAMES McGARRIE	SCOTS GUARDS

HENRY McHARRIE	ROYAL SCOTS FUSILIERS
ROBERT McM McKIE	SCOTS GUARDS
WILLIAM W McLAGAN	ARGYLL & SUTHERLAND HIGHs
JAMES McLELLAND	SCOTS GUARDS
JOHN McMEEKIN	28th CANADIANS
JOHN NEVILLE	ROYAL HIGHLANDERS
ROBERT G REID	SCOTS GUARDS
JOHN SLAVEN	KINGS OWN SCOTTISH BORDERERS
ANDREW SMITH	ROYAL SCOTS
GEORGE McD SMITH	SEAFORTH HIGHLANDERS
JAMES B SMITH	ROYAL IRISH LANCERS
DANIEL TORRANCE	ROYAL MARINE LIGHT INFANTRY
JAMES WILSON	LOVATS SCOUTS

THEY NEVER FAIL WHO DIE IN A GREAT CAUSE. THEY BUT AUGMENT THE DEEP AND SWEEPING THOUGHTS WHICH OVERPOWER ALL OTHERS AND CONDUCT THE WORLD AT LAST TO FREEDOM. GREATER LOVE HATH NO MAN THAN THIS, THAT A MAN LAY DOWN HIS LIFE FOR HIS FRIENDS.

Pte. Thomas Brown, S/21753.
7th Battalion Cameron Highlanders.
Killed in action 17th August 1916.

Thomas was the only son of Sergeant and Mrs Brown of Castle Kennedy village. He was 23 years old when he was killed in a major offensive from Gommencourt to Maricourt. The Somme saw huge losses and every building, landmark and foot gained, was battled over.

Thomas had enlisted in November 1915 having previously been employed as a blacksmith with Mr Wood of Haplandmuir, Dunlop.

He was the first soldier connected with the Inch congregation to be killed in the war. A service was conducted by Rev. David Hair at Inch on Sunday 17th September in which he said:

"We meet today under a distinct sense of sorrow and loss...he was until recently a member of this congregation, one known to us all. When the call came for men to join the Army he willingly enlisted and, after little more than three months in France, he has made the supreme sacrifice. Today, as we recall his happy face, we give God thanks for his life. We remember his cheerfulness, his helpfulness, his kindness and now by his death he has set a crown upon his life...Our tenderest thoughts gather round the bereaved home. To his father, mother and sisters we offer our respectful sympathy."

Thomas is commemorated alongside 72,000 others with no known grave on the Thiepval Memorial.

Corp. John Fagan, 34093.
16th Battalion Royal Scots.
Killed in action 22nd October 1917.

John was the son of Edward and Annie Fagan who had lived at Lochans Mill before moving to 8 George Street, Stranraer. John had been awarded the Military Medal for conspicuous bravery in the field.

He had worked in Liverpool in a chain grocery store owned by a Mr Hughes in Liverpool.

John was 22 years old when he was killed. The weather was by this time very cold and the battle along Ypres Salient very drawn out. He is commemorated on the Tyne Cot memorial to the missing. Tyne Cot marked the furthest point reached by Commonwealth forces until almost the end of the war. John is also on Stranraer War Memorial.

Pte. Alexander Fleming, M2/193628.
729th Mechanical Transport Coy, Army Service Corps.
Died 22nd January 1917.

Alexander was the son of Mr and Mrs Robert Fleming of Whiteleys, later of Bridgebank, Stranraer. He was 20 years old when he died of dysentery in 40 General Hospital, Basra and he is buried in Basra War Cemetery.

When his death was intimated in the local paper his parents, brothers and sisters inserted the following poem;

Past his suffering, past his pain
Cease to weep, for tears are vain;
Calm the anguish of the breast,
For the sufferer is at rest.
He is sleeping, sweetly sleeping,
And on earth will never awake
Although hearts are over him breaking
And in anguish almost break.
His lips are sealed in silence
For ever hushed their tone
Oh! It is bitter parting
To know that he is gone.
We will meet our darling son
In that world of worlds the best
Where the blessed cease from trouble
And the weary are at rest.

The headstones in Basra were deteriorating rapidly by 1935 and were removed then. Though the graves remain, the names of those who are buried there are now on a screen wall.

Pte. Andrew Forrester Forster, 174.
11th Battalion Australian Infantry.
Killed in action 17th May 1915.

Elder brother of the below named William Forster and second son of Ellen and the late William Forster of Mains of Larg, New Luce. Andrew was born in Cumberland, and then educated at Stranraer High School. Both he and his brother emigrated to Australia, where they enlisted. Andrew was an engineer and he had undergone training for that role in Glasgow prior to emigrating.

Andrew was in the same battalion as George Bell, who is not on any local war memorial, but is listed under New Luce as a "Son Remembered". They boarded the same troopship on the same day when they went to war, and surely must have known one another.

Andrew was killed at Gallipoli in the area known as Anzac in fierce fighting. He was 27 years old and is buried in Lone Pine Cemetery, Anzac, Turkey, grave reference I.H.3. He is also commemorated on the Australian War Memorial.

Lieut. William Forster, 21st Battalion Australian Infantry. Killed in action 3rd May 1917.

Youngest son of the Ellen and the late William Forster, William was born in New Luce. He was educated in New Luce Public School and the Ewart Institute, before becoming a medical student at Edinburgh University. He also attended Edinburgh University Officers Training Corps.

He emigrated to Canada and for a short time was in the Canadian Ordnance Survey Service before emigrating to Australia. There he joined the Field Ambulance Section of the Australian Imperial Force. He was swiftly promoted to Sergeant Major and fought in Egypt and Gallipoli, where he was badly wounded in action. He was invalided home but on his recovery joined the Australian Imperial Force Infantry Battalion receiving a commission. He was sent to France in July 1916 fighting in the Somme. The local newspaper reported that for his bravery he received a Military Medal and a second star, though Australian records show his recommendation for a Distinguished Conduct Medal read:

> *"For most valuable service in action at Pozieres in charge of stretcher bearers. He has proved himself a gallant soldier and his set a fine example of endurance and devotion to duty to his men, whose work was uniformly of the highest character."*

His Battalion Commander sent a letter to William's mother:

> *"Lieut. Forster was a gallant and fearless officer who had gained the respect and confidence of every member of his unit. He died a soldier's death, being killed instantaneously while leading his men into action at Bullecourt."*

William was 25 when he was killed. He is commemorated on the Australian War Memorial and on the Villers-Bretonneux Memorial, Somme.

Pte Thomas J Hamilton, 16089.
6th/7th Battalion Royal Scots Fusiliers.
Killed in action 29th December 1916.

Tom Hamilton had been employed by Mr Hugh Chalmers, Chlenry before he enlisted in 1914. At the time of his death his parents were living at High Mye Farm before moving to Eldrick Hill, Lochans. He was their eldest son.

He was a machine gunner for almost two years and would have been a prime target for the opposition. Tom died age 23. While the local newspaper listed his date of death as 31st December, the CWGC lists it as 29th December 1916. His friends Sergeant Alex. Baillie, who was wounded, and Jane Baillie of High Auchneil, Leswalt placed the following poem in the local newspaper on his death:

I little though his time so short
When he on furlough came;
Back to the front he proudly went.
Ne'er to return again.

With no known grave, Thomas is commemorated on pier and face C of Thiepval Memorial.

Pte. William Hill, 10458.
2nd Battalion Royal Scots Fusiliers.
Killed in action 31st October 1914.

Before enlisting the young William Hill had worked on the Blair, Stoneykirk. He had served five years in the Army and was stationed with his regiment in Gibraltar when war broke out.

His mother, Mrs Alexander Hill of Cults, Castle Kennedy did not receive official notice of his date of death until January 1916. He fought in the Ypres Salient and is commemorated on the Menin Gate Memorial to the missing panel 19 and 33. He was 21.

His mother inserted the following poem with his death notice in the newspaper:

When on the field of battle
He calmly took his place
He fought and died for Britain
And the honour of his race.

Pte. John Swan Jess, 38373.
3rd/8th Battalion Scottish Rifles (Cameronians).
Killed in action 1st August 1918.

John was the eldest of seven sons of Joseph and Elizabeth Jess (nee Swan). In 1911 the family were living at Little Clendrie Stranraer where his father was a ploughman and uncle helped on the farm. John enlisted at Dunragit. When he was killed he was barely 18 years old, and is commemorated on Soissons Memorial as one of 4000 men with no known grave who died in the Battles of Aisne and Marne in 1918.

Pte William Kennedy, 42430.
10th/11th Battalion Highland Light Infantry.
Died from wounds 24th March 1917.

William Kennedy was one of four brothers who enlisted when war broke out. He was married to Annie Gibb and lived at Cairney's Corner, Inch. Before he enlisted he was employed at Aird Donald Parks.

William died of wounds in 37 Casualty Clearing Station which was situated Avesnes-le-Comte and he is buried in the communal cemetery extension there, grave reference III.C.1.

Pte. Charles Kerr, 8110.
5th Battalion Royal Scots Fusiliers.
Killed in action 31st December 1915.

Charles Kerr was the son of Mrs Hamilton of Deerpark, Castle Kennedy (later Mrs Slavin). Before the war he was employed by Joseph Johnson of Deerpark. He was a native of Leswalt.

Charles Joined the RSF in November 1914 and fought at Gallipoli. His mother received notice that he had been injured on the 30th December, but a comrade wrote a letter which suggested he was either killed on that date or died the following day from wounds:

"A few lines to say I have been wounded and lying in St Andrew's Military Hospital, Malta. I was wounded in the face by the bursting of a bomb, but cheer up and don't worry, for I will soon be all right again. I am very sorry to say Charlie Kerr was killed beside me the same day as I was hit. That was on December 30th. He was hit on the head and back. He died about half an hour afterwards. I spoke to him then but he could not answer me. He was then carried away for there was a heavy bombardment on at the time, and the shells were flying all around us. It was a pure hell all that day, so Charlie was hit with a piece of one of the shells. I don't know how I missed some of them. There is only a hundred of us left now, so I consider myself very lucky that I got through it with what I got, and I have myself to blame for it, for I volunteered to do a thing, and that was when I got hit."

Lieutenant J.M. Kerr (named on Portpatrick War Memorial) also wrote to Mrs Hamilton about the death of her son:

"We were very sorry when we learned that you son, Private Charles Kerr, No. 8110, had died of the wounds he received in action on 30th December, and his Company Officer has asked me to write expressing our deep sympathy with you in your bereavement. As he was not in my platoon, I had not a great deal of opportunity of coming in touch with him, but I know he was respected in the Company as a good and brave soldier, and he – like other good fellows from Stranraer, who fell in the closing days of 1915 – coolly laid down his life in a successful and important action. His own Platoon Officer, Mr McNaughton, also died of wounds on the same occasion. He was wounded by a shell, but it will be a relief to you to know that he became unconscious, and was spared any suffering which otherwise he might have had."

Charles is buried in Lancashire Landing Cemetery, Turkey, grave reference J.78. He is also commemorated on Leswalt War Memorial.

Pte. William Kilgallen, 7877.
1st Battalion Royal Scots Fusiliers.
Died from wounds 17th June 1915.

William had worked for Mr J.B. Chalmers of Barsolus prior to enlisting. He was a National Reservist and had previously served in the Connaught Rangers. His wife was living at Barsolus at the time of his death in 1917.

Bedford House, Ieper, Belgium was an area used as headquarters and a base for field ambulances. The house itself and surrounding trees were destroyed during fierce fighting by shellfire.

William is buried at Bedford House Cemetery, enclosure number 2, grave reference IV.B.3. He is also on the memorial at Sandhead.

Pte. James R. Marchbanks, 4383.
1st/5th Battalion King's Own Scottish Borderers.
Killed in action 19th December 1915.

Born in Newton Stewart, James' last name is listed correctly on the war memorial at Inch and on his medal index card but listed as Marchbank with the CWGC.

James' father was George Marchbanks, a gamekeeper, and more than likely it was his uncle who was the gamekeeper or factor at Lochinch and it is probable that he spent much of his time growing up on the estate.

James was killed in action at the Dardenelles and is buried in Redoubt Cemetery, Helles, Turkey, grave reference XI.A.8.

Pte. James Martin, 260258.
1st/5th Battalion Seaforth Highlanders.
Killed in action 23rd July 1918.

James Martin was the youngest son of Mr and Mrs John Martin, Low Barnultoch. Prior to enlisting he was an apprentice blacksmith with Mr John O'Hare of Castle Kennedy.

He enlisted on the 12th July 1915 and had been on active service in France for thirteen months prior to his death aged 19. He is buried in Marfaux British Cemetery, Marne, grave reference III.I.8.

Pte. Thomas Milroy, 252132.
49th Battalion Canadian Infantry.
Died 30th October 1917.

Born on 7th August 1886 in Stranraer the third son of Thomas and Mary Milroy (nee Murray) of High Mark, New Luce. Thomas was almost 30 years old when he enlisted in Canada in 1916. He had a dark complexion, dark hair and blue eyes. He was 5 feet 8 inches tall and had a long scar on his left hand.

He is buried in Poelcapelle British Cemetery, Belgium, grave reference XIX.B.8. Thomas is also on the war memorial at New Luce and the one at Cairnryan. He is also named on the family headstone in New Luce Kirkyard.

Robert Mitchell, Royal Scots. Unknown date of death.

I was unable to establish which of the Robert Mitchells who served in the Royal Scots, was the one named on the memorial. There were six listed with the SNWM. I could find no reference to his death in the local newspaper other than a small suggestion that he was likely to be the son of Robert and Annie Mitchell, who may have lost a son in the war – but no first name or regiment was given. If it is this man then his father was a slater and Robert was born at Station Place, Stranraer. The 1911 census only lists one Robert Mitchell as living in Wigtownshire and because of his age, it is unlikely to be the same man.

Pte. John McCarlie, 8779.
King's Own Scottish Borderers.
Killed in action 14th August 1917.

John was the eldest son of James and Margaret McCarlie (nee Glen), of Craigcaffie. He had a sister Isabella, who died in infancy and another sister Jane. He was married to Mary Moffat from Waterside Cottage, Kettleholm. He was 31 years old when he was killed.

John had been sent to Gaza where he was engaged in fierce fighting. He is buried in Gaza War Cemetery, Israel, grave reference VII.D.9. John is also named on the family headstone in Inch Churchyard.

Pte. Peter McClymont, 31492.
15th Battalion Royal Scots.
Killed in action 28th April 1917.

Peter's wife lived at Balcraig Moor Portwilliam and his parents lived at Boreland Glenluce. He was one of five brothers all on active service in the war.

Before enlisting Peter had been employed by Mr William Millar, Cults, Castle Kennedy. Initially he was reported missing on 28th April but within two months his death was confirmed to his family. He is commemorated at Lieven Communal Cemetery Extension, France, grave reference V.B.2.

Gunner Walter McCrae, 125684.
A Bty. 307th Brigade Royal Horse and Field Artillery.
Killed in action 10th May 1918.

Spelt McRae on the SNWM and CWGC. Walter was born in Aberdeen to Alexander and Barbara McRae.

Whatever his local connection I was unable to trace it. There was a Mr John McCrae who lived in High Street Stranraer during the war and he was perhaps related or he may have worked or settled here before the war.

Walter is Buried at Vieille-Chapelle New Military Cemetery, grave reference VII.E.11. He was 27.

Pte. James McGarrie, 12386.

1st Battalion Scots Guards.
Killed in action 27th September 1915.

James enlisted in November 1914 and completed basic training prior to being sent to France in May 1915. He was employed at Balker Home Farm and lived there with his parents prior to enlisting.

His parents later received further communication from the Scots Guards Record Office stating he was buried between Lone Trees and Chalkpit Wood Vermeilles, despite this he has no known grave. James is commemorated on Loos Memorial.

Pte. Henry McHarrie, 32193.
1st Battalion Royal Scots Fusiliers.
Killed in action 26th September 1917.

Henry was one of four sons of Mr and Mrs John McHarrie, Kirminnoch, Dunragit all on active service. Henry was the youngest brother and was 19 when he was reported missing, having only been in France for four months. His parents were later living at High Mark Leswalt.

Of the six McHarrie names listed as killed with the CWGC in the war three are from the Rhins and are likely to be related. He had a namesake from Glenluce, likely to be a relative, possibly a cousin, whose name is missing from the war memorial at Glenluce.

With no known grave he is commemorated on Tyne Cot Memorial.

Gdsm. Robert McKie, 14235.
2nd Battalion Scots Guards.
Killed in action 5th August 1917.

Robert was married and lived with his wife Elizabeth McCrory and young son and daughter at Cairney's Corner, Inch.

Before the war he had worked for Mr J.B. Chalmers of Barsolus. Robert was previously wounded on 25th September 1916 but had recovered enough to be sent back to Belgium.

With no known grave, Robert is commemorated on the Menin Gate Memorial, he was 32. On his death his wife inserted the following poem in the local newspaper:

He sleeps beside his comrades
In a hallowed grave unknown,
But his name is written in letters of love
On the hearts he left at home.
Sleep on, dear daddy, and take your rest,
They miss you most who loved you best.

Pte. William M. McLagan, 12261.
14th Battalion Argyll and Sutherland Highlanders.
Killed in action 26th September 1917.

On the outbreak of war William immediately volunteered but he was rejected twice on medical grounds. He was accepted for enlisting on his third attempt. Williams father was the schoolmaster at Inchparks. Before enlisting William had worked at the draper shop of Messrs Craig and Kyle in Stranraer. His parents Robert and Jane later lived at Aldouran View, Leswalt.

When informed of his death, his parents were told that he was killed instantly when returning to the trenches after having carried a wounded man to the first-aid station. He was 21 years old.

William is buried at Fins New British Cemetery, Sorel-Le-Grand, grave reference I.AA.17.

Pte. James McLelland, 13316.
2nd Battalion Scots Guards.
Died from wounds 1st December 1917.

Son of Mrs A McLelland, Culhorn Mains. James died from wounds at No 9 General Hospital France. He was 39 years old. His mother later moved to 8 Greenvale Street, Stranraer.

James is buried at St Sever Cemetery Extension, Rouen, grave reference P.V.C.5A.

Lance Corporal John McMeekin, 424307.
28th Battalion Canadian Infantry.
Killed in action 1st August 1917.

John's last name is spelt at least three different ways on three different memorials. Spelt as above on Inch memorial, McMeeken on the CWGC. McMeckan on Kirkcolm War Memorial and McMeekan with the Canadian Archives. To add to the confusion it is spelt McMeikan in the local newspaper report of his death. He was the son of Mr and Mrs Alexander McMeekin of Aird Farm and was born on 22nd July 1892.

Originally a farm labourer, John had emigrated to Canada. He had previously served for two years with the Royal Scots before enlisting in May 1915. John was reported as wounded in 1916 and treated in the 8th

Stationary Hospital Winnereux. He was awarded a Military Medal for gallantry in the field.

John had a fair complexion with blue eyes and brown hair. He is buried in Lapugnoy Military Cemetery which contains many graves of those killed during the Battle of Arras. His grave reference there is V.A.12.

Pte. John Neville, 41748.
8th Battalion Black Watch.
Died from wounds 21st October 1918.

Son of Mr W. and Maria Neville of Aird Cottages, Castle Kennedy, John's brother was serving in the Highland Light infantry. John was invalided home suffering from Trench Fever in 1917; it was the second time he was sent to the 1st Scottish Hospital in Aberdeen.

Mr and Mrs Neville received word that both of their sons were injured and had been hospitalised with wounds within three days of each other on 22nd and 25th March 1918. John and his brother both recovered. On October 21st of the same year John was injured a fourth time from which he did not recover. He died at 36 Casualty Clearing Station and is buried at Duhallow Advance Dressing Station, Belgium, grave reference IV.G.8. John Neville's death plaque is held in the archives of Stranraer Museum.

Pte. Robert Gunion Reid, 12725.
3rd Battalion Scots Guards.
Died 26th January 1915.

Robert was born at Barnultoch on 15th October 1878. He was the son of William and Grace Reid (nee McMaster) who farmed Barnultoch. His father died at Mahaar in 1916, siblings in the family were spread out locally at Barsolus, The Grange, and Low Knockglass.

Robert died at Caterham Surrey aged 35. His body was returned to Castle Kennedy Station and the hearse was escorted by three local men from his Company. All three of those men lost their lives later in the war. The men were R. McCracken (Stranraer War Memorial), J. Tully (Portpatrick and Stranraer Memorials), and M. Hunter (Stoneykirk Memorial). Although Robert does not have a military headstone, he is named on the family headstone in the churchyard.

Corporal John (Jack) Slaven, 2nd Battalion King's Own Scottish Borderers. Died from wounds 6th October 1917.

Jack Slaven was the fourth son of John and Martha Slaven (nee McWilliam) of Borland Dairy, Inch. His father had been the dairyman at Barscarrow some years previously. Jack had a teenage sister, Agnes, who had died in 1912. His brother Edward was a carter on the farm at Barscarrow at the time of the 1901 census, when another brother, Fergus, and sister Maggie were listed as scholars. Through the following years the family continued to have strong connections with both Stoneykirk and Castle Kennedy.

The National Bible Society had been giving copies of the New Testament to troops before they went to the trenches. They wrote to Rev. Hair from Inch and enclosed a copy of their bible with a bullet hole in it. The letter went on:

> *"This one saved the life of the lad whose name it bears. The bullet penetrated as you will see, so far into the Testament, and then glided off and wounded him in a less serious place. He was carrying it in the front of his top left hand pocket, but for it he would have been shot through the heart. I gave the lad a new copy of the Testament. One of your ones, and he willingly gave me this most interesting one, which, with his heartiest consent and thankfulness to God for such a gift that saved his life, I now send to you, knowing that you will be interested to have it. The lad is progressing favourably, and I believe, now out of danger. He just received the New Testament the night before he went to the trenches. He comes from Inch near Stranraer and is a fine Christian lad."*

The name written inside the bible was Jack Slaven. Jack recovered from this injury, which happened on 12th July 1915. He went on to be awarded a Military Medal for conspicuous bravery in capturing seven Germans single handed in a dug-out in an attack on Vimy Ridge.

Later in the war, he died at a casualty clearing station from wounds received the previous day. He was 22 years old. Jack is buried at Godeswaersvelde British Cemetery, France, grave reference I.N.50. He is named on the family headstone at Stoneykirk Churchyard.

Jack's sister, Maggie, married Hugh McCormick in 1919 after the "war to end all wars" was over. Both of their sons Hugh and Robert, fought in the Second World War. Leading Stoker Robert was killed off the coast of North Africa on 10th November 1942 when HMS Martin was torpedoed by a U-Boat. A farming diary belonging to the Slaven family is held in the archives of Stranraer museum.

Pte. Andrew Smith, 17239.
15th Battalion Royal Scots.
Killed in action 28th May 1917.

Andrew was a gamekeeper and before the war he was living at the kennels in the grounds of Lochinch. In the 1911 census it gives his age as 29 and head of the household. Two other estate workers John Hyslop and John Keenan were also living at the kennels in 1911, both later served in the war. Andrew is buried at Roeux British Cemetery, grave reference D46.

Pte. George McDowall Smith, 74.
1st Battalion Seaforth Highlanders.
Killed in action 19th January 1916.

George was the son of William and Sarah Smith (nee McDowall), Corner House, Lochans.

On the outbreak of war George was already serving with his regiment in India. He was posted immediately with his regiment to the Western Front where he engaged in heavy fighting.

Later he was sent to the Persian Gulf and it was there he was killed aged 26 and having served over seven years in the army. He is commemorated on Basra Memorial panel 37 and 64. George is named on the family headstone in the Glebe Cemetery.

Pte. James Beattie Smith,
5th Royal Irish Lancers.
Killed in action 7th February 1917.

With thousands of J.Smith names on the CWGC, James proved very difficult to trace. His date of death on the SNWM is listed as above but it is recorded as 5th February 1917 with the CWGC.

His local connection is not known and indeed this may well be a different man to the one named on the memorial. This James was born in Little Geoch, Ireland.

He served with the 5th Lancers and the Queens Royal West Surrey Regiment. He is buried in Gosforth St. Nicholas Churchyard.

More will be known about James once the 1911 census is available to the public, unless an ancestor can come forward with additional information.

Pte. Daniel Torrance, CH/2420(S).
1st Royal Marine Battalion Royal Naval Division.
Killed in action 2nd September 1918.

Eldest son of Mr and Mrs Daniel Torrance of Innermessan. Daniel was described as a promising young student at Stranraer High School and was attending university in Edinburgh when he reached the age for enlisting.

He was 19 years old when he was lost in the period leading up to armistice. Daniel has no known grave and is commemorated on the Vis-En-Artois Memorial, France. He is also named on Stranraer War Memorial.

Lance Corporal James Fleming Wilson, 203954.
Lovats Scouts/ 6th Battalion Cameron Highlanders.
Killed in action 28th March 1918.

James was the son of Joseph and Elizabeth Wilson (nee Jess), late of Mains Over Airies Whauphill. The couple had five children who died before the age of three. James had a sister Jeanie and a brother, Fred (Robert Frederick). James had for some years been in the service of the Earl of Stair before the war.

He is buried in Feuchy Chapel British Cemetery Wancourt France. He is also named on the family headstone in Inch as is his brother, Fred, who was killed in action 9th May 1918. His mother lived through the sorrow of having outlived seven of her children. James is also on Old Luce War Memorial.

Sons of Inch Remembered

The following men and women are included here because they had a connection with Inch, for some it would be their final resting place, others are named in the cemetery, and some are those who survived.

I have omitted the following men as they are named on other local memorials, or have stronger connections to another local parish: Jack Lees and his brother William are both buried in the churchyard at Inch, but Jack is named on Stoneykirk Memorial, Peter Monteith is named on the family headstone here but is also named on Leswalt Memorial, John McClymont is interred at Inch but is named on Stranraer Memorial, John Marshall is named on the family headstone here but again he is named on Stranraer Memorial.

John James Dalrymple, 12th Earl of Stair.
Survived.

John Dalrymple received a D.S.O. early in the war for his part in the capture of around 200 Germans near Ypres. Not long afterwards, his Company were surrounded during the retiral from Mons in 1914. He had leant his Burberry greatcoat to another officer who was killed in the action. Although not seriously injured, John had been blown up and partially buried before being unearthed by those who became his captors. His sister, Marjorie Dalrymple, recalled in her memoirs;

> *"For once we had obvious reason to be truly thankful for the Sabbatarian strictness of our part of Scotland. My sister-in-law was shut away at home and, as it was Sunday, she mercifully never got the "wounded and missing, believed killed" message till word came through to her that he was in German hands."*

The Castle Kennedy postmistress had refused to call a telegram boy out to deliver the message on a Sunday so the message was not relayed.

Whilst he was still in captivity, his father died in December 1914 and John became the 12th Earl of Stair. His time in captivity was spent at Crefeld in North Germany. He had an astigmatism and due to the conditions of his confinement it was feared he would go blind. He was released as a gesture of goodwill through Switzerland. Amazingly his wife and children were able to travel across the Western Front through the frontlines by train to visit him in Switzerland. A gentleman's agreement on both sides meant that the train would not be fired on by either side as it travelled through countryside and battlefields.

It is well worth mentioning the particularly great effort of his wife during the war. Lady Violet Dalrymple suggested that Lochinch Castle could become Lochinch Auxiliary Hospital for convalescing soldiers who had been injured. She perhaps thought it better that the children would be able to go to Switzerland in their holidays and visit their father, than remain at the castle with physically and mentally scarred convalescing soldiers. Indeed in a diary was kept at Lochinch with group photos of every batch of soldiers who stayed. Each soldier was named – with the occasional and sometimes witty comment about the man. Against a few of the names there is a later note added in which intimates that the soldier died or was missing later in the war. Only a few of the men named are local, two from the Rhins – John Norris of the Seaforth Highlanders from Stranraer and Thomas Milroy of the RFA from Portpatrick.

The men were well looked after in the stable block, with full access to the grounds, and fishing on the lochs. In almost every weekly newspaper Lady Violet has thanked individuals for their kind donations of foodstuffs and necessities such as razorblades which assisted the men in their recovery.

The Earl's sister Marjorie nursed at the Front, and on her return to London, she devised fitted temporary false limbs, which aided shrinkage and healing. Beatrice, Lord Stair's other sister, Marjorie and a large group of ladies started to make these limbs in a shop in London. With the large numbers of limbless men returning from the war, they were in great demand.

Convalescing soldiers with VAD nurses at Lochinch Castle

Daniel Hart, Bank Agent. Died from the effect of the 1914-1918 war 20th December 1937.

Daniel is named on a headstone in the cemetery, he was 54 when he died and presumably was injured in the war and never fully recovered. Whatever the effect was that the war had on him, he must have suffered for almost twenty years after the war was over. His cause of death was listed as an embolism.

He was married to Jane Hogarth. In a cruel blow for Jane, their son, Colin died in the Second World War at Hiroshima. He had been aboard the Lisbon Maru which was sunk in the Pacific in 1942 by an American submarine. The submarine was targeting Japanese Troops. What the Americans did not know was that there were 1800 British Prisoners of war aboard and around 1000 perished. Colin had been a prisoner of war and was kept in terrible conditions then finally entombed in the ship, unable to escape.

Pte. Andrew Johnson,
19th Battalion Australian Infantry Forces.
Killed in action 3rd September 1915.

Andrew was the son of William and Jane Johnson (nee Jolly). He had a sister also named Jane. His parents had lived at 6 Clifton Terrace, London Road, Stranraer.

Andrew had emigrated to Australia and it was there he enlisted. His brother John had emigrated some time before him. He boarded the transport ship Ceramic on 25th June 1915. He was part of the Australian Forces landing in Gallipoli. Andrew is buried in 7th Field Ambulance Cemetery, Turkey, grave reference IV.A.6. He is also named on the family headstone in Inch Churchyard. His name does not appear on any Rhins War Memorial.

Rev. Heggie in a sermon shortly after Andrew's death spoke about the loss:

> *"You will all be sorry to learn of the death of Andrew Johnson, who, before going to Australia, was a member of this church, and whose mother is known to you all. Andrew Johnson was a young man of modest and unassuming manners. True-hearted and steady, and when he left the old country some three years ago for Australia, all who knew him predicted for him real success. When the Great War began, he, along with*

his brother John enlisted, and came to Sydney for training, subsequently sailing for the Dardanelles, where some of the fiercest fighting of the war has taken place. He had offered for country and for King, for honour and justice, the best and supreme sacrifice of his life. The sad news was communicated to his mother by his brother John, and I am sure I voice your feelings when I say we lay on his far-off grave the wreath of our warm regard and pride, and assure his mother and the members of the family our deepest sympathy in their sorrow."

Pte. James Scott,
5th Battalion Royal Scots Fusiliers.
Killed in action 6th November 1917.

James was a son of Alexander and Elizabeth Scott (nee Fleming) late of Carthlearie and then Mains Cottage, Ballantrae. He was married to Sarah and they had lived at Kirkbride Kennels, Crosshill.

James is buried in Beersheba War Cemetery as he was killed in Palestine. He is also named on Ballantrae War Memorial and he is on the family headstone of his parents in Inch Churchyard.

Leswalt and Inch soldiers in the Argyll and Sutherland Highlanders waiting to leave for France. Left from the back: Pte. McLagan, Inchparks Schoolhouse, Pte. Reid, Challoch, Pte. Davis, Lochnaw Lodge, Lance Corporal Myles, Larbrax School, Pte. McLagan.

KIRKCOLM WAR MEMORIAL

In July 1919 a group of demobilised men met to discuss planned Victory celebrations in Kirkcolm. The Victory celebrations had been advertised in the local paper and included a Victory Picnic, and entertainment. The men swiftly reached a unanimous vote that they would take no part in the celebrations. They wanted to make their feelings heard and felt very clearly that until there were plans in place for an appropriate memorial to their fallen comrades, there would be no celebration. Public opinion in Kirkcolm was that an appropriate memorial should be raised, but no officials it seems, had, at the time of the Victory celebrations, made any plans. It was another two years before Kirkcolm's men were honoured.

Kirkcolm war memorial was unveiled on a sunny Sunday on 26th May 1921 to a very large audience who arrived, walking, riding, by cart and by car. After a service in the church the congregation came out into the graveyard where largest crowd the parish had ever seen had gathered. They were in fields, on the road and up embankments as well as in the graveyard and on the walls. After a dedication by Rev. Martin, Colonel Arthur Buchanan MP unveiled the memorial.

The Celtic cross of Creetown granite, which had been transported by local carrier W. Simpson, looked out over green pastures and on towards Lochryan. Many of the onlookers placed floral wreaths and tributes at the base, including relatives of those who were lost, the Earl of Stair, and the Misses Buchanan of Corsewall estate. At end the ceremony, Capt. McLauchlin led a march-past of the ex-servicemen who all saluted the memorial on their way. The parish had never before seen such a huge crowd in its midst.

The inscription on the front reads:

DEDICATED IN HONOURED MEMORY OF THE GALLANT MEN OF THE PARISH OF KIRKCOLM WHO FOUGHT AND DIED IN THE GREAT WAR 1914-1918. "THEIR NAME LIVETH FOR EVERMORE".

Panel two:

GNR. JOHN KYLE	R.G.A.
PTE. HUGH ROSS	G.H.
PTE. JAMES HAWTHORN	S.H.
PTE. WILLIAM MORROW	A.E.F.
PTE. HENRY STEWART	R.S.F.
PTE. HUGH STEWART	R.S.F.
PTE. DAVID WALLACE	A. & S.H.
PTE. JOHN McR. SIMPSON	H.L.I.
L.STR. WILLIAM WALLACE	R.N.
D.K.H. JOHN PALMER	R.N.R.

Panel three:

CPL. THOMAS GRAHAM	G.H.
CPL.ALEX. McCREDIE	A. & S.H.
LCE. CPL. ALEX. W. CRAIG	S.H.
LCE. CPL. HUGH LIGHTBODY	G.H.
LCE. CPL. HUGH McGIBNEY	R.S.F.
LCE.CPL. JOHN McMECKAN. M.M.	C.E.F.
BOM. ALEX. PATERSON	R.G.A.
GNR. JOHN McINTYRE	R.G.A.
PTE. DAVID KILPATRICK	G.H.
PTE. SAMUEL A. KILPATRICK	C.A.M.C.
PTE. ALEX. GIBSON	K.O.S.B.

Panel four:

"GREATER LOVE HATH NO MAN THAN THIS; THAT A MAN LAY DOWN HIS LIFE FOR HIS FRIENDS."

Lieut. John S. Kyle, 174931.
253 Siege Bty. Royal Garrison Artillery.
Killed in action 3rd November 1918.

John was the fourth son of Alex and Lizzie Kyle, Drumdow, Kirkcolm. Aged 21 John died in the clearing of the forest at Nord. He was buried by 17th, 33rd and 38th Welsh Divisions at Forest Communal Cemetery Nord, grave reference D.9.

John died very close to Armistice and his death notice was not in the local newspaper until 28th November. It is likely his family were not informed of his death until after Armistice was declared. John is also named on Stranraer War Memorial.

Pte. Hugh Ross, S/22836.
1st Battalion Cameron Highlanders.
Died 30th December 1916.

Hugh was the adopted son of Thomas and Grace Henderson (nee Tweedie) from High Clachan and Kirranrae. The couple had four children who died very young, two of whom had died on the same day.

Hugh was 22 when in France when he became acutely unwell. He died at Rouen Hospital in France from acute appendicitis.

He is buried at St. Sever Cemetery Extension, Rouen, grave reference O.IV.E.9. Hugh is also named on the family headstone in Kirkcolm churchyard.

Pte. Wm. James Hawthorne, 202603.
1st/4th Battalion Seaforth Highlanders.
Killed in action 9th April 1917.

Born in Bellamore, Armagh, and known to his wife as Jim he was killed at the age of 24. Before the war he had been working for Mr Cochrane, Heighton, Kirkcolm. His wife was Bessie Hamilton and she was living at Mahaar while he was serving abroad.

William was buried at Roclincourt Military Cemetery, Pas de Calais, grave reference I.B.39

When he died, his wife Bessie inserted the following poem in the local newspaper:

He died at his post, like a soldier brave,
He answered his country's call;
He sleeps far away in a hero's grave,
For his country's cause he did fall.
I loved him in life, I love him still
Too dear for his memory to fade,
And my sad thoughts often wander to the spot
Where my dear Jim is laid.

Pte. William Morrow,
109 Infantry, 28th Division, 159th International American Expeditionary Force.
Died from wounds 17th October 1918.

The family headstone in Kirkcolm lists William's date of death as 17th October 1918, as does the American records. He is not on the CWGC, which is rightly so as America is not in the Commonwealth, however he is also not on the SNWM.

William was the third son of William and Margaret Morrow, Weirston, Kirkcolm. At some stage William must have emigrated to America and enlisted there. He was 32 when he died from wounds at Base Hospital France. He is buried at Meuse-Argonne American Cemetery, Romagne, France, the headstones there are plain white crosses. He is also named on the memorial there.

Pte. Henry Stewart, 12599.
2nd Battalion Royal Scots Fusiliers.
Killed in action 28th September 1915.

Henry was born in Kirkcolm and worked in Kilmarnock at Glenfield Engineering Works. He was married and lived with his wife in Kilmarnock. His father was Hugh Stewart who was a mason in Kirkcolm.

Henry enlisted on 30th August 1914 and after training at Fort Matilda he was posted to the Front on 14th May 1915.

Though the following letter gives a different date of death from that listed on the CWGC website, Henry's wife received this from his Sergeant after his death:

> *"It is with much sympathy I inform you of your husband's death. On Thursday night, 30th September, after the great offensive, my platoon was detailed to reinforce D Company. We occupied a RAP (Regimental Aid Post) leading to the German trench, which had been taken from D Company. It was there he fell in his main endeavour to do his bit for his country and his home. I have always been with his platoon, except for a period of three weeks, when I was with No.6. Although he belonged to the Grenade Company, he was more or less under my command, and he proved a very willing and able soldier. I was greatly surprised to know he lived in "Killie" and so near to my place. I greatly sympathise with you in your great loss.... I shall conclude with my kind regards, and trust that God will bless you in your hour of great need."*

With no known grave, Henry is commemorated on Loos Memorial. Although not a brother of the below named Hugh, they are likely to have been closely related.

Pte. Hugh Stewart, 20402.
1st Battalion Royal Scots Fusiliers.
Killed in action 28th March 1918.

Hugh was the son of William and Mary Stewart (nee McKie) His parents had already lost twins and one other child in infancy. They later moved to Ecclefechan though when there were family deaths they were returned 'home' to be interred in Kirkcolm cemetery.

Hugh was 22 when he was killed, and he is commemorated on Arras memorial as well as the family headstone in Kirkcolm cemetery.

Pte. David Wallace, S/8094.
11th Battalion Argyll and Sutherland Highlanders.
Killed in action 23rd March 1918.

David was born in Glenluce, the fourth son of Mr and Mrs John Wallace of Clashmahew. His brothers also served in the war including William, named below. His cousin Tom Wallace is named on Stranraer Memorial. Another family photograph of David shows him standing with three braided white stripes and a black piece of material on his left forearm. These white braided stripes are believed to be wound stripes. The wound would likely have to be more than a flesh wound before the stripes were given, and it means that David was fairly seriously injured on at least three occasions.

With no known grave David is commemorated on Arras Memorial.

Pte. John McRobert Simpson, 471.
9th Battalion Highland Light Infantry.
Killed in action 15th July 1916.

John was born in Glasgow and was married to Minnie Murray. The couple lived at 26 Hunter Street, Scotstoun. He was called after his father who was also John McRobert Simpson of Kirkcolm. John is commemorated on Thiepval Memorial, pier and face 15C.

Fireman/Trimmer William Wallace,
SS Sycamore, Merchant Navy.
Killed in Action 25th August 1917.

William was the son of John and Helen Wallace and was born in Stranraer. He was married to Nellie McKay of North Park, Kirkcolm. He was a brother of David Wallace who is named above and a cousin of Tom Wallace who is named on Stranraer Memorial.

SS Sycamore was sunk by UB-61 with Commander Theodor Schultz in charge of the u-boat. There were 11 killed on the steamer, including William. His death notice in the local newspaper inserted by his wife intimated that he had drowned. He was just 35 and is commemorated on Tower Hill Memorial.

Deck Hand John Palmer, HMS Vivid, Royal Naval Reserve. Died 16th December 1915.

John was the son of Samuel and Annie Palmer (nee Cunningham). He died at Haslar Naval Hospital, Gosport, aged just 37. His two brothers, William and James had both died in infancy.

In what must have been a dreadful time for his mother, John's father died around ten weeks after him. His body was returned home and he is buried in the family plot in Kirkcolm Parish Churchyard. It is likely that he is the same John Palmer as the man named on Stranraer War Memorial.

Corp. Thomas Graham, 7907. 1st Battalion Queens Own Cameron Highlanders. Killed in action 25th September 1914.

Thomas was born in Stoneykirk and is more than likely one of three sons of Mr and Mrs James Graham of Glengyre who were all serving at the same time.

With no known grave he is commemorated on La-Ferte-Sous-Jouarre Memorial, Seine et Marne.

Lance Corp. Alexander McCreadie, 201577. 1st/5th Battalion Argyll and Sutherland Highlanders. Killed in action 8th November 1917.

Alexander was the son of James McCreadie of Kirkcolm. He had enlisted in February 1915 and had been on active service for more than two years. His name is spelt McCredie on the memorial in Kirkcolm.

The Third Battle of Gaza ended on 7th November the day before Alexander was recorded as having died. The troops that captured the city began the burials. Alexander is buried in Gaza War Cemetery, grave reference XII.E.14.

Alexander with his wife Nell on their wedding day.

Lance Corp. Alexander William Craig, 202702.
6th Battalion Seaforth Highlanders.
Killed in action 9th April 1918.

Alexander's wife was living at Merslaugh, Ervie when she received news he had been killed aged 23. He was the son of Agnes and Thomas Craig and stepson of Helen Craig. Before Alexander enlisted he worked for Mr Thomas Robertson, Clendrie, Kirkcolm. Alexander is commemorated on Loos Memorial, panel 112-115.

Lance Corp. Hugh Lightbody,
42nd Battalion Canadian Infantry.
Died of wounds 2nd May 1917.

Born in Stranraer on October 6th 1885, Hugh was the second son of James and Mary Lightbody, Glen Cottage, Awhirk. His mother was living in Dunoon at the time he enlisted. Hugh's brother was living in High Curghie Farm, Kirkmaiden where there used to be ancient standing stones.

Hugh emigrated to Canada about 1912 after having worked for some time for Mr Crichton of Drumdow. When he enlisted in Canada on 2nd September 1915, Hugh listed his trade as a shipper. He was 5 feet 8 inches tall with light brown hair, a fair skin and blue eyes. Hugh had tattoos on each forearm. Both his photo from the Free Press above and the War Memorial in Kirkcolm seem to suggest that Hugh was in the Cameron Highlanders, whatever regiment he served with, he paid the ultimate price.

Hugh was seriously wounded and died at the Military Hospital, Hampstead. He is buried at Brookwood Military Cemetery, Surrey, grave reference IX.E.8.

Lance Corp Hugh McGibney, 15577. 2nd Battalion Royal Scots Fusiliers. Died from wounds 24th April 1917.

Called after his father, Hugh lived with his parents and family at Mahaar. His sister Elizabeth was married to William Calderwood and they lived at Auchneil. In a very sad time for his mother, his sister died in 1911 followed by his father in 1915.

Hugh McGibney had been wounded twice previously when he was once again wounded in April 1917 aged 20. He was removed to hospital but died from his injuries. An army chaplain wrote to his mother in Kirkcolm to break the sad news.

Hugh had enlisted in November 1914 and was sent to France the following May, his father had just died a few days before he was sent to the front. When he was killed his mother inserted the following poem in the local newspaper:

He marched away so bravely,
His head so proudly held;
His footsteps never faltered,
His courage never failed.

When on the field of battle
He calmly took his place,
And fought and died for Britain
And the honour of his race.
Not far behind the firing line,
Within the sound of guns,
A wooden cross is the only sign,
Neath the rays of the setting sun,
To denote the resting place of one,
Who did his duty well;
Facing the dangers as each day dawned,
And like a hero fell.

Hugh is buried at Bucquoy Road Cemetery, Ficheux, grave reference I.C.20. He is also named on the family headstone in Kirkcolm Churchyard.

Lance Corporal John McMeckan, 424307.
28th Battalion Canadian Infantry.
Killed in action 1st August 1917.

John's last name is spelt at least three different ways on three different memorials. Spelt as above, on Kirkcom War Memorial, McMeeken and on the CWGC, McMeekin on Inch War Memorial and McMeekan with the Canadian Archives. To add to the confusion it is spelt McMeikan in the local newspaper report of his death. He was the son of Mr and Mrs Alexander McMeekin of Aird Farm and was born on 22nd July 1892.

Originally a farm labourer, John had emigrated to Canada. He had previously served for two years with the Royal Scots before enlisting in May 1915. John was reported as wounded in 1916 and treated in the 8th Stationary Hospital Winnereux. He was awarded a Military Medal for gallantry in the field.

John had a fair complexion with blue eyes and brown hair. He is buried in Lapugnoy Military Cemetery, grave reference V.A.12., which contains many graves of those killed during the Battle of Arras.

Gunner Alexander Paterson, 61089.
184th Siege Bty. Royal Garrison Artillery.
Killed in action 4th June 1917.

Alexander was the son of Samuel and Sarah Paterson, High Mark, Leswalt. He was born in Portpatrick, his family later moved to (the) Lochans. Before the war Alexander had worked as a dairyman. He enlisted in 1915 and had been on service abroad for almost two years.

Alexander is buried at Vlamertinghe Military Cemetery, Belgium. Alexander is also on the war memorial at Leswalt. His name is spelt Patterson on the CWGC. He is named on his grandparent's headstone in Portpatrick Cemetery.

Gunner John McIntyre, 129593.
346th Seige Bty. Royal Garrison Artillery.
Died of wounds 15th August 1917.

John was the twin son of Mr and Mrs McIntyre of Dally Bay. He was married to Elizabeth Geddes who later lived in Foundry Lane, Stranraer, and the couple had four children. Before the outbreak of war John worked for Mr Clement the baker in Stranraer for 12 years as a van driver.

John was 42 when he was badly injured and died at No.7 Casualty Clearing Station, France. His parents, brothers and sisters inserted the following poem in the local newspaper when he was killed:

No mother's care did him attend,
Nor o'er him did a father bend;
No sister by to shed a tear,
No brother by his words to hear.
Sick, dying in a foreign land,
No father by to take his hand;
No mother near to close his eyes-
Far from his native land he lies.

John is buried at Noex-Les-Mines Communal Cemetery, France, grave reference II.H.34. He is on Kirkcolm and Stranraer Memorials.

Pte. David W. Kilpatrick, 7799.
2nd Battalion Gordon Highlanders.
Killed in action 25th September 1915.

David was from Kirkcolm and at the time of the 1901 census he was one of eight siblings living at Kirkbryde with their parents John and Mary.

Stranraer man James McCormack who was in the Scots Guards had a letter home published in the Free Press about a chance encounter with David.

> *"Last night Joe Irons and I were walking along the street of a village where we are presently billeted when we met a party of the 2nd Gordons. Sure enough Stranraer was represented among them in the person of Pte. D. Kilpatrick, Kirkbryde, Kirkcolm, who was in the Commercial Bank*

(Mr Paton's). You should have seen his face when I shouted "How's the Clayhole?" Further along the street, Kilpatrick met a school chum of his named Spence, also of Kirkcolm, who is in the Scots Guards bomb throwers. We had a long talk about dear old Stranraer. Kilpatrick was telling me he had met J.Wyllie, senr (horse breaker) further along the line. The 2nd Gordons were with us in the charge on Sunday morning and they suffered. Joe says he would rather charge Sandy Little of Dunragit in the semi-final of the Junior League, than charge Mr Alleman! I guess the boys who used to entertain us in the summer evenings in Stair Park are pretty well scattered now. And I daresay many of them are taking part in the rough game out here. Well good luck to them all."

David is mentioned in another of James McCormack's letters which is included at the end of the Stranraer section, because it names several local men.

Sadly for the Kilpatrick family, two sons were lost as David was a brother of the below named Samuel. David has no known grave and he is commemorated on Loos memorial.

Pte. Samuel Alexander Kilpatrick, 33680.
3rd Field Ambulance Canadian Army Medical Corps.
Killed in action 27th September 1918.

Samuel was born in Kirkcolm on 19th February 1891. He was a dairyman to trade, though he had emigrated to Canada. He was a son of John W. Kilpatrick, Kirkbryde, Kirkcolm. When he enlisted in Canada in September 1914, he was described as being six feet tall with black hair a dark complexion and brown eyes.

Samuel's brother David is listed above. Samuel is buried in Sans-Les-Marquion British Cemetery, France, grave reference I.D.27.

Pte. Alexander Gibson, 27112.
6th Battalion King's Own Scottish Borderers.
Killed in action 3rd May 1917.

Born in Ecclefechan, Alexander was the son of William and Sarah Gibson of Cairngarroch. Aged 28 when he was killed, and with no known grave Alexander is commemorated on Arras Memorial.

Sons of Kirkcolm remembered

Two men named here had Kirkcolm connections but are not on any local memorial, and another man, David Govan, is named on the family headstone in the churchyard, but is named on Stranraer memorial. I have also included in this section a short story on Kirkcolm man, John McDowall, who survived the war.

Pte. Robert McDonald, 23831.
6th Battalion King's Own Scottish Borderers.
Killed in action 30th September 1918.

Before the war Robert was employed by Mr Cochrane Kelly of Southwick Dumfries. His parents were Charles and Agnes McDonald of Kirkcolm and his sister who was named as his next of kin was Mrs Geddes of Boreland. He had two brothers also serving with the Colours at the same time.

Robert is buried in Dadizeele New British Cemetery, Belgium, grave reference V.D.7. He is not named on any local memorial.

Sergeant James Lees, 1653.
9th Battalion Highland Light Infantry.
Killed in action 8th November 1916.

James was the only son of William and Agnes Russell Hodge Lees of 3 Mauldslie Street, Partick. James' grandfather and family were native to Ervie, Kirkcolm, and James had been called after his grandfather.

James had been wounded and taken to hospital where he subsequently died of his wounds. He is buried in Etretat Churchyard, Seine Maritime, grave reference II.B.14.

Pte. John McDowall, 208048. Scottish Rifles. Survived.

John was born in Sandhead, in 1904 he married Jessie McAllister in Stranraer. The couple lived in Portencallie Farm, Kirkcolm and they had four sons and four daughters.

John enlisted around 1916 and was sent to the front. He was captured in the Somme area in 1917 and sent to work in the salt mines. He was reported missing and his wife received a postcard in July 1918 from the Red Cross which stated:

> *Dear Madam,*
>
> *In reply to your enquiry concerning Pte. John McDowall, Scots Rifles, we herewith beg to inform you that his name has not yet appeared on the Lists of Prisoners, received from Germany. When it does so, we shall let you know as soon as possible. As we find that many enquirers forward us photographs of their missing relatives or friends, we would mention that these are of no use to us in our investigations. There are no charges in connection with your enquiry...*

Later after his wife had been notified he was a prisoner, a letter was to arrive from the prisoner of war camp at Stendal:

> *My Dear Wife and All,*
>
> *Just a line to let you know that I am well and hope you are all in good health. Well dear I had your letter yesterday and was glad to see it – you had written it on the 23rd July. Well I see by it that you had a call of Polly Mann but she will just be the same yet, had you Bob up seeing you and how is his wife keeping? You can tell him I was asking for them all... Well how is Johnnie and Nellie getting on? You can tell them I am always thinking of them and you will be sending Nellie to School... Thank Mr Martin for the money he sent me I had it the day I was taken a prisoner.... Lots of love and kisses from your loving husband.*

John spent almost two years in captivity, but he returned home to Portencallie Farm and was to celebrate both his Golden and his Diamond Wedding Anniversary with Jessie and their family.

LESWALT WAR MEMORIAL

Leswalt new cemetery gates were opened in 1916. When the cemetery opened, Sir Andrew N. Agnew, of Lochnaw suggested to the council that a space should be reserved in the middle of the cemetery so that a memorial to those who had died during the war might be erected when the war was over.

The Rev. Wilson and Rev. Robertson combined congregations in Leswalt U.F. Church for the first Armistice Sunday anniversary. After the service, the large congregation with many men in uniform walked to the cemetery to watch the dedication and unveiling of their new war memorial.

Sir Andrew N. Agnew made a speech before the unveiling in which he said:

> *"These names will remain with us henceforth.....and when we are gone it will remain as a reminder to those who come after us that if they enjoy quiet and prosperity at home, if they see peace and goodwill spreading through the world, they owe these blessings to the Glorious Dead, to whom we reverently dedicate this memorial."*

The 16 feet high freestone obelisk was sculpted by Mr Nish from Stranraer. There are four highly polished granite panels around the obelisk. Three of the panels contain the names, rank and regiment of the thirty eight men who died in the Great War. On the facing panel the inscription reads:

TO THE HONOURED MEMORY OF RESIDENTS IN THE PARISH OF LESWALT WHO LAID DOWN THEIR LIVES FOR THEIR COUNTRY IN THE GREAT EUROPEAN WAR 1914 TO 1918 AND WHOSE NAMES ARE HERE INSCRIBED.

THIS MONUMENT IS ERECTED IN TOKEN OF ADMIRATION AND GRATITUDE BY THEIR FELLOW PARISHIONERS.

Transcription, clockwise, first panel:

LCE CPL	JOHN MILROY	R.S.F.
PTE	WILLIAM ALEXANDER	"
"	JAMES BURNS	"
"	SAMUEL CALDWELL	"
"	WILLIAM DORANS	"
"	GEORGE ESPIE	"

"	JAMES HARVEY	"
"	JOHN LEES	"
"	JAMES WATSON	"
GDSM	JOHN CALDWELL	S.G.
"	WILLIAM McNAUGHT	"
GNR	JAMES BAILLIE	R.F.A.
"	J.D. JENKINS	"
BOM	PETER REID	"

Second panel:

CORP	ROBERT RICHARDSON (D.C.M.)	G.H.
PTE	JAMES RICHARDSON	C.H.
"	P.A. MONTEITH	C.A.N.E.F.
"	J.A. MURRAY	"
"	ALEX RENNIE	"
"	ROBERT MILROY	M.R.
"	J. CRAIG	AUST. I.F.
"	DAVID MONTEITH	R.F.
"	CHARLES KERR	R.S.F.
"	ROBERT McCUBBIN	"

Third panel:

PTE	THOMAS SMALL	B.W.
GNR	JAMES RENNIE	R.G.A.
"	ALEX PATERSON	"
"	JOHN WITHER	"
PTE	ROBERT McNEILLIE	K.O.S.B.
LCE CPL	WILLIAM McKILLOPS	G.H.
PTE	WILLIAM HARVEY	"
"	WILLIAM MUIR	S.H.
"	ALEX McCARLIE	"
"	THOMAS GRACIE	"
"	A.A. LITTLE	A.S.C.
"	WILLIAM TRUEMAN	"
"	JAMES HERDSMAN	"
"	SAMUEL COOK	R.S.

Lance Corporal John Milroy, 14571.
8th Battalion Royal Scots Fusiliers.
Died 20th December 1918.

One of three sons of Mrs Sarah Logie of Balgracie, Leswalt, later East Freugh. John was born at Dindinnie. All three brothers were serving in the forces. His brother James was wounded on the same day that his other brother, Robert, was reported missing. Robert was killed on the day he was reported missing and is named below. John's two brothers had been in Canada on the outbreak of war. John enlisted in October 1914.

John was wounded earlier in the war, but he returned to fight again. Like so many thousands of soldiers who had come through the fighting and the armistice, John caught 'Spanish Flu', developed pneumonia and died before he could return home.

He is buried in Dedeagatch Cemetery, Greece, memorial reference 45. His brother Robert is listed below.

Brothers, John who was killed and James who was injured.

Pte. William Alexander, 19773.
1st Battalion Royal Scots Fusiliers.
Died from wounds 14th July 1916.

William was born in the Parish of Stoneykirk. He was the son of Mr Alexander of Kirkland Hill, Leswalt. Before the war William had worked for Mr Lees of Ervie.

William enlisted on 22 July 1915 and died when he was 19 years old. He is commemorated on Thiepval Memorial.

Pte. James Burns, 10th Battalion Royal Scots Fusiliers.
Killed in action 15th September 1917.

James was the eldest son of William and Jane Burns. His father had died before him and his mother had remarried and moved to Glasgow. Whatever his connection locally his death notice was in the Free Press.

His mother was told he had been killed instantaneously. He was 19. He is buried in Belgian Battery Corner Cemetery, grave reference I.L.12.

Pte. Samuel Caldwell, 8177.
1st/5th Battalion Royal Scots Fusiliers.
Killed in action 12th July 1915.

Samuel was the fourth son of Mrs Agnes Caldwell (later Mrs Edgar) of Dhuloch Mains and High Mark, Leswalt. All four brothers enlisted in the army in November 1914. Samuel's brother, John, listed further below, was in the Scots Guards and had been killed only a few weeks before him. Before the war Samuel had been employed as a farm servant by Mr Cochran at Northcairn.

Samuel was first reported as missing in Gallipoli on 12th July and his mother placed an appeal in the local newspaper for anyone with information to contact her. When the news came it was not good. He is commemorated on Helles Memorial, panel 72 to 75.

Corp William Dorans, 6954.
1st Battalion Royal Scots Fusiliers.
Killed in action 13th November 1914.

William Dorans was a reservist who was called up immediately on the outbreak of war. He had worked for Mr Fraser of Craigenholly and lived there with his wife and two children. William was the eldest son of Mr and Mrs Dorans of Larbrax.

William is commemorated on the Menin Gate Memorial to the missing. Although his rank is listed as a Private on Leswalt memorial he is listed as a Corporal with the CWGC. His name is also on Glenluce Memorial, and there is a photograph of him in that section.

Pte. George Sproat Espie, 14936.
6th/7th Battalion Royal Scots Fusiliers.
Killed in action 31st July 1917.

George was married and lived with his wife at Kirminnoch, Ervie. He enlisted on the outbreak of war and after training was sent to France, where he had been serving for around a year and a half. George is commemorated on the Menin Gate Memorial panel 19 and 33.

Pte. James Harvey, 12539.
1st Battalion Royal Scots Fusiliers.
Killed in action 16th June 1915.

James was born in the parish of Inch. He worked as a farm hand and continued to do this when he moved to Ayrshire.

He was first reported missing then presumed killed on the above date. James is commemorated on the Menin Gate. He is not the same man as his namesake buried in the Glebe Cemetery, Stranraer.

Pte. John Skimming Lees, 7030.
1st/5th Battalion Royal Scots Fusiliers.
Killed in action 14th July 1915.

John was born in Leswalt. His parents were Mr and Mrs David Lees of Burgess Cottage, Leswalt. He is on Larbrax School Roll of Honour as being in the Gordon Highlanders, but must have transferred to the R.S.F.

He was 18 when he took part in horrendous fighting at Gallipoli. He is commemorated on Helles memorial, panel 72 to 75. John is also on Stranraer Memorial.

Pte. James Watson, 10859.
2nd Battalion Royal Scots Fusiliers.
Killed in action 31st October 1914.

I could find out very little else about James Watson from the local newspaper which could confirm the background details of this man.

He is most likely to have been the adopted son of Mrs Dougan 27 Sheuchan Street, Stranraer. Mrs Dougan had four sons, her adopted son and her son-in-law all serving in the forces at the same time. He was born in the parish of Inch and had already been wounded in the left shoulder at Ypres.

He has no known grave and is commemorated on the Menin Gate panel 19 and 33.

Gdsm. John Caldwell, 11960.
2nd Battalion Scots Guards.
Died from wounds 19th May 1915.

Brother to the above named Samuel Caldwell, John's mother had remarried and moved from Leswalt area to Mull Farm in Drummore. John had two other brothers serving, William was also in the Scots Guards.

John had been a farm worker and was employed at High Mark before the war. He is buried in Bethune Town Cemetery, grave reference III.D.73. He was 21.

Gdsm. William McNaught, 12611.
2nd Battalion Scots Guards.
Killed in action 29th September 1915.

William was the youngest son of James Kerr McNaught and Janet Todd McNaught of Lochnaw. Prior to the war he was second engineer on board the Anchor liner Transylvania. He was a good school friend of James McCormack the coal merchant's son and James wrote home the story of the circumstances of William's death. The full letter is included at the end of the Stranraer section. According to the letter, one of his last acts was one of kindness to an injured comrade who was lying in the open. William risked his life to take him water.

Aged 28 when he was killed, he is commemorated on Loos Memorial, panel 8 and 9.

Gunner James Osborne Baillie, L/7006.
210th Brigade Royal Field Artillery.
Killed in action 26th March 1918.

James was the eldest son of John and Mary Baillie (nee Lauchlin) of High Auchneil, Leswalt. He was one of five brothers all serving the Colours at the same time. James' brother William was badly wounded on 18th October 1918 and was admitted to hospital to recover from his injuries. Alex Baillie had lost his good friend Thomas Hamilton (Inch Memorial), and another brother, Hugh had written home in a letter:-

> *The town we are in is nothing but a mass of ruins. When I saw those ruins I could picture myself in the nice, quiet homesteads which they were a year ago. Splendid churches have been knocked down and even the graves in the churchyards have been blown to pieces. No-one at home can realise the conduct of the Germans towards the poor Belgians, unless they see the state of the country for themselves. If the enemy lands on the shores of England, the fate of the people there will be similar.*

When James was killed his father inserted the following poem in the local newspaper:

Sleep on, dear son, and take your rest,
They miss you most who loved you best.

James was married to Grace Neville, Aldouran Bridge, Leswalt. He was 37 when he was killed and he is commemorated on Arras memorial. He is also named on the family headstone in Kirkcolm churchyard.

Gunner John D. Jenkins, 250547.
50th Brigade Royal Horse and Field Artillery.
Killed in action 11th October 1918.

Born in the Parish of Inch, John was the only son of William and Isabella Jenkins of Cairnbrock, Leswalt.

Aged 20 when he was killed he is commemorated on Tyne Cot Memorial, panel 4 to 6 and 162.

Gunner Peter Reid, 646671.
74th Brigade Royal Field Artillery.
Killed in action 18th September 1918.

Peter was the second son of Ivie and Colina Reid of the Challoch. He was brought up in Glasserton, with his siblings.

During the war his elder brother served with the Royal North Lancs and became a 2nd Lieutenant, while a sister was doing munition work.

Aged 21 when he was killed, he is buried at Lagnicourt Hedge Cemetery, grave reference I.B.2.

Corp. Robert Tennyson Tarbert Richardson, 266937.
6th Battalion Gordon Highlanders. D.C.M.
Killed in action 23rd March 1918.

Robert Richardson was eldest son of John and Jane Richardson of High Barbeth, Leswalt and later Weirston, Kirkcolm. Brother to the below named James.

Before the war he had been a gamekeeper at East Wemyss, Glenapp Castle and Dunskey Estate.

He had received a D.C.M. for gallantry in the field, his citation read:

> *"Lance-Corporal Richardson displayed great courage and determination during a bombing attack against the enemy, and materially assisted in the success of the operation."*

He was wounded in the Battle of Loos in September 1915, but had recovered and returned to the trenches. He had only been back around ten days when he was returned to hospital in Cardiff with frostbite. He remained in hospital for four months to recover.

He was 28 when he was killed and like so many others has no known grave. He is commemorated on Arras Memorial.

Pte. James Brydson Richardson.
6th Battalion Cameron Highlanders.
Killed in action 29th September 1917.

Brother to the above named Robert, James was killed a few short months before his brother. He is buried at Duisan British Cemetery, Etruin grave reference V.B.41. This was close to a Casualty Clearing Station.

James is named on the family headstone in Leswalt Old Kirkyard.

Pte. Peter Agnew Monteith, 154349.
1st Battalion Canadian Pioneers.
Killed in action 13th June 1916.

Peter was eldest the son of the late Robert and Mrs Mary Monteith (nee Agnew), he was born on 4th September 1877 in Stranraer. His father was a farmer who had died in 1901 leaving his mother to raise him with his six brothers and sisters. When he emigrated to Canada he listed his mother as his next of kin and recorded that she was still living at the Knock and Maize, Portpatrick.

Peter was a joiner who had learned his trade with Alex McLauchlin of Stranraer. He had worked for a while at Ailsa Shipbuilding Yard at Troon, and at the carriage works of the Glasgow and South Western Railway, Kilmarnock.

He had spent a year in the Galloway Rifle Volunteers before emigrating in around 1904 to what was hoped to be a new life in Canada. He had spent a long time visiting all around America and Canada before deciding to settle in Vancouver Island.

He was 5 feet 7 inches tall with a dark complexion, dark brown hair and grey eyes. Peter passed as medically fit for service in September 1915.

The Monteith family from left to right: Alexander, Christine, Agnes on her mother Mary's knee, Maggie, Ross, Marjory, Tom on his father Robert's knee, Peter. Robert junior is sitting at the front and Mary junior is standing at the back.

Peter's mother received the following letter on his death:

> *"It is my very sad duty to write to you and inform you of the death of your son Peter, who was killed in action on the night of the 12th. He was my best friend in our whole Company, and some time ago he gave me your address, and asked me to write to you if anything should happen to him. There was some very fierce fighting, and part of our Company was in the worst of one of the fiercest bombardments we have had on this front, and it was there that Peter met his death. There is one, and only one, comforting thing about it, and that is that he was killed at once and did not suffer. His body was recovered after the fighting and buried near the front line. It will comfort you in time to know how highly he was thought of by all his comrades. He was always the same, always willing to help any one of the boys. He was my greatest chum, and I shall miss him at every turn I make, and I think he is missed more than any of the others we lost. This had been a hard letter for me to write, and I hope you will find some comfort in the fact that he was so highly thought of, and that he did his duty like a man."*

He was killed in action near Zillebeke and is named on the Menin Gate Memorial and the family headstone at Inch. His mother, Mary, outlived three of her children.

Pte. James Agnew Murray, 8894.
1st Battalion Highland Light Infantry.
Died of wounds 18th April 1915.

Whilst Leswalt memorial has listed James as being in the Canadian Expeditionary Forces, they made this assumption based on the fact that James had emigrated with his parents, Mr and Mrs Thomas Murray to 44 Fairfield Avenue, Greenfield Park, Montreal. James married Marion Train in 1903 at Mauchline, Ayrshire before he emigrated.

Either his parents had belonged to Leswalt or James had worked locally there at some time. Whatever his local connection, his death announcement was in the local newspaper.

Whilst James is listed with the SNWM he is not on the CWGC, and although his final resting place is not recorded, his death announcement in the local newspaper announces he died of wounds in the Persian Gulf at Mesopotamia.

Pte. Alexander Rennie, 319875.
51st Battery, Canadian Field Artillery.
Died 22nd May 1916.

Alex Rennie was born in Leswalt to David and Catherine Rennie. The couple had a large family and in the 1901 census they were living at Leswalt with their 10 children. He married Margaret Little in 1914, at Whithorn. Alex' and his wife and parents seem to have emigrated to Canada at some stage, and it would have been there he enlisted.

Alex' records are not available online unlike almost all other Canadian military records for the Great War. Whatever the cause of his death, injury or illness, Alex died at home in Canada, and is buried at Ottowa, Beechwood Cemetery, grave reference D.R.24.4.

Pte. Robert Milroy, 42506.
Canadian Mounted Rifles.
Killed in action 15th September 1915.

Brother to the above John Milroy. Robert was one of three sons of Mrs Sarah Logie of Balgracie. Born in Glasgow in 1897, he was in Canada on the outbreak of war with his brother James and they both enlisted there. A farm labourer to trade, Robert cited his mother as his next of kin when he enlisted. He was 5 feet 4 with a fair complexion, brown hair, and brown eyes. Brother James had also been wounded and had rejoined his regiment at the time their mother was informed of Robert's death. He is commemorated on Vimy Memorial.

Pte. John Craig, 5672.
25th Battalion Australian Imperial Forces.
Died from wounds 17th October 1917.

John Craig was native to Leswalt. About 1907 John had emigrated to Australia. There he had bought and run a farm. On the outbreak of war he sold his farm and joined the services in Australia. His sister was Mrs Caughie from Knocknain. His brother-in-law Robert Caughie inserted his death notice in the local newspaper.

John was taken to 12th General hospital on the outskirts of Rouen when he was wounded. He is buried in St. Sever Cemetery Extension, grave reference P.III.J.10A.

Pte. David Monteith, 66100.
10th Battalion Royal Fusiliers.
Killed in action 9th March 1918.

David Monteith had lived with his family at Auchentibbert, and must have been familiar with three other men who are named on local memorials all from 'The Kibbert'. They include, the Todd brothers on Stoneykirk Memorial, and James McCrorie on Glenluce. Other men from Auchentibbert also served including Pte. McGrady and Pte. McCulloch who are both mentioned in newspaper reports.

When David died his mother and siblings inserted the following poem into the local newspaper:

Duty called, and he was there
To do his bit and take his share;
His heart was good, his spirit brave
His resting place a soldier's grave.
We miss him, yes, we miss him!
Hiss loss we are left to mourn;
It's hard to sit at times and think
He never shall return.

He is buried at Hooge Crater Cemetery, Belgium, grave reference XI.F.10. David is named on Leswalt and Stoneykirk Memorials.

Pte. Charles Kerr, 8110.
5th Battalion Royal Scots Fusiliers.
Killed in action 31st December 1915.

Charles Kerr was the son of Mrs Hamilton of Deerpark, Castle Kennedy (later Mrs Slavin). Before the war he was employed by Joseph Johnson of Deerpark. He was a native of Leswalt. Charles Joined the RSF in November 1914 and fought at Gallipoli. His mother received notice that he had been injured on the 30th December, but a comrade wrote a letter which suggested he was either killed on that date or died the following day from wounds:

> *"A few lines to say I have been wounded and lying in St Andrew's Military Hospital, Malta. I was wounded in the face by the bursting of a bomb, but cheer up and don't worry, for I will soon be all right again. I am very sorry to say Charlie Kerr was killed beside me the same day as I was hit. That was on December 30th. He was hit on the head and back. He died about half an hour afterwards. I spoke to him then but he could not answer me. He was then carried away for there was a heavy bombardment on at the time, and the shells were flying all around us. It was a pure hell all that day, so Charlie was hit with a piece of one of the shells. I don't know how I missed some of them. There is only a hundred of us left now, so I consider myself very lucky that I got through it with what I got, and I have myself to blame for it, for I volunteered to do a thing, and that was when I got hit."*

Lieutenant J.M. Kerr also wrote to Mrs Hamilton about the death of her son:

> *"We were very sorry when we learned that your son, Private Charles Kerr, No. 8110, had died of the wounds he received in action on 30th*

December, and his Company Officer has asked me to write expressing our deep sympathy with you in your bereavement. As he was not in my platoon, I had not a great deal of opportunity of coming in touch with him, but I know he was respected in the Company as a good and brave soldier, and he – like other good fellows from Stranraer, who fell in the closing days of 1915 – coolly laid down his life in a successful and important action. His own Platoon Officer, Mr McNaughton, also died of wounds on the same occasion. He was wounded by a shell, but it will be a relief to you to know that he became unconscious, and was spared any suffering which otherwise he might have had."

Charles is buried in Lancashire Landing Cemetery, Turkey. He is also commemorated on Inch War Memorial.

Pte. Robert McCubbin, 20338.
1st Battalion Royal Scots Fusiliers.
Killed in action 14th July 1916.

Born in Stranraer in 1898. Before the war Robert was assisting with the dairy at High Mark, Leswalt. He would therefore have known the Patersons very well, including the below named Alexander.

When Robert joined the army he completed a short period of training before being sent to the front. He is commemorated on the Thiepval Memorial, pier and face 3C.

Pte. Thomas Small, 7524.
1st Battalion Black Watch.
Killed in action 11th November 1914.

Thomas was born in Leslie, near Glenrothes, and was resident for a time in Kirkcaldy. Already a member of the forces Thomas had spent 12 years in India before returning home. By the time he married Bridget Campbell in 1908, he listed his usual address as Burgess, Leswalt and he was a postman there. By 1911 he was living in Rose Cottage, Leswalt.

Had he not been a reservist, he would not have been called up until 1916, however he was one of the first to be called up when war broke out. He left behind his wife and six children all of whom were under the age of six; the youngest born the year he was killed. With no known grave, Thomas is commemorated on the Menin Gate panel 37. His brother John, was killed the following year, he too has no known grave.

Gunner James Rennie, 301706.
3rd Mountain Bty., Royal Garrison Artillery.
Killed in action 28th November 1917.

James was the son of David and Kathleen Rennie. He was married to Agnes Blair and they lived at 29 Agnew Crescent, Stranraer.

Gunner Rennie wrote a lengthy letter home to the Rev. J Heggie:

> *Your welcome letter to hand. I should have written sooner. You have no idea how we long to hear from friends at home. When the mail gets dished out, and nothing for you- well, you go to bed, such as it is, very crestfallen. You say I must have seen a lot of fighting. I have had my share. We had a big scrap on the 25th September. No doubt you will have read about it. We were at it for a week before the real thing came off. We fired every day over 200 rounds. The day our men charged it must have been over 3000. We captured three lines of trenches with two battalions of infantry, and about 300 prisoners. The Germans brought up about 40,000 men from Lille – in fact, all the garrison there – and our men were forced to retire after destroying all the gun fortifications. It has rained for over a week, and our lines are something dreadful; in fact it is nearly impossible to get about. It the mud gets any worse they will have to supply us with flying machines. We never suffered anything like this last winter. It seems very strange that I have never met in with any Stranraer lads. I see their deaths in the "Free Press," and I know they have been out here, but of course we have a long line, say, about from Stranraer to Newton Stewart. It is difficult to find any one you know, as we are never much more than a mile on each side of our billet; but I am always enquiring, and I have hopes that I will run across a Stranraer Chiel before long. I saw a flying machine brought down one morning about two months ago by one of our daring flyers. The German aviators are no match for our men. After they were brought down, they opened their machine gun on our infantry that went to take them prisoners. I am pleased to say they will fire no more machine-guns, as they got their just deserts. Our men brought another one down near Sallie. About one mile on the right of our battery. He hadn't a chance to use his gun as he turned turtle. Both machines were very little damaged, and I have seen them flying over the Huns, which must make their hearts sore. I have just received word about my brother in law being dead. There will be many sad homes in Stranraer and district, but I would rather be where they are than have it said I was afraid to enlist (Shirkers, take note!) I expect to be in Stranraer shortly for a short leave, and I may be able to explain more fully about all my adventures abroad among the muck.*

James became ill and died of fever at Quetta Hospital, India, aged 39 years. He is buried in Quetta Government Cemetery Ref 2925. He is commemorated on Delhi Memorial.

Gunner Alexander Paterson, 184th Siege Bty. Royal Garrison Artillery. Killed in action 4th June 1917.

Alexander was the son of Samuel and Sarah Paterson, High Mark, Leswalt. His family later lived in Lochans. Before the war Alexander had worked as a dairyman. He enlisted in 1915 and had been on service abroad for almost two years.

Alexander is also on the war memorial at Kirkcolm, and his photograph is included in that section. Alexander is named on the headstone of his grandfather in Portpatrick Cemetery. His name is spelt Patterson on the CWGC.

Gunner John Wither, 107438. 1st Highland Heavy Bty., Royal Garrison Artillery. Died 9th April 1919.

There are two men listed as having been killed in the war with the name John Wither. Both are local, the other is on Sandhead War Memorial.

John could not have died in Scotland as his death is not registered there. John was 27 when he died. His body was returned home and he is buried in Leswalt Old Kirkyard.

Pte. Robert McNeillie, 202656. 2nd Battalion King's Own Scottish Borderers. Died from wounds 27th October 1917.

Robert was the youngest son of Robert and Catherine McNeillie and was born in Leswalt. The family lived in a few dairies including Mark, Balcarry in Glenluce and Ballaird in Colmonell. Robert had worked the dairy with his father before he enlisted. He had only been in the army for five months when he was killed. He was 19.

His parents inserted the following poem in the local paper:

His King and coutry called him,
So he took his only chance
To show his grit. He did his bit
And fell "somewhere in France".

He is buried in Lijssenthoek Military Cemetery, Belgium, grave reference XXII.F.1A.

Lance Corp. William McKillops, 7339. 8th/10th Battalion Gordon Highlanders. Died from wounds 2nd May 1917.

William McKillops was born in Portpatrick. His parents lived at High Craichmore, Leswalt. He was married to Janet McNaughton, who later moved to Perth. Before the war he had worked for the Portpatrick and Wigtownshire Joint Railway Company at Dunragit Station.

He had been in France since June 1915 and had seen very fierce fighting. He was attached to the Light Railway Operating Company there. Whilst working on the railway he received severe injuries through a railway accident. William died from his injuries at a Dressing Station. He was 29.

He is buried at Duisans British Cemetery, Etrun, grave reference II.Q.10. There is another man with the same name on Stranraer memorial and it is more than likely that the men were related.

Pte. William J. Harvey, 9675. 2nd Battalion Gordon Highlanders. Killed in action 29th October 1914.

William had been a ploughman with Mr Hunter of Whiteleys before joining the army around 1904. He had been in India for eight years before the outbreak of war and was immediately posted to Cairo. One of William's brothers, John, had also been in the army for a number of years and was a Sergeant first with the 21st Fusiliers then with the Territorials. Another brother Robert lived at Little Lochans, and sister Mary lived in Glasgow.

William's brother-in-law Mr Peter Ramsey from Mains of Airies Farm received a letter notifying the family that William was missing. The letter from the Adjutant of the Company stated that William had gone missing with many others who had been in a trench to the right of the battalion. The comrades had been completely cut off and the Company were making enquiries in Berlin as to their fate. It was possible they had been taken prisoners and the Adjutant stated they could only hope for the best. News was later received that William had been killed on that day. William is commemorated on the Menin Gate Memorial.

Pte. William Muir, 6777.
7th Battalion Seaforth Highlanders.
Killed in action 12th October 1916.

William was born in Creetown. He was married to Isabella and she lived in Sword Street, Glasgow. Before the war William worked for William Adair, Newfield, Leswalt. William is buried in Warlencourt British Cemetery, France, grave reference V.G.14.

Pte. Alexander McCarlie, 241436.
1st/4th Seaforth Highlanders.
Killed in action 20th July 1918.

Alexander was married to Helen King from Kirkland Cottage, Lochnaw, they had four young children and he worked for Sir Andrew Agnew. His parents lived at 5 Queen Street, Stranraer. He had a brother on active service and sisters at home.

Alexander had been on active service for fourteen months. He had previously been admitted to No.22 General Hospital France suffering from trench fever. He was 31 when he was killed. His parents inserted the following poem in the local newspaper when he died:

We cannot forget him, we loved him too dearly
For his memory to fade from our lives like a dream
But our lips need not speak when our hearts mourn sincerely,
For grief often dwells where it seldom is seen.

Alexander is buried in Marfaux British Cemetery, Marne, grave reference VIII.D.5. He is also named on Stranraer War Memorial.

Pte. Thomas Gracie, 241868.
5th Battalion Seaforth Highlanders.
Killed in action 6th September 1917.

Thomas was the youngest son of Mr and Mrs Samuel Gracie of Little Airies, Ervie. He had two brothers who were both on active service. Before the war Thomas had helped his father on the farm. After a short period of training Thomas was sent to France. He had only been there for three months when he was killed. He was 20.

He was the namesake of one of the Heart of Midlothian Football Players of the famous McCrae's Battalion who was killed in the war.

Thomas is commemorated on Tyne Cot Memorial, panel 132 to 135 and 162A.

Pte. Alexander Little, 30280.
5th Brigade Canadian Field Artillery.
Killed in action 28th October 1917.

Alexander was the 31 year old son of Nathan and Elizabeth Little of High Balyett. He had emigrated to Canada and enlisted there on 24th September 1914. On his Canadian attestation papers he recorded that he had served a year in Stranraer Artillery 1905-1906, and the Hamilton Ontario Militia 1912-1913. He was described as 5 ft 5 inches, with a dark complexion, brown eyes and dark brown hair.

Alexander's photo had appeared in the local newspaper just a few months before his death as he had won a Military Medal for bravery in the field. In the local newspaper his rank was recorded as Lance-Corporal. Perhaps there was insufficient time to record his promotion or perhaps there was an error in either the newspaper or the CWGC in recording his rank.

Alexander is buried in Vlamertinghe New Military Cemetery, Ieper, grave reference IX.E.5.

Pte. William Trueman, 331969.
1st Base Mechanical Transport Dept. Army Service Corps.
Died from wounds 27th August 1918.

William was the first of the three Trueman brothers to be posted abroad. Before the war he was a dairyman for Mr Hannay at the Challoch. William was 19 when he died from tetanus after being wounded in action. He is buried in St Sever Cemetery Extension, Rouen, grave reference Q.V.H 16. He died the same day as his brother.

William's sister, Annie Trueman is listed on the second Cairnryan Memorial of those who served their country. She enlisted in the WRAF on 1st October 1918 and was stationed at RNAS Luce Bay. When she enlisted, she would have known that all three of her brothers had already been killed in the war. William and his two brothers are on Cairnryan War Memorial, and a photograph of him is printed in that section.

Pte. James Herdsman. 295416.
12th Battalion Royal Scots Fusiliers.
Killed in action 21st April 1917.

James Gorman Herdsman was born on the 24th November 1894 to Agnes Herdsman at Greenfield, Leswalt; his father was not named when his birth was registered, although his mother was from Meikle Galdenoch, Leswalt. The local paper reported that he had been killed in action in Egypt. He had originally enlisted in the Ayrshire Yeomanry in 1915 but was transferred to the Imperial Camel Corps. He had also worked at Meikle Galdenoch before the war.

It is possible that James Herdsman is the same man who tried to rescue his friend, Andrew Murray from the River Cree either when he was home on leave or before he enlisted. It is an unusual name in the area and it is more than likely the same man. James did manage to recover his friend from the water, but he had already died. Andrew Murray's brother is listed on Stranraer War Memorial.

There is no record with the CWGC or SNWM of a James Herdsman as having been killed in the war; however a death announcement in the local newspaper for a man killed on the same date offers sympathies to Mr and Mrs Herdsman on the death of Pte. James Alexander although it does not suggest they are his parents. He is named as James Alexander on the 1911 census and living with his aunt and uncle John and Jane Herdsman and he may well have been raised by them. It is more than likely that James Herdsman is the same man who is named as James Alexander on Stranraer War Memorial.

If it is the same man then, James is buried in Gaza War Cemetery, grave reference X.E.2.

Pte. Samuel Cook, 20750.
2nd Battalion Royal Scots.
Killed in action 12th July 1916.

Samuel was the son of Joseph and Annie Cook (nee Waterson) from Carscreugh, later Ernespie Lodge. He was killed in the Battle of the Somme aged 20.

Samuel is commemorated on Theipval Memorial and is named on the family headstone in Glenluce Cemetery.

Sons of Leswalt remembered

For whatever reasons long forgotten, some men who seem to have connections with an area are not named on the local war memorial. For a few, it may have been an oversight, perhaps for others it was a choice not to have their name on the memorial, or perhaps the men did not meet the criteria set by that particular war memorial committee.

Serg. Alexander Beggs Torrance.
1st/14th Battalion London Scottish.
Killed in action 1st July 1916.

Alexander was called after his father who had lived and worked at the Calcutta Inn, Whithorn. He is named on the family headstone in Leswalt Old Kirkyard, which also has the names of generations of Torrances from Leswalt.

Alexander was the recipient of a Military Medal for bravery in the field. He is commemorated on Thiepval Memorial. Alexander was 26. He is not named on any other local memorial.

Pte. George Anderson, 40881.
2nd Battalion Cameronians.
Killed in action 29th June 1917.

George was born in Wigtown although at the time of his death his parents gave their address as 188 Holm Street, Anderston, Glasgow. His father and two other brothers were all serving at the same time.

Before the war George was working on the farm of High Craichmore and his sister and brother-in-law lived at Sheuchan Lane, Stranraer.

George is buried in Perth Cemetery (China Wall), Ieper, grave reference I.B.7. He is not named on any local war memorial.

NEW LUCE WAR MEMORIAL

New Luce memorial was unveiled by the Earl of Stair on a calm Sunday morning in May 1920. A large congregation attended the service conducted by the Rev. Alexander and the Rev. Graham, in what appears to have been a very lengthy sermon. Rev. Graham's son Second Lieutenant Gerald Francis Graham had been awarded a Military Cross for "conspicuous gallantry and devotion to duty whilst acting as a forward observation officer". In his speech at the unveiling ceremony Lord Stair remembered being in a village in Belgium called Zandvoorde, Flanders. Two German shells had arrived, hitting the church tower. Within a short time the whole village had been in ruins. Many civilians had been killed and the Earl remembered at least one man from New Luce was amongst those fighting there to defend the people.

The memorial is a tall Celtic cross on a stepped base designed by James Miller, a Glasgow architect. It was constructed by Glasgow buiding contractor Mr S. Smith. The idea and organisation of the memorial had been that of Mr John McWhirter of Barlure and he received due praise for all his efforts at the ceremony. The memorial is in the standing at the side of the road at the front of the village church, in the church wall. The inscription reads:

1914 – 1918 TO THE GLORY OF GOD AND IN LOVING MEMORY OF THE MEN CONNECTED WITH THIS PARISH WHO FELL IN THE GREAT WAR.

JAMES HEWITSON, 1/8TH A. & S. HIGHS. KILLED 17TH MARCH 1917.

JAMES KEATINGS, 15TH H.L.I. KILLED 7TH MAY 1916.

W.J. McLEAN, ROYAL ENGINEERS. KILLED 19TH NOVEMBER 1917.

ROBERT McMEEKING, R.F.A. KILLED 12TH JUNE 1917.

WILLIAM McMEEKING, 2ND H.L.I. KILLED 28TH APRIL 1917.

ROBERT McWHIRTER, 7TH CAMERON HIGHS. KILLED 25TH SEPTEMBER 1915.

THOMAS MILROY, 49TH CANADIANS. KILLED 30TH OCTOBER 1917.

JOHN MURRAY, 1ST BLACK WATCH. KILLED 25TH SEPTEMBER 1916.

THOMAS NISH, ROYAL SCOTS FUSILIERS. DIED 26TH JANUARY 1917.

On a stone set into the wall behind the memorial is inscribed:

THEIR NAME LIVETH FOR EVERMORE.

Private James Hewitson, 301456.
1st/8th Argyll and Sutherland Highlanders.
Killed in action 17th March 1917.

Eldest son of Robert and Grace Hewitson. Before the outbreak of war he had been a shepherd in the service of the Duke of Argyll at Campbellton. James had previously been a shepherd to the Earl of Stair at the home farm of Balker. His father had been a shepherd for over twenty years at Darnimow. The family had lived at Awies, New Luce and later moved to Shennas, Ballantrae.

James' Company Commander wrote to express his sympathies and referred to his expert violin playing:

> *"He was a wonderful fiddler, and used to come round and play to us after dinner. He also played so well that we found it hard to let him go, even at a late hour."*

James was 23 when he was killed. He is buried at Roclincourt Cemetery in France, grave reference II.E.15

Pte. James Keatings, 13837.
15th Highland Light Infantry.
Killed in action 7th May 1916.

The Galloway Advertiser and Wigtownshire Free Press records refer to a military honour being bestowed on James Keating. Unfortunately the date recorded is incorrect and I was unable to trace anything further about his award. The CWGC lists his date of death as 8th May 1916. He is buried in Authuile Military Cemetery, Somme, France, grave reference A.11.

Pioneer William Jackson McLean, 41864.
14th Division Signal Coy. Royal Engineers.
Died of wounds 19th November 1917.

Originally from New Luce, William had moved to Glasgow where he was a constable in the Eastern Division before enlisting. He lived with his wife and three children at 2 Yate Street, Glasgow. He was 29 when he died.

He was buried at Duhallow Advanced Dressing Station, Ieper, where he died from wounds. His grave reference there is III.C.1.

Gunner Robert McMeeking, 951578. Royal Field Artillery. Killed in action 12th June 1917.

Youngest son of William McMeeking of Waterfoot, New Luce. His mother had died aged just 31 in 1891. Robert had left the area to work with the Glasgow Corporation on the tramway service.

Robert was serving at the same time as his two brothers James and William. His brother William had been posted missing since April 1917 and no official confirmation of his death came through until after Robert's death.

Robert's father was informed of his death by letter from a chaplain serving with the forces. He was 29 when he was killed. He is buried in Anzin-St. Aubin British Cemetery, France, grave reference III.C.17. He is named on the family headstone in New Luce Kirkyard where his name is spelt McMecking.

Lance Corporal William McMeeking, 35161. 2nd Highland Light Infantry. Killed in action 28th April 1917.

Elder brother to the above Robert McMeeking, William was married to Mary Ann Matthews McMeeking of Stairdam, Murthly, Perthshire.

William had served his apprenticeship as a gardener at Lochinch Castle and after a number of important appointments had become head gardener at Craigie House Ayrshire before enlisting.

William had passed exams for signalling to gain his rank in the army. He was first posted as wounded and missing and his father was notified, but it was not until April 1918 that his father was informed of his death. He was killed in the planned offensive at Arras in April 1917. He is commemorated on Arras Memorial. As with his brother Robert his last name is spelt McMecking on the family headstone in New Luce Kirkyard.

His remaining brother, James, survived the war.

Private Robert McWhirter, S/13661.
7th Cameron Highlanders.
Killed in action 25th September 1915.

Son of John McWhirter of Barlure, who played a leading role in having a memorial in New Luce, and stepson of Jessie McWhirter. Robert was originally posted as missing and his parents informed.

The 25th September was the first day of the Battle of Loos where the British forces outnumbered Germans 7 to 1. The battle was a disaster for the British, lack of shells, a planned gas release that killed and injured their own soldiers and lack of covering fire meant that the German machine guns could kill the British forces by the thousand.

Robert is commemorated on Loos Memorial, France.

Private Thomas Milroy, 252132.
49th Battalion Canadian Infantry.
Killed in action 30th October 1917.

Third son of Thomas and Mary Milroy (nee Murray), High Mark, New Luce. Thomas was a farmer and was 31 when he was killed. He had been born on 7th August 1886 in Stranraer.

Thomas enlisted in Canada on 21st January 1915. He was five feet eight inches tall with a dark complexion, blue eyes and brown hair. He also had long scar on his left hand.

He is buried at Poelcapelle British Cemetery, Belgium, grave reference XIX.B.8. Thomas is also on the war memorial at Inch and Cairnryan. He is also named on the family headstone in New Luce Kirkyard.

Private John Murray, S/40297. 1st Black Watch. Killed in action 25th September 1916.

Son of the local blacksmith at The Smithy, New Luce, John Murray, called after his father, was educated in New Luce Public School before he went on to work on farms. When he was twenty years old he joined Glasgow's Police Force and was promoted to plain clothes detective in a few years.

He joined the Scottish Horse and underwent training before being transferred to the Black Watch and posted to France in August 1916. He was only in France for six weeks when he was killed.

John was killed in the Battle of the Somme and like thousands of others he is commemorated on Thiepval Memorial to the missing.

Private Thomas Nish, 33377. 10th Battalion Royal Scots Fusiliers. Died 26th January 1917.

Born on 21st September 1879 in New Luce, Thomas was the son of James Nish, a well known local joiner. His father had died before 1901 and he lived with his mother, Mary, brothers Robert and John, and sister Mary in Main Street New Luce. Thomas was an agricultural labourer whilst both his brothers had followed in his father's trade as joiners.

Thomas died of pneumonia in Dumfries Infirmary aged 38. He is buried in New Luce Parish Churchyard. His younger brother Robert registered his death.

Sons of New Luce remembered.

Not on the war memorial, but named in the churchyard is the below named George Bell, and the story of David McLean who survived the war.

Pte. George Bell,
11th Battalion Australian Infantry Forces.
Killed in action 25th April 1915.

George was a grandson of the late John Bell of Glenwhilly. He had emigrated to Australia and it was there he enlisted. The family headstone in New Luce Kirkyard records his age as 28. George was a cousin of Tom McGill who is named on the war memorial at Glenluce.

He was in the same Battalion and went to war aboard the same troopship on the same day as Andrew Forster, who is named on the War Memorial at Inch. They surely must have known one another.

George was first reported missing and the Red Cross did what they could to find out what had happened to him. It emerged that when the forces landed on the beach they came under fire. Sgt. Chamberlain was in charge of the group of men George was with. Shortly after landing they were not seen again. It later emerged that Sgt. Chamberlain had been taken prisoner and this gave hope to George's family. However some time later a comrade told how George was shot in the thigh and was bleeding very heavily. His comrades got to him and bound his wound, but under very heavy fire they had to leave him.

He buried is in Plugges Plateau Cemetery, Anzac, grave reference B.6. He is commemorated on the Australian War Memorial. His aunt, mother of Tom McGill, filled in his records for the Australian forces after his death.

Pte. David Baird McLean, 16th Battalion Highland Light Infantry. Prisoner of War, survived.

Born in New Luce in 1897 and named after his father, David was taken prisoner on 20th November 1916. He had been injured and captured alongside a number of others. Despite his injuries, the men had been forced to walk some distance with the aid of a rifle butt in the neck.

David recalled that he had his wounds dressed fairly quickly though others had to wait days before getting any sort of medical attention. He was confined outdoors in a wire cage, with no shelter or bedding. Sometime later he was transferred to Delbruck where he was employed on a farm ploughing with oxen and doing general farm work. He was allowed a Sunday off unless the farm was busy.

For two years, ten French prisoners, one Englishman and he were all confined to sleeping in a very small room, so small that when they were all lying down there was no room for any of them to stand up or move around. The sanitation was non-existent and whilst he was there he became seriously ill with influenza. No medical attention was given and his French comrades brought him the little food that was allowed. This diet consisted of coffee and black bread at breakfast, and lunchtime they had soup made from water and unwashed vegetables. David recalled that "You could see the dirt and feel the sand grating on your teeth." Supper was described as "a view of the scenery by moonlight."

The men were all glad that they were allowed to receive parcels from home and he admitted that they would have starved had they not raided hen houses and dairies for additional sustenance.

David survived the war and recovered from the wounds and his influenza. I was saddened to discover that the death of a David Baird McLean was recorded in New Luce as a result of precognitive drowning, however the date of death in 1917 meant it could not be the same man, sadly for his mother however, the man was his father. David would still have been in captivity at the time.

The McCredie Family, Church Cottage, New Luce.

Four sons and a nephew of Mr and Mrs McCredie all were able to return home after the war was over. The Free Press featured them as 'doing their bit' in the army.

From the top: Pte Andrew McCredie, RGA., Pte. Jas McCredie, 1st Scots Guards, Pte Charles McCredie, 10th Gordon Highlanders, Pte. Robert McCredie, RGA, and Pte Jas. McGuire, 2nd Gordon Highlanders.

PORTPATRICK WAR MEMORIAL

Around one thousand people were thought to have attended the unveiling of Portpatrick War Memorial on Sunday 6th November 1921. The Parish Church did it's best to accommodate the huge crowd, where the Rev. James R. Kennedy gave a short address, followed by Rev. John Brownlie who was in army uniform.

A procession walked from the church, led by Stranraer Town Band, with relatives of the deceased, ex-servicemen led by Major James McLean, Craigmount V.A.D. Nurses, and school children, to the main road where Portpatrick War Memorial stands.

The relatives were given a place within the memorial enclosure, while the surrounding throng were on the road and stood on the high ground to get a good view. The memorial was shrouded in a large Union Jack. General Sir Charles Fergusson Brt., K.C.B., K.C.M.G., D.S.O., M.V.O. then unveiled the memorial after an appropriate speech. Numerous wreaths were laid. Mr Neil Shaw conveyed the thanks for the unveiling.

Many dignitaries were in attendance and one lady in attendance, who was 90, had also been to the opening of the Parish Church in 1842.

The tall Celtic cross was made from Dalbeattie grey granite and sculpted by D., H., & I. Newall of Dalbeattie. It was designed by local architect James Torrance. The railings (now gone) around the memorial were sculpted by Messrs. C & A Hunter, Foundry Lane, Stranraer. There are 18 names from the Great War. The inscription reads:

TO THE GLORY OF GOD AND IN HONOUR OF THE MEN OF THIS PARISH WHO GAVE THEIR LIVES IN THE GREAT WAR 1914-1918.

CORPL.	ANDREW ANDERSON	WILTS REGT.
L. CORPL.	JOHN ANDERSON	R.S.F.
LIEUT.	ANDREW A. CUMMING	R.S.
PTE.	ROBERT DRYNAN	K.O.S.B.
PTE.	JAMES ECCLES	H.L.I.
PTE.	WILLIAM KELLY	GORDON HIGHRS.
LIEUT.	JAMES MELROSE KERR	R.S.F.
PETT. OFF.	WILLIAM MCCULLOCH	H.M.S. "ALBACORE"
SERG.	CHARLES M. McGREGOR	A & S HIGHRS
SERG.	JAMES M. McGREGOR	N.S.W.I.
PTE.	SIMON G. McGREGOR	C. VICTORIA RIFLES
PTE.	ALEXANDER McKENZIE	R.S.F.
PTE.	NEIL SHAW	CHESHIRE REGT.
STOKER	JOHN SMITH	H.M.S. "CRESSY"
PTE.	JOHN SMITH	S.R.
PTE.	JOHN SMITH	R.S.F.
PTE.	GILBERT THOMSON	CANADIAN REGT.
PTE.	JAMES WITHER TULLY	SCOTS GUARDS.

"DULCE ET DECORUM EST PRO PATRIA MORI"

The last line translates as "It is a sweet and right to die for one's country." Before the war it had often been quoted, but when written in the poem by Wilfred Owen it is referred to as "the old lie".

Corporal Andrew Anderson, 33091.
7th Battalion Wiltshire Regiment.
Killed in action 10th February 1917.

Andrew was a son of Andrew and Jeanie Anderson of Portpatrick. He had two brothers who were also in the army and had grown up at Auchtermacain. Before the war he had been a gamekeeper and had learned the job working at Dunskey estate, he then worked in the service of Lord Stair at New Luce for three years. Following that Andrew worked at Carlock for the late Mr J.H. Stock of Glenapp. Mr Stock had a son who was serving in the war and also died.

Andrew was married to Isabella and had two small children. He was 28. As he had been in the Galloway Rifle Volunteers before the war, on the outbreak of war he felt it was his duty to rejoin.

He is buried at Doiran Military Cemetery, Greece, grave reference III.B.14. A memorial service was held for him in Glenapp Church. His brother John is named below.

Lance Corporal John Anderson, 23804.
1st Battalion Royal Scots Fusiliers.
Killed in action 28th March 1918.

Brother to the above named Andrew, John also grew up at Auchtermacain. Aged 24 he was youngest of the three brothers who were serving in the army. Before the war he had worked for Mr McLean at Killantringan. At the time of his death, the third brother, and only survivor of the three was injured and hospitalised.

John is commemorated on Arras Memorial.

Second Lieut. Andrew Alexander Cumming,
4th Battalion Royal Scots.
Died 5th February 1918.

Andrew was the son of the proprietor of the Crown Hotel in Portpatrick. He had for a number of years been associated with the Ayr and Galloway Artillery. He was an exceptional shot and had won many competitions and distinctions. He then took an interest in the welfare of the local company of the Royal Scots Fusiliers and is likely to have known James Melrose Kerr very well as he had an interest in recruiting for the company.

When war broke out he enlisted and served as an N.C.O on the 5th K.O.S.B. He then received a promotion being commissioned due to good and faithful service and was positioned in the Royal Defence Corps. On his death certificate he was recorded as being in the 4th Reserve Battalion of the Royal Scots.

Andrew had a perforated ulcer and was taken for treatment to the Military Hospital at Craiglockhart in Edinburgh. He died almost four months later from an abdominal abscess as a complication of the ulcer.

Andrew never married and seems to have devoted his life to the military. He does not have a military headstone, but is buried in Portpatrick cemetery and named on the family red granite headstone there. His death certificate records his death as the 6th February, although the stone and CWGC records his death as the 5th

Pte. Robert Drynan, 40863.
1st Battalion King's Own Scottish Borderers.
Killed in action 4th October 1917.

Robert was the son of Grace Drynan, 11 Hill Street, Portpatrick. Before the war he worked for the Parish Council.

He was seriously wounded in April 1917 and was sent back to North Evington Hospital, Leicester to be treated. Early in October of the same year he was posted as missing. A Chaplain had been trying to find out what had happened to him and discovered that Robert and another man were taking a message to Battalion Headquarters when a shell had exploded. The comrade was badly injured but did not see Robert again. It was assumed he had been killed on that day.

Robert is buried in Poelcapelle British Cemetery, Belgium, grave reference XLVII.C.7.

Private James Eccles, 42097. 17th Battalion Highland Light Infantry. Died from wounds 8th March 1917.

James was the third son of Mr and Mrs James Eccles from Maxwell Road, Govan then 94 McLellan Street, Plantation, Glasgow. His family had previously lived at Colfin and he had worked with Messrs. Gibb Brothers, drapers in Stranraer.

James had originally enlisted in the Scottish Rifles, 23679, but afterwards transferred to the Highland Light Infantry. He was around 20 when he was killed and is buried at St. Sever Cemetery, Rouen, grave reference O.VI.E.4. It is more than likely James was related to the Eccles family of Drummore. Two of them were also called James and are on the Kirkmaiden Memorial in Drummore.

Pte. William Kelly, S/14968. 8th/10th Battalion Gordon Highlanders. Killed in action 11th April 1917.

William was the only son of Mrs Susan Drysdale Kelly of Enoch, Portpatrick, later Galdenoch Mill, Leswalt. Before enlisting William had worked for Mr Douglas, Portree.

His mother inserted the following poem in the local newspaper:

Duty called him. He was there
To do his bit and take his share;
His heart was good, his spirit brave,
His resting-place a soldier's grave.

Aged 26, William has no known grave and is commemorated on the Arras Memorial.

2nd Lieut. James Melrose Kerr, 1st/5th Battalion Royal Scots Fusiliers. Died 3rd September 1916.

James Melrose Kerr had for a number of years assisted his uncle, James Purves who was the factor for Dunskey. Previously he had trained as a banker in the Royal Bank of Scotland branches at Ecclefechan then Edinburgh. While he was staying in Portpatrick, James had taken a keen interest in the local community. He had been the honourable secretary to the R.N.L.I. and had become well known in the village because of his good work.

James enlisted on the outbreak of war and he received a commission. As part of his duties he asked if he could be sent to Wigtownshire to help with recruitment to the Royal Scots Fusiliers and from the number of men who served locally in the R.S.F., he appears to have been excellent at recruitment.

Having been posted abroad, it was James who wrote to the mother of Pte. Charles Kerr who is on Inch Memorial when her son was killed. As a local officer, James wrote many more of the letters to Wigtownshire families offering sympathy whenever one of his men was killed.

He was posted to Gallipoli in October 1915 where he saw fierce fighting. He then was in Egypt where once again he was involved in very heavy fighting. He was taken to a hospital base in Port Said suffering from an injured ankle. While recovering he decided to go for a swim nearby. In what appears to have been a tragic accident. James drowned.

The CWGC lists James as the son of William and Eliza Purves Kerr from Lockerbie. It is likely his mother had remarried as the newspaper of the time lists his parents as Mr and Mrs Kerr, Schoolhouse, Middlebie. James is buried at Port Said War Memorial Cemetery.

Chief Stoker William McCulloch, 28877.
Royal Navy HMS Albacore.
Killed in Action 9th March 1917.

Born on the 27th September 1874 in the parish of Stoneykirk. William was a son of James and Mary Heron McCulloch of Dunragit Home Farm and Stoneykirk. He was married to Annie Wallace, Enoch, Portpatrick. When William joined the navy he had brown hair, grey eyes, a fresh complexion, a burn scar on his head and another scar on his lower jaw. He was 5 feet 7 inches tall. While he served on a few different ships during the war he was paid an additional gratuity. William was one of three brothers all on active service at the same time. The local newspaper later suggests a fourth son was also serving.

Though the CWGC lists his age as 33 when he was killed it also spells his name McCullock, it is spelt correctly on his naval records. William joined the Royal Navy aged 21 and had served at sea for 21 years until his death. He had served in the Battle of Jutland. HMS Albacore suffered an explosion on the 9th March 1917 though the cause was not identified at the time, she may have hit a mine. William's wife received the following letter:

> *"I deeply regret to have to inform you that telegraphic information has reached this department to the effect that William McCulloch, chief stoker, belonging to HMS Albacore, was killed yesterday (9th March), when that vessel was damaged by explosion."*

William is also on Glenluce War Memorial as is his brother, David and their photographs can be seen in that section. It can be assumed William would have known the above named William Kelly well because of them both having lived at Enoch.

Serg. Charles M. McGregor,
1st Battalion Argyll and Sutherland Highlanders.
Killed in action 16th April 1915.

Charles was difficult to find additional details on. He was born in Blairgowrie, and may have been related to James McGregor listed below.

Charles has no known grave and is commemorated on the Menin Gate Memorial panel 42 and 44.

Sergeant James K. McGregor, N.S.W.I. Killed in action, unknown date.

Sadly I was unable to trace James through the very well kept Australian records. There are many James McGregor names, few who were of the rank Sergeant. If the assumption is made that he was a brother of Charles listed above, since there were few people with that surname in the Rhins area, then there is one Sergeant who was born in Brechin which is fairly close to Blairgowrie where Charles was born. However that one sergeant served with the Scottish Horse and yet another assumption would have to be made that he had transferred from the Australian Forces. Simon listed below has the same last name, but I was unable to link him with either James or Charles, and had they been closely related, their names would have perhaps also been on that family headstone in Portpatrick Cemetery.

More may be found out about James and Charles once the 1911 census is made available to the public.

Pte. Simon Grant McGregor, 24th Battalion Canadian Infantry. Killed in action 10th February 1916.

Spelt MacGregor on the CWGC. Simon was the son of John and Annie M. Grant McGregor. He was born at Ballikinrain, Balfron, Stirlingshire. His parents were listed as living at Dunskey, Portpatrick. He was 27 when he died. He is buried in La Laiterie Military Cemetery, Belgium.

Both of Simon's parents died at Dunskey Lodge, and their headstone is in Portpatrick Cemetery. There are no other family names on the stone.

Pte. Alexander McKenzie, 240805. 1st/5th Battalion Royal Scots Fusiliers. Killed in action 26th August 1918.

Alexander was bowman of Portpatrick Lifeboat before the war. He was the third man to lose his life from the lifeboat crew. He was married to Sarah and they had two children who lived in 13 Hill Street, Portpatrick.

Alexander had already come through very heavy fighting having fought at Gallipoli and Egypt; he had only just been transferred to the Western Front.

Alexander is commemorated on Vis-En-Artois Memorial.

Pte. Neil Shaw, 74010. 11th Battalion Cheshire Regiment. Killed in action 3rd May 1918.

Born in Govan. Neil was the only son of Neil Shaw, of the Commercial Hotel, Portpatrick and Sandringham Terrace, Largs. Neil had also lived in Pollockshaws Road, Shawlands, Glasgow.

It was Neil's father who was in the War Memorial Committee for Portpatrick and had given the thanks after the unveiling. With no known grave, Neil is commemorated on Tyne Cot Memorial. He was 26 years old.

1st Class Stoker John Smith, K/13677. H.M.S. Cressy, Royal Navy. Killed in action 22nd September 1914.

John was the son of James and Minnie Ann Smith of 8 Hill Street, Portpatrick.

HMS Cressy was a large armoured cruiser and was travelling with another two ships when they were attacked by submarine U9 off the Dutch coast. The other two ships were sunk first and Cressy stopped to lower lifeboats in a desperate attempt to save the men as there were lots of them struggling in the water. When she stopped and began to lower her lifeboats, the uboat which had been waiting out of sight, fired a torpedo and the ship sank within fifteen minutes. Over 500 men were killed.

John is commemorated on Portsmouth Naval Memorial.

Pte. John Smith, 9th Battalion Cameronians (Scottish Rifles). Killed in action 22nd October 1915.

John was the son of Mrs Violet McGury (formerly Smith), who lived in 9 Hill Street, Portpatrick. Interestingly all three John Smith's listed on the memorial came from Hill Street in Portpatrick. A fourth John Smith not on the memorial was from the Colfin, he enlisted in Canada and was also killed.

John Smith named here, was 20 when he was killed and he has no known grave and he is commemorated on the Menin Gate.

Pte. John Smith, 62601.
3rd Battalion Royal Scots Fusiliers.
Died 28th May 1919.

John was the youngest son of John and Mary Smith of 6 Hill Street, Portpatrick. He was a fisherman to trade, though at the time of his death he was still attached to his battalion.

John became acutely unwell 10 days before his death. He died in Stobhill Hospital of meningitis and is buried in Glasgow Western Necropolis Cemetery. He was 18 years old, and his sister Jeanie McLean registered his death.

Pte. Gilbert Thomson, 72124.
6th Canadian Light Trench Mortar Battery.
Killed in action 20th April 1918.

It is likely that Gilbert was the nephew of Jane Gilmour of Creechan Park, Kirkmaiden who was aged around 10 at the time of the 1901 census. From the details on the census of Thomson or Thompsons living in Portpatrick he is likely to have had relatives living there whose occupations are given as servants. He is further likely to have emigrated to Canada and enlisted there.

Although it was difficult to establish any local connection, I believe he could be the above man who listed his occupation on his attestation papers as a chauffeur. His date of birth fits in with the boy on the 1901 census. He may have worked on the Dunskey estate prior to emigrating.

If it is the man listed above, he is buried at Wailly Orchard Cemetery, Pas de Calais, grave reference II.E.2.

Pte. James Wither Tully, 12382.
1st Battalion Scots Guards.
Killed in action 27th March 1916.

James Wither Tully was the son of William and Agnes Jane Tully of Colfin. He had a brother who had died aged just four and a half years. His niece would have been Barbarah Hannay who ran a very well known shop in Castle Steet, Stranraer for many years. Before the war James was serving an apprenticeship at the Union Bank in Stranraer. He enlisted in November 1914 and undertook training before being sent to France. He had written home to friends and family at Colfin asking them not to worry about him.

James and two other comrades had returned home to carry the coffin of their comrade Robert Gunion Reid, who is buried in Inch Churchyard.

> *"Don't fret too much about me. I am going out to do my duty, and I shall do it. I won't shrink from anything that's got to be done, and if I am killed it will be while doing my duty."*

His parents were told he was mortally wounded when he had been on guard duty. He had died within five minutes of being shot by a sniper.

A service which gave thanks for his life was held in Ivy Place Church, Stranraer by the Rev. James Salmond and his name alongside many others is on a brass plaque inside the church which is currently known as the Town Kirk.

John is buried in Potijze Chateau Wood Cemetery, Belgium, grave reference A.17. He is named on the family headstone in Portpatrick Cemetery.

Sons of Portpatrick remembered.

Two of the men whose names are listed below are likely not named on the memorial as they were not local men, but they have perhaps established themselves locally as Portpatrick has been their resting place for almost a century and it was here their bodies were found.

Corp. Frank Thomas Myall, 3048.
5th Battalion King's Own Scottish Borderers.
Died as the result of an accident 5th March 1915.

Frank's usual address was given as 37 Port Street, Annan. He was 36 years old and married, and for whatever reason he was at the busy resort of Portpatrick.

On the night of 5th March 1915, at around 9pm, Frank accidentally fell into the pier at Portpatrick. He was unable to be rescued from the water and drowned. His body was not recovered until it was found in the water at the harbour on the 19th April. Frank is buried in Portpatrick cemetery.

Pte. Philip O'Brien, 24677.
6th Battalion Royal Dublin Fusiliers.
Killed in action 10th October 1918.

The body of 23 year old Philip O'Brien was found on the shore at Larbrax on the morning of November 18th at around 9.30am. He was known to have been missing from 10th October. Samuel Johnston the police constable arranged for the body to be examined and the cause of death was recorded as drowning.

Whatever the circumstances of his death, it was not recorded in the Register for Corrected Entries, however Constable Johnston had already dealt with the body of James Duller aged 42, which had washed up only two days beforehand. James' date of death is the same as that of Philip, so it can perhaps be summised that both men were drowned in the same incident. James Duller was in the Ayrshire Yeomanry, and he is buried in Whittlesey Cemetery, Cambridgeshire, where perhaps he had family. Philip is buried in Portpatrick Cemetery.

The local newspaper reported that Philip was on his return journey from Tipperary to France but does not mention the ship. The Leinster was sailing from Dublin to Holyhead on the date both Philip and James were reported missing. The vessel was sunk by the uboat UB123 with the loss of 530 people on the date both Philip and James were killed. It is likely they were killed when that vessel was sunk.

Frederick Miller, S/9480.
9th Battalion Black Watch.
Killed in action 11th February 1918.

Although Frederick's parents lived in Dorset, he was the grandson of Mr and Mrs William McWhirter of Lagganmore. Aged only 18 he died at Loos and with no known grave he is commemorated on the Loos Memorial.

Frederick is named on his grandparent's headstone in Portpatrick Cemetery.

Pte. Robert Smith, S/1956.
8th Battalion Gordon Highlanders.
Killed in action 25th September 1915.

Robert was born at the Colfin and I have been unable to find any reason why neither he nor his brother listed below, are on Portpatrick War Memorial. These two local men are not named on any other local memorial.

Robert joined the army the day after war was declared. His father was the late John and Agnes Conchie Smith of the Colfin, and Robert had left to seek work, which he had found with the Glasgow Tramway Department before he enlisted.

With no known grave, Robert appears to be one of the forgotten men. He is commemorated on panel 115 to 119 of Loos Memorial.

Pte. John Smith, 772282.
1st Battalion Canadian Infantry.
Died from wounds 24th April 1917.

Although there are three John Smiths on Portpatrick Memorial, this man is not one of them. He was the brother of Robert named above. Born on 1st September 1886 at the Colfin to the late John and Agnes Conchie Smith, John had emigrated to Canada, and it was there he enlisted in 1915.

He was described as 5 ft 7 inches tall with a dark complexion, blue eyes and dark hair. When he enlisted there he gave his brother Hugh's name as his next of kin. At the time Hugh was also living in Toronto. His occupation was given as a farmer.

He was wounded during the fighting for the capture of Vimy Ridge by the Canadians and likely returned to the 42nd Casualty Clearing Station. John is buried in Aubigny Communal Cemetery Extension, grave reference II.D.66.

Ordinary Seaman William M. McRobert, J/67975.
HMS Vivid, Royal Navy.
Died 18th April 1917.

William's parents lived at the Knock, Portpatrick. He had a sister, Annie, who was living at home and a brother, James, who was a Lieutenant in the R.A.F. William was only 18 and he died of measles and pneumonia in the Royal Naval Hospital in Plymouth. Some war memorials include the names of those who died on service, whether it was through illness or injury. It seems sad for his family in particular that William was in the services during the war, died, and is not on the War Memorial.

When he died his parents and siblings inserted the following poem into the local newspaper:

Honest and just in all his ways,
True and faithful to the end of his days,
Forgotten to the world by some he may be,
But dear in our memory he'll ever be.

The lines seem particularly poignant since he is not on any local war memorial. William is buried at Ford Park Cemetery, Devon, grave reference S.4.15

STONEYKIRK WAR MEMORIAL (SANDHEAD)

A very large congregation attended the service before the unveiling ceremony for Stoneykirk Parish War Memorial on 18th December 1921. The service took place in the Drill Hall, Sandhead as it had been anticipated there would be a large crowd. The Drill Hall could not pack everyone in, so the attached schoolroom was also used, but even then large numbers of people were standing outside.

The service was led by Rev. Lowrie and Rev. Barr. Afterwards the congregation followed three pipers who led a procession to the War Memorial.

In drizzling rain Rev. Robertson whose son was the first name on the memorial, introduced Lord–Lieutenant of Wigtownshire, Sir Herbert Maxwell who made a fittingly solemn speech before releasing the Union Jack which had been draped around the memorial. The thirty nine names were then read out by Mr J. Muir. After the laying of many wreaths, Mr T.B. Wright of Auchleach thanked Sir Herbert on behalf of the relatives of the fallen men.

The tall granite Celtic cross which stands on Motte Hill has a cast bronze plaque with thirty nine names on it. Perhaps through some oversight, two names appear to have been missed off and not referred to at the unveiling. The additional names have been added in lead lettering beneath the bronze plaque. There are forty one names on the memorial. To the side of the memorial is a bench with a plaque which reads:

PRESENTED BY THE EX-SERVICEMENT OF STONEYKIRK IN MEMORY OF THEIR COMRADES WHO GAVE THEIR LIVES IN THE GREAT WAR 1914-1918.

The inscription on the memorial reads:
IN ENDURING MEMORY OF THE GALLANT MEN OF THIS PARISH WHO GAVE THEIR LIVES IN THE GREAT WAR 1914-1919.

LIEUT. G.H.M.ROBERTSON, NGN. REGT.	LIEUT. PETER McCAIG, R.A.F.
LIEUT. A. HUNTER, K.O.S.B.	LIEUT. S.HOUNAM, ROYALHRS.
LIEUT. PETER MILROY, K.O.S.B.	SERGT. ADAM HOLMES, SEA.HRS.
SERGT. R. McDONALD, K.O.S.B.	SERGT.J. McCARLIE, R.SCS.FUS.
PTE. W. AGNEW, D.C.M., R.S.F.	PTE. J. CUNNINGHAM, SC.GDS.
RFLN. R. FLEMING, K.R.R.CORPS.	PTE. J. GRAHAM, AUS. EX.FORCE.
PTE. ALEXr. GRAHAM, R.S.F.	PTE. T.K. HAINEY, K.O.S.B.
PTE. M. HUNTER, SCOTS GUARDS	PTE. R.McD. HOLMES, R.S.F.
PTE. A. JOHNSTONE, D.W.R.	PTE. J. JOHNSTONE, R.S.F.
F.C.,W.G. KENNEDY, R.A.F.	PTE. ARCHd. KELLY, N.&D.R.
O.S. JACK LEES, ROYAL NAVY.	PTE. W. KILGALLEN, R.S.F.
DRIVER J. LOGAN, A.S.C.	PTE. JOHN MARTIN, R.S.F.
PTE. D. MONTEITH, R.FUS.	PTE. D. McCULLOCH, A.I.Y.
PTE. J. McCLYMONT, AUS.I.F.	PTE. ALEXr. McDONALD, H.L.I.
PTE.A. McKERROW,CAM.HRS.	PTE. D.R.McLEAN, SCOTS GUARDS.
PTE. J. McCLELLAND, H.L.I.	PTE. H. PATON, SCOTS GUARDS
PTE. QUINTIN RANKIN, R.S.F.	PTE. J. RILEY, SCOTS GUARDS.
PTE. T. RILEY SCOTS GUARDS.	O.S. T. ROBBINS, R.NAV.RES.
GUNNER C.TODD, CAN.G.A.	GUNNER S.TODD, CAN.G.A.
PTE. J. WITHER, H.L.I.	

"THEIR NAME LIVETH FOR EVERMORE"

L/CPL. BLAIN RANKIN,..........R.S.F.
PTE. JOHN RANKIN, ... BLACK WATCH.

Lieut. George Hawthorn Minot Robertson.
13th Battalion Nigeria Regiment, W.A.F.F.
Died 10th March 1919.

Son of the Rev. George Robertson and Martha Hawthorn Urquhart Robertson, George was 33 when he died. He had been working for six years in the Colonial Civil Service and was recalled from Military work in Africa in 1919.

George's father introduced Sir Herbert Maxwell at the unveiling of the war memorial at Sandhead. He is buried in Portpatrick Cemetery. He is also named on the Singapore War Memorial.

Lieut. Peter McCaig,
54th Sqn. R.A.F.
Killed in action 27th September 1918.

Peter had enlisted in the Scottish Horse but was transferred to the fairly newly formed 54th Squadron, a fighter squadron at the Western Front.

He was the son of Lieut. Col. John and Grace McCaig (nee Ralston) of Altogue, and High Mye, Stoneykirk. Peter's mother Grace had died before the war. His father remarried and Peter's stepmother died in 1916.

Peter's father John died just over two weeks after him. It is likely he had been told of his son's death.

The local newspaper twice records Peter as being named Patrick, but it is recorded in his service record as Peter.

On the day Peter was killed, the 1st Canadian and 11th Divisions took Haynecourt, in very fierce fighting. Peter is buried in Haynecourt British Cemetery, Nord, grave reference I.B.25. He is also named on the family headstone in Stoneykirk Churchyard.

2nd Lieutenant Archie Hunter,
King's Own Scottish Borderers.
Died 15th September 1919.

Archie was a farm assistant and of Thomas and Janet Hunter (nee McDowall). His father was a blacksmith to trade. Archie had served in the war but fell ill on his return home.

When he was in the Post Office at Stoneykirk he took suddenly ill and collapsed. Dr Dunlop was sent for from Sandhead but Archie did not regain consciousness and died. He had diabetes for which there was no treatment in those days. Archie is buried in Stoneykirk Parish Churchyard, he was 20 years old.

2nd Lieutenant Samuel Wolves Hounam, 11th Battalion Black Watch. Died 2nd June 1918.

Samuel was the son of John and Marion Hounam (nee McGill). He was born in Gilnockie Schoolhouse, Canonbie on the 20th April 1896, his father was the teacher there. His parents were married in Stoneykirk in September 1894. Samuel's mother died just over a year after he was born and she is buried in Kirkmadrine cemetery next to several generations of McGill's dating back to 1723.

Samuel attended Dumfries Academy and Edinburgh University where he was a Student of Arts 1914-1915, before he enlisted. Samuel's father remarried again and his second wife also died, as did another son aged only 16. Samuel's father remarried for a third time.

Though Samuel served in the war his cause of death was a brain tumour, he was 22. He died at home at Kildonnan. Samuel is also on his mother's headstone at Kirkmadrine – though the name is spelt Hounan on the stone.

He is on the war memorial at Canonbie, at Gilnockie School where he was born, and at Edinburgh University. His obituary was published in the Eskdale and Liddesdale Advertiser shortly after his death. His death is not recorded with the CWGC.

Lieut. Peter Milroy, S/26932. 1st Battalion King's Own Scottish Borderers. Killed in action 30th November 1917.

Peter had been the proprietor of a drapery business in London before he enlisted. His parents lived in Low Mye, Stoneykirk.

He was reported to his parents as being missing from 3rd December. There had been very fierce fighting for days around the time Peter was killed. He is commemorated on Cambrai Memorial which has the names of over 7000 men with no known grave.

Farrier Quartermaster Sergeant Adam Holmes, 1427.
1st/3rd Scottish Horse .
Died 6th October 1915.

Father of the below named Pte. Robert Holmes, Adam lived with his wife and large family at Drumbreddan. The family knew very little about where he had been sent. They thought it may be the Dardanelles.

Adam became unwell with dysentery he was taken to Alexandria but he died with a very high temperature. Adam is buried in Alexandria (Chatby) Military Cemetery, Egypt, grave reference F.34.

Though the memorial states "Sea. Hrs." it is possible someone got the abbreviation for Scottish Horse mixed up, and since the names on the memorial are a cast bronze plaque it would be impossible to correct any errors. Adam is also named on the memorial inside Ardwell Church.

Sergeant Robert McDonald,
1st/5th Battalion King's Own Scottish Borderers.
Died 24th October 1915.

Robert's parents lived at Awhirk. Before the war Robert had worked on the railway in Hamilton, but he had been in the Territorials and volunteered for Foreign Service at the beginning of the war.

Robert fought at Gallipoli, but be became very unwell and was invalided home. Robert died in Redlands War Hospital in Reading. There were very many war hospitals there, taking care of wounded soldiers returning from the field. Roberts cause of death was recorded as acute dilatation of the heart.

His body was returned to Stranraer Station by train from Reading. It was accompanied by Officers and men from the Royal Scots Fusiliers who had travelled from Ayr to form a firing party. The procession was watched by a large crowd in Stranraer as it made its way along Edinburgh Road and Dalrymple Street before proceeding out to Stoneykirk. He is buried in the Churchyard there.

Sergeant John McCarlie, 8779. 1st Battalion Royal Scots Fusiliers. Killed in action 11th November 1914.

John was born in New Luce on 22nd October 1887 at Knockibay shepherds house. His parents were James and Elizabeth McCarlie (nee Kelly). By the 1901 census his father had died, and since the house was tied to the job, the family moved. John is then recorded as living with his mother, brother, two sisters and his niece at Port O'Spittal cottage, Stoneykirk parish.

Having just turned 27, John was killed. He is buried in Tyne Cot Cemetery, grave reference XLIII.E.9.

Pte. William Agnew, 16270. 2nd Battalion Royal Scots Fusiliers. Killed in action 12th October 1916.

William was the son of William and Maggie Agnew (nee Stewart) from Knockencule.

He had already received a Distinguished Conduct Medal. At the time of his award of the medal he had been serving with the 7th Battalion and they had taken heavy losses. The citation for his medal read:

> *"For gallantry and devotion to duty in holding with Cpl. Mackay a barricade for twenty-four hours. Out of a party of twelve these two alone survived. 24.6.16."*

Within four months of receiving his award and aged just 19 he was killed in action. William is commemorated on the Thiepval Memorial and is also on the war memorial at Portwilliam.

Guardsman John Cunningham, 11512. 1st Battalion Scots Guards. Killed in action 10th June 1915.

John Cunningham was born and enlisted in Stranraer. He was the son of Joseph and Sarah Cunningham (nee Paul) of Port O'Spittal, Lochans. John married Grace Heron on the 3rd April 1914 at Kirkmaiden. He worked as a ploughman at Droughduil, Dunragit and lived at Cowans, Portlogan.

Captain Cuthbert who commanded John's company sent the following letter:

> *"It is with deepest regret that I have to inform you that your husband, who was in my Company, was last night, about 7.30, struck by a bomb from a trench mortar, which hit him in several places, so that he died, but very bravely, without a grumble. He was one of the best men in my Company, and I am extremely sorry to lose him. He will be buried with all due respect in this village, about half a mile behind the trenches. I am truly sorry to give you such sad news."*

A further letter from Sergeant Savage stated that:

> *"Private Cunningham was wounded at 7pm, that he died about an hour afterwards, and that he was one of the best in the section, always merry and smiling."*

John is buried in Vieille-Chapelle New Military Cemetery, Lacouture, France, grave reference II.A.3. He is also named on Drummore War Memorial.

Rifleman Robert Fleming, 43682.
King's Royal Rifle Corps.
Killed in action 28th August 1918.

Robert was the eldest son of Mr and Mrs Robert Fleming from Drumbreddan Dairy. He is named on the memorial inside Ardwell Church, but is not the same man as the one named on Glenluce Memorial.

The London Division of the K.R.R.C. were part of a push to recapture Croisilles on the day Robert was killed. The mission was seen as successful. Aged 24 he is buried at Croisilles, grave reference V.E.18.

Pte. John Graham,
Australian Expeditionary Force.
Unknown date of death.

Another man who was difficult to research because of the numbers of men with the same name. From the newspaper reports around that time, I feel that he was the son of William Graham of Cairnhandy, and brother to the below named Alexander. John had emigrated to Australia and it was there he enlisted. John is named on the memorial inside Ardwell Church.

Pte. Alexander Graham, 241195.
1st/5th Royal Scots Fusiliers.
Killed in action 1st October 1918.

Before the war Alexander had worked for more than five years at Barnsallie, Glenluce for Mr John Fisher. His parents William and Jeanie Graham (nee Muir) lived at Cairnhandy, Ardwell. Alexander's eldest brother John had emigrated to Australia and enlisted there, he had not been heard from since the first Australian landings at Gallipoli and was feared killed or drowned.

Alexander had enlisted in July 1915 and spent over two years in Egypt. He had been allowed a brief leave home before being sent to France. His father received news his 24 year old son was missing before it was officially confirmed that he had been killed.

Alexander is commemorated on the Vis-En-Artois Memorial, France. He is also named on Old Luce Memorial in Glenluce, the memorial inside Ardwell Church, and on the family headstone in Stoneykirk Churchyard.

Pte. Thomas K. Hainey, 26974.
2nd Battalion King's Own Scottish Borderers.
Killed in action 4th October 1917.

Thomas' parents had once been in Moorpark Dairy but later moved to High Ardwell. They had two sons both on active service in the war.

With no known grave, Thomas is commemorated on Tyne Cot Memorial. He is also named on the memorial inside Ardwell Church.

Pte. Murray Hunter,
1st Battalion Scots Guards.
Died from wounds 17th July 1915.

Murray was the youngest son of William Hunter of Garthland Mains. Murray was very involved with his farming before the war. He regarded his chief hobbies as Ayrshires and Clydesdales, preferring the Clydesdales.

He was educated at Lochans Public School and Stranraer High School and then took a course at Kilmarnock Dairy School. He assisted his father with the management of the farm. He had four siblings who had died in their childhood, and at least two other siblings.

Murray enlisted in November 1914 and after a period of training was sent to the front where he took part in heavy fighting. He had returned home during the war to carry the coffin of his comrade, Robert Gunion Reid who is named on Inch memorial and buried in the churchyard there. He was severely wounded by shrapnel in the knee and hip and taken to a casualty clearing station, but he did not survive. Murray is buried in Lillers Communal Cemetery, grave reference II.A.40. He is named on the family headstone in Stoneykirk Churchyard.

After his death his father received a letter from Captain Hamilton of Dalzell offering his regrets and condolences.

Pte. Robert McD Holmes, 24976.
2nd Battalion Royal Scots Fusiliers.
Killed in action 31st July 1917.

Son of the above named Sergeant Adam Holmes, Robert had lived with his family at Drumbreddan. Before the war be was employed in Eldrick, Portlogan by Mr McMurray.

His Aunt, Mrs McGeoch from 25 St Andrew Street, Stranraer had received the following letter from his Commanding Officer:

> *"It is with deepest regret I have to inform you that your nephew, Pte. R. Holmes, was killed in action on July 31st. He was in the attack on that day, and was shot through the head by a bullet from a German machine gun, death immediately ensuing. He did his bit nobly, and has made the supreme sacrifice for his country's sake. He was a splendid fellow, always willing and eager in his work, and I know the officer to whome he acted as orderly thought highly of him. This officer was wounded by the same bullet. I know no words of mind can heal this wound to you, but I wish to assure you of my heartfelt sympathy in your sad loss."*

Robert is commemorated on the Menin Gate Memorial and on the memorial inside Ardwell Church.

Pte. Alexander Johnstone, 26290.
Duke of Wellington's West Riding Regiment.
Killed in action 27th March 1918.

Son of Robert and Annie Johnstone of Port William, late of Culmore. Born in Stoneykirk parish, Alexander was one of four brothers serving at the same time. When his brother James, named below was killed, his parents had still not received confirmation of his death, just that he was missing. With no known grave Alexander is commemorated at Arras, bay 6. His photograph is beside those of his three brothers, below.

Pte. James Johnstone, 241052.
1st/5th Battalion Royal Scots Fusiliers.
Killed in action 5th September 1918.

Brother to the above named Alexander Johnstone, James was born in the Parish of Kirkmaiden. He had been on active service for nearly three years in Egypt when he was drafted to France in April 1918. The third brother of James and Alexander was discharged from service in 1916, having been wounded. A fourth brother, William was serving with the Canadian Expeditionary Force.

Before going to the army James had been a rabbit trapper in Stoneykirk district. He was married to Margaret Wilson and they lived at Culmore.

James was 28 when he was killed and he is buried in Queant Road Cemetery, Buissy, grave reference III.F.34.

Four Johnstone brothers who served at the same time. Robert who was wounded and invalided home, William served with the Canadian Forces, and Alex and James who lost their lives.

Flight Cadet William Gardner Kennedy, 202414.
Royal Air Force & 1st/5th Battalion Royal Scots Fusiliers.
Died from wounds 6th November 1918.

William enlisted in the Royal Scots Fusiliers, but was transferred to the R.A.F. and sent to train.

William was at a training school of the Royal Air Force in Egypt when he received his injuries. Flying was relatively new and often very dangerous. He was taken to Ismailia Military Hospital but did not recover.

Before the war he had worked for Mr Neil of Kilbreen. His father had been a farmer at the Meoul and had died in 1905.

Aged 23, William is buried at Ismailia War Cemetery, Egypt, grave reference Q.72. He was named on the family headstone in Stoneykirk Churchyard which has since fallen.

Pte. Archibald Johnston Kelly, 112907.
11th Battalion Nottingham & Derbyshire Regiment (Sherwood Forresters).
Killed in action 23rd October 1918.

Archibald was married to Mary Kelly of Garthland Mains, Lochans. I could find out very little additional information on him.

Archibald is buried in Highland Cemetery, Le Cateau, grave reference IV.D.8.

Ordinary Seaman Jack R. Lees.
HMS Benbow, Royal Navy.
Died 20th February 1919.

Although Jack is buried in Inch cemetery he is not on the war memorial there. His parents are in the plot next to him in the cemetery and a third family headstone belonging to Jack's brother, William, stands beside theirs.

Jack's brother William was in the Royal Fusiliers and he was badly injured by shrapnel in the right arm and leg, and admitted to hospital in Nottingham. William served in Gallipoli, Egypt and Palestine before being transferred to the front in France, where he was injured. William recovered from his injuries and came home from the war. I believe he was then employed by Mr John Rankin, farmer of Portpatrick. In 1925 a ship, the Claremorris was wrecked at the coast close to the farm. In almost hurricane conditions John Rankin and five of his employees including William helped to get some of the men ashore at considerable risk to themselves of being washed into the sea. The men who took part in the rescue, received a reward of £3 each for their bravery.

During the war, Jack and William's parents were living at East Galdenoch, Stoneykirk. Jack became ill and died aboard HMS Benbow. The ship had taken part in the Battle of Jutland and had patrolled home waters during the war.

Pte. William Kilgallen, 7877. 1st Battalion Royal Scots Fusiliers. Died from wounds 17th June 1915.

William had worked for Mr J.B. Chalmers of Barsolus prior to being called up. He was a National Reservist and had previously served in the Connaught Rangers. His wife was living at Barsolus at the time of his death in 1917.

Bedford House, Ieper, Belgium was an area used as headquarters and a base for field ambulances. The house itself and surrounding trees were destroyed during fierce fighting by shellfire. It is there at Bedford House Cemetery that William is buried. He is also on the memorial at Inch, and there is photograph of him in that section.

Driver James Logan,
Royal Army Service Corps,
& 8th Battalion the Border Regiment.
Killed in action 5th August 1917.

James was a son of William and Annie Logan (nee Wright) of the Blair, Stoneykirk, formerly Boreland, Inch. Before the war he worked for Mr McCulloch of Cairngarroch. He had four sisters and one brother who all died in infancy. Other siblings survived, though his parents both died within two years of each other after the war.

He was 29 when he was killed and he is commemorated on the Menin Gate. James is named on his parent's headstone in Stoneykirk Churchyard.

Pte. John Martin, 22929.
2nd Battalion Royal Scots Fusiliers.
Died from wounds 23rd April 1917.

John was born and raised in Stoneykirk. His parents, John and Elizabeth lived there in Sunnyside Cottage. It is very likely John is related to James Martin who is listed on Inch Memorial. Before the war John had worked for the Rhins District Committee.

He is buried with 22 other British soldiers at Signal Trench Memorial 4 in Wancourt British Cemetery. The area had seen very fierce fighting and it was there John was badly injured. He died from his wounds that day.

Pte. David Monteith, 66100. 10th Battalion Royal Fusiliers. Killed in action 9th March 1918.

David Monteith had lived with his family at Auchentibbert, and must have been familiar with three other men who are named on local memorials all from 'The Kibbert'. They include, the Todd brothers on Stoneykirk Memorial, and James McCrorie on Glenluce. Other men from Auchentibbert also served including Pte. McGrady and Pte. McCulloch who are both mentioned in newspaper reports.

When David died his mother and siblings inserted the following poem into the local newspaper.

Duty called, and he was there
To do his bit and take his share;
His heart was good, his spirit brave
His resting place a soldier's grave.

We miss him, yes, we miss him!
Hiss loss we are left to mourn;
It's hard to sit at times and think
He never shall return.

He is buried at Hooge Crater Cemetery, Belgium, grave reference XI.F.10. David is named on Leswalt and Stoneykirk Memorials.

Pte. David McCulloch, 295353.
12th Battalion Royal Scots Fusiliers.
Killed in action 8th December 1917.

David was born in Maybole. The 12th Battalion was also known as the Ayr & Lanark Yeomanry, (A.L.Y). It does say A.I.Y on the memorial. The name proved too difficult for me to find his local connection as there are and were many McCulloch families in the area.

He is buried in Jerusalem War Cemetery, Israel, grave reference X.56.

Pte. James McClymont, 4745.
19th Battalion Australian Infantry.
Died from wounds 8th January 1917.

James was born in Barnhill, Ardwell. After attending Ardwell Public School, he became a gardener. He was single and emigrated to Australia, leaving his mother behind. She was Isabella McClymont of Kirkmabreck.

He enlisted in Australia and his battalion set sail from Sydney on 13th April 1916. He was sent to the Western front where he was badly injured. He died from his wounds and is buried in St Sever Cemetery Extension, Rouen, grave reference O.IV.I.12. He is also named on the memorial inside Ardwell Church, he was 32.

Pte. Alexander McDonald, 43420.
12th Battalion Highland Light Infantry.
Killed in action 10th April 1917.

Alexander was born at (the) Cults. He was serving in the HLI as he had been transferred from the Ayrshire Yeomanry.

Alexander is buried at Duisan British Cemetery, Etruin, grave reference II.F.4.

Pte. Andrew McKerrow, S/20945. 7th Battalion Cameron Highlanders, Killed in action 28th June 1916.

Born in Milton, Kirkcudbrightshire, Andrew was the son of Robert and Sarah McKerrow (nee Kirk) from Kirkmabreck Dairy, Sandhead. Before the war he had helped his father with the dairy herd. The family were later in Damhouse, Kirkcolm.

He enlisted on 27th September 1915 and underwent basic training before being sent to the front. He was 19 when he was killed and is buried at Bois-Carre Military Cemetery, Haisnes. He is named on the family headstone in Stoneykirk Churchyard, and on the memorial inside Ardwell Church.

Pte. David Ritchie Williamson McLean, 1st Battalion Scots Guards. Killed in action 31st July 1917.

Born in the parish of Kirkmaiden, David was the son of John and Della McLean (nee Martin) of Barnhill, Ardwell. David's older brother Jacob had died before the war.

David was married to Ann, and he is named on the family headstone in Stoneykirk Churchyard, and on the memorial inside Ardwell Church. He is also commemorated on the Menin Gate.

Pte. James McClelland, 13664. 14th Battalion Highland Light Infantry. Killed in action 28th November 1917.

James served under the name James Johnston. He was the son of Mrs Janet McClelland of Danevale Crossing, Crossmichael.

James is named on the memorial inside Ardwell Church. 22 when he was killed, he is commemorated on Cambrai Memorial. I was unable to trace his local connection, but the surname McClelland has strong local connections in both the Machars and the Rhins.

Pte. Henry Paton,
1st Battalion Scots Guards.
Killed in action 4th March 1917.

Henry was one of four brothers all serving in the army at the same time. His brother William was a piper in the Seaforth Highlanders and had already been serving for seven years. On the outbreak of war his unit was moved from India to France and he was wounded twice. Brothers James and John were in the Ayrshire Yeomanry. Their father had been in the army for 21 years.

Henry Paton with his brothers, James, John and William.

Before the war Henry had worked for Mr McDowall at High Three Mark where the family lived. He enlisted on 15th February 1915. Henry is buried at Guards Cemetery, Combles, grave reference II.C.6. He was 21.

Pte. Quintin Dick Rankin, 240328.
5th Battalion Royal Scots Fusiliers.
Died 25th June 1918.

Quintin was the fourth son of John and Margaret Rankin of Kildrochet. He had come through the horrors of the war to succumb to pneumonia following the influenza virus.

He died at 57th Casualty Clearing Station, France aged 21. He is buried at Aubigny Communal Cemetery Extension, grave reference IV.L.51.

Pte. James Riley, 13210.
Scots Guards.
Died 12th February 1915.

Elder brother to the below named Tom Riley, James was the son of James and Maggie Riley from Low Ardwell, later Drumbreddan. He had enlisted and was undergoing training at Caterham when he became ill. The cause of death was recorded as pneumonia secondary to pleurisy. Although James did not see battle in the trenches, he had been prepared to fight for what he thought was right. He was 21.

His body was returned to Stoneykirk and is buried in the churchyard. His father was to die shortly afterwards, and his younger brother was killed later in the war. A service was held in Ardwell Church by Rev. Barr where sympathies were offered to his mother and siblings. He is also named on the memorial inside Ardwell Church.

Pte. Tom Riley,
1st Battalion Scots Guards.
Killed in action 10th August 1916.

Tom had enlisted aged only 16. He underwent training and had been in the army for around 19 months when he was killed. His commanding officer wrote to his mother to say that he had been asleep in the trench when a mortar hit him. His death was instantaneous.

In an eighteen month period Mrs Riley of Low Ardwell had lost her husband, Tom and his brother. She was left with a large young family to raise.

Tom is commemorated on Thiepval Memorial. His brother is listed above. He is also named on the memorial inside Ardwell Church.

Ordinary Seaman Tom Robbins.
Royal Naval Reserve. H.M.M.L. "247".
Died 29th September 1918.

Tom was the son of Mrs E. Robbins (later Mrs Weir) of Sandhead. He was married and his wife then lived at Newlyn, Penzance, and then later moved to Littlehampton.

Tom was working with H.M. Trawler Section. The ship he was on was lost in hurricane force weather. It hit rocks off the coast of St. Ives and was reported to have exploded. All but one of the crew were lost in the explosion, or drowned.

Pte. Crawford Todd, 303021.
1st Battalion Canadian Garrison Artillery.
Killed in action 9th August 1917.

There were two Todd families who lived in Auchentibbert which is locally known as the Kibbert. They had moved over from Larne before the turn of the century. In total there would have been around fourteen children. By the 1901 census some of the family included Mary, Patrick, Hunter, Irvine and David.

At some stage, brothers Samuel and Crawford had moved over to Canada and when war broke out they enlisted into the same battalion on the same day. The local newspaper in Stranraer was proud of the patriotism shown by the Todd family who had six brothers all serving at the same time.

His attestation papers when he enlisted confirm that Crawford was born on 26th February 1892, in Larne. His medical inspection form described him as having dark hair, dark complexion and grey eyes.

The two brothers who had enlisted on the same day were also to die on the same day, by the same shell, at Vimy Ridge. They are buried in the same row of Bully-Grenay Communal Cemetery, British Cemetery. Crawford's grave reference is III.E.6. and his brother is buried in the same row.

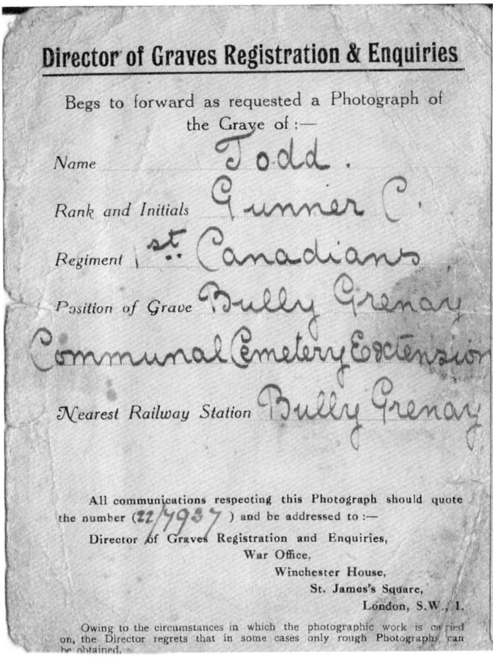

Director of Graves Registration & Enquiries

Begs to forward as requested a Photograph of the Grave of :—

Name Todd.

Rank and Initials Gunner C.

Regiment 1st Canadians

Position of Grave Bully Grenay Communal Cemetery Extension

Nearest Railway Station Bully Grenay

All communications respecting this Photograph should quote the number (22/7937) and be addressed to :—

Director of Graves Registration and Enquiries,
War Office,
Winchester House,
St. James's Square,
London, S.W. 1.

Owing to the circumstances in which the photographic work is carried on, the Director regrets that in some cases only rough Photographs can be obtained.

Family card and photo showing the original grave of Crawford Todd.

Brothers Robert (Bob) Todd of the Ayrshire Yeomanry, and Irvine Todd A.S.C. survived the war.

Gunner Samuel Todd, 303022.
1st Bty. Canadian Garrison Artillery.
Killed in action 9th August 1917.

Samuel was born in Larne in 1878 and was called after his father; the family lived in Auchentibbert (the Kibbert). His father was the blacksmith there for more than 20 years employed by Mr Cochran. Samuel was married to Mary Mitchell (Preston), a widow who had lived in Castle Douglas before marrying Samuel, their address when he was killed was given as Cairnhandy.

Samuel had emigrated to Canada with his brother Crawford and it was there they enlisted in October 1915. He was described as having a fair complexion, fair hair and grey eyes. He was 5 feet 9 ½ inches tall.

He was 32 when he was fatally injured and taken to No.7, Casualty Clearing Station at Vimy Ridge and he is buried in Bully-Grenay Communal Cemetery, British Cemetery in the same row as his brother, grave reference III.E.14. He is also named on the memorial inside Ardwell Church.

When Samuel Died his widow inserted the following poem in the local newspaper:

Sleep on, dear Sam, in a foreign grave,
In a grave we shall never see,
But as long as life and memory last
We will remember thee.

He sleeps beside his comrades
In a hallowed grave unknown,
But his name is written in letters of love
On the hearts he left at home.

Samuel had a sister named Martha Lynch and she recounted to her daughter Mary the story of how she had six brothers serving in the Great War at the same time. In 1978 Mary with her husband Malcolm made the trip to France to the cemetery where she knew her two uncles were buried. It was an emotional experience, the men lie only seven graves apart. Mary and Malcolm have visited the graves every year since that first visit.

James (Jim) Todd and William (Bill) Todd of the R.F.A., surviving brothers of the above Samuel.

Pte. John Wither, 40774.
Highland Light Infantry, & 2nd Battalion K.O.S.B.
Killed in action 26th October 1917.

Two men named John Wither were killed in the Great War and they are both local. The other man is buried in Leswalt Old Kirkyard.

This John Wither was the youngest son of John Wither of Float Bay, Sandhead. Mr Wither had just heard another son had been injured for the second time and was in hospital in Sheffield when the news came through about his youngest.

Before the war young John had worked for Mr J. Gibson, Butnow, Ardwell.

John is commemorated on Tyne Cot Memorial, and on the memorial inside Ardwell Church.

Lance Corp. Blain Rankin, 12905. 7th Battalion Royal Scots Fusiliers. Killed in action 26th September 1915.

One of two names that seem to have been added on to the war memorial at a later date. Blain was a son of James and Mary Rankin of Sandhead, later James Rankin moved to Vernon, British Columbia. Blain was born in Sandhead and had grown up there. His sister was Mrs Annie Downie who inserted the following poem in the local newspaper when her brother was killed:

Sleep on, dear brother, in a foreign grave,
Your life for your country you nobly gave;
No friend stood near you to say good-bye,
But safe in God's keeping now you lie.
I little thought, when we parted last,
He would no more return;
He slumbers now in a soldier's grave,
And I am left to mourn.
I cannot say, I will not say,
That he is dead, but just away.

Blain is commemorated on Loos Memorial. His brother John is listed below.

Pte. John Rankin, S/6270. 8th Battalion Black Watch. Died from wounds 9th July 1916.

Younger brother of the above named Blain, John was also born and raised in Sandhead. A third brother, the eldest, James, served with the Canadian Mounted Rifles and was a Quartermaster Sergeant.

His brother James had moved to West Kilbride where he was employed in farm service. Like so many other men, John enlisted on the outbreak of war and had gone to France in April 1915.

He is buried at Peronne Road Cemetery, Maricourt, grave reference IV.C.36.

Sons of Stoneykirk Parish remembered

The following men all have connections in some way to Stoneykirk, but for reasons long forgotten; they are not commemorated on a local war memorial.

2nd Lieut. John Watson McIntyre, 4th Battalion King's Own Scottish Borderers. Killed in action 30th March 1917.

John was the son of Andrew and Jane McInyre of Braeside, Pinmore. His father was the only son of John and Mary McIntyre (nee McCracken). For many years John's grandfather had been working for James McDouall of Logan and must have been very highly regarded as the McDouall family erected his headstone. John's brother is listed below.

John was 25; he is buried at Fabourg D'Amiens Cemetery, Arras, and is named on his grandparent's headstone in Stoneykirk Churchyard. His brother was also killed and is named below.

Pte. James Riggs McIntyre, 16th Royal Scots. Killed in action 1st July 1916.

James was killed on the first day of the Battle of the Somme. That day Britain was to lose more than half of its officers and more than 20,000 men. The men had gone over the top and were mown down by German machine gun fire.

James was 21, in that futile battle which continued until November, over a million men died from all sides. Like too many others, James has no known grave and he is commemorated on Thiepval Memorial. He is also named on his grandparents headstone alongside his brother named above, in Stoneykirk Churchyard.

Pte. Joseph Murray, 27180.
Royal Scots Fusiliers.
Latterly 42475 10th/11th Battalion Highland Light Infantry.
Accidentally killed 29th May 1917.

Joseph Murray was born in the parish of Stoneykirk and prior to enlisting he was working for Mr Marshall at Bridgebank, Stranraer. Joseph joined up in September 1916 and while he was away his wife was living in Rankinstone, Ayr.

He had been twice wounded in action, but was captured and taken prisoner on 9th April and made to work in Germany. Reports did not say what type of work he was made to do, but his wife received word he had been accidentally killed whilst working on 29th May.

Although Joseph is easily found on the SNWM lists I could not find him on the CWGC, and do not know where his final resting place is. It seems particularly sad that a man who died in captivity during the war is not commemorated on a local memorial.

Serg. John Hannah, 38th Battalion Machine Gun Corps. Died 24th June 1919.

John is not on any local war memorial, although he does have a military headstone. His story is particularly sad. He was in the Machine Gun Corps, and was a prime target for the enemy. Somehow he came through the war without being killed and during the course of the war had won a Military Medal for conspicuous bravery in the field.

When he returned to work as a farm servant he had only been back from the war for a short time.

On the morning of Friday 20th June, Robert Erskine of Salchrie farm had been sent by his father to get the help of John Hannah and John Drysdale to take some cows down the farm road to the field where the bull was. The bull was let out of the field and it seems it took some time for the men to separate it from the cows. John was leading the bull when it rushed at him unexpectedly from behind, catching him with his horns and tossing him at least three times. Dr Andrew McCreadie of Stranraer was called out to the farm and summised from the injuries that John would die. It took four days for him to finally succumb to the injuries.

His funeral took place two days later. The cortege stopped at the Wigtownshire Creamery where members of the local Comrades of the Great War draped his coffin with a Union Jack. The procession of friends and military then continued walking out to Stoneykirk Churchyard where he was interred.

John had come through some of the bloodiest and fierce battles of the war then returned home to his usual 'safe' job, and was killed when it was least expected.

STRANRAER WAR MEMORIAL

Stranraer war memorial in Lewis Street was unveiled on Sunday 5th March 1922 at 2p.m. by The Right Honourable Sir Herbert E. Maxwell, Bart of Monreith, Lord-Lieutenant of Wigtownshire. The programme for the event was printed by the Free Press. After a service in the Parish Church the large procession made their way to the new memorial for the unveiling. Sir Herbert addressed the crowd before unveiling the memorial and Provost Dyer read out all the names in "The Last Roll Call".

Further inscriptions were added to include the dates and names from the Second World War and other conflicts.

When first unveiled, the inscription on the memorial read:

TO THE GLORY OF GOD AND IN MEMORY OF THE MEN FROM THE ROYAL BURGH OF STRANRAER WHO GAVE THEIR LIVES FOR KING AND COUNTRY IN THE GREAT WAR 1914 -1918. THEIR NAME LIVETH FOR EVERMORE

Wm. M. Adair
James Alexander
Wm. Alexander
Alex. Allan
Hugh Allison
Robt. Auld
Chas. Baird
Thos. Baird
John Ballantyne
Robt.Bodle
James Boe
James Bradford
James Brown
Thos Bryden
Richard Cairney
Roland Caldwell
Samuel Caldwell
Wm. H. Caldwell
Samuel Campbell
Wm. Campbell
John Caughie
Peter Collins
Robt. N. Collins
Matthew Cook
Edward C. Crawford
Adair D. Davidson
Alex. Davidson
John Davidson
Thos. Dewar
Wm Diamond
John Dougan
Herbert Dunn
James Emerson
Robt. Espie
John Fagan
Alex. Findlay
Wm. Flanagan
Wm. Forsyth
Duncan M. Fraser
Wm. Fraser
Wm. Galloway
Adam Gibb
David Gibb
Wm. Gibson
John Gillespie
David Govan
David Hall
James H. Hall
John C. Hall
James Halliday
Alex. Hamilton
John Hamilton
Thos. Hamilton
James Hannah
Harry Harvey
John Higgins
Chas. Hollis
George S.L.Hood
John Houston
John P. Hughan
David H. Johnston
James Johnston
Saml. Johnston
Tom S. Keenan
David Kelly
Hugh Kirkwood

John S. Kyle
John Laidlaw
James Laurie
John S. Lees
Robt. M. Little
Alex. G. Lock
Wm. Logie
John Mann
John W. Marshall
Wm. Monteith
James Morgan
Wm. Morrison
Wm. Morrison
Robt. Murchie
David Murdoch
George Murray
John B. Murray
Joseph McCabe
Saml. McCandlish
Wm. McCandlish
Alex. McCarlie
Wm. H. McCash
Matty. McClumpha
Wm. McCluskie
John McClymont
Wm. McClymont
Robt. McCracken
Robt. L. McCrea
John F. McCredie
Harry W. McDowall
Thos. McGeoch
John McGivern
Robt. McHarrie
John McIntyre
Hugh J. McKay
Robt. McKenzie
David McKie
James McKie
John McKillops
Wm. McKillops
Kenneth McLennan
Donald J. McMillan
James McWhinnie
Wm. J. McWhirter
David B. McWhirter
Wm. McWilliam
Gilbert Neil
Hugh Neil
Chas. McD. Nelson
Robt. Nish
Chas. O'Keefe
Robt. W. Ormiston
Uri B. Ormiston
John Palmer
Wm. Paterson
Wm. Patrick
John Pirrie
John Pirrie
Colin Porteous
Alex. Rennie
Robt. Rennie
Wm. Rennie
James Richardson
John C. Robertson
Joseph Robinson
Thos Robinson
John P. Ross
James Rowden
Thos. Russell
Alex. Saul
Edwin Small
Hugh Small
Andrew K. Smellie
Hugh Snodgrass
Hugh Stewart
Neil Thom
Alex. Thompson
Alex. F. Thomson
James Thomson
Wm. Thomson
Daniel Torrance
James W. Tully
David Tunnock
Thos. Wallace
Alan H. Whyte
John Wilson
Wm. A. Wilson
John Williamson
Fred M. Wood
Sam. Wood
John Wyllie

Celebration then commemoration, a victory parade passing through Station Street in Stranraer; below crowds at the unveiling ceremony.

Able Seaman William Miller Adair, HMS Watchman, J/47150. Died 27th October 1918.

Aged 22 when he died in City Hospital Edinburgh. William's death is recorded on the Marine Register.

He was the only son of James and Agnes Adair, 13 Agnew Crescent Stranraer. His body was returned home and he was buried in Sheuchan cemetery.

Originally his headstone was a white stone cross which was once lying against the church wall in the cemetery. Perhaps it had been broken at some time previously, and removed there. William now has a war grave – but on visiting it in 2010 a piece of white stone about an inch in diameter was just visible under the grass. My son and I pulled back the turf and there flat on the ground on the top of the grave was the original cross. Though some of the lead lettering had been damaged probably through grass cutting, it was still possible to make out the inscription:

William Miller Adair. A.B. Royal Navy died on active service 27th October 1918. A token of respect and esteem from his shipmates of HMS Watchman. It was the time of sunset for him and he went west into the glory and not into the dark.

Pte. James Alexander, 295416. 12th Battalion Royal Scots Fusiliers. Killed in action 21st April 1917.

James was called after his father who had lived at 35 Sheuchan Street, Stranraer. I believe from the records he was raised as James Herdsman at Leswalt. His death announcement in the local newspaper however offered sympathies to Mr and Mrs Herdsman of Meikle Galdenoch, Leswalt. It is my belief that this is the same man who is named as James Herdsman on Leswalt War Memorial.

Aged 21 when he was killed, James is buried in Gaza War Cemetery, grave reference X.E.2.

Lance Corp. William Alexander 13507. 15th Battalion, Highland Light Infantry. Killed in action 8th September 1916.

William Alexander was a baker to trade and worked in for the local bakers and grocers in Stranraer Mr John Clement.

He was the eldest son of Mr and Mrs James Alexander of 35 Sheuchan Street, Stranraer.

Gilbert Neil, also named below, wrote home to his own mother:

> *"I was looking for William Alexander today, as his company came out of the trenches a few days ago, but I got a great surprise. I was taken into headquarters, and the chaplain was busy writing to inform his father that he had been killed in the trenches with a minewerf. I felt very sad when he told me, as everywhere I went – even in the trenches – we used to meet each other and talk about home, and I always kept the 'Free Press' for him. He was well liked by all in his company, always very cheery and frightened of nothing. He was well known at home by all the footballers and played in the League matches. His platoon sergeant was telling me he was very sorry to lose him, as he was not only his bosom pal, but he was a fine soldier also. He seemed very sorry when he was telling me how it happened. I had just seen him a few days previous - when he told me he was the first man to go on leave when it started."*

William had been an excellent goal scorer in Stranraer Junior League and was very well known playing centre forward. He had also a good singing voice and was a member of the Sheuchan Parish Choir. He was 23 when he was killed.

He is buried in Cambrin Churchyard Extension, grave reference R.8. A different local man with the same name is on Leswalt War Memorial.

2nd Steward Alexander Allan, Merchant Navy, SS Powhatan. Lost at sea 6th April 1917.

Born in Dumbarton, Alexander, known as Alec, was the son of Robert and Mary Allan of 8 St John Street, Stranraer. Alexander was married to Martha Harper.

SS Powhatan was carrying fuel and was around 25 miles from the Outer Hebrides when she was sunk by the German U-boat U66. Alexander was one of the 36 crew who lost their lives, while the Captain was taken prisoner.

Alexander was 30 at the time of the sinking of his ship. He is commemorated on Tower Hill Memorial, London.

Pte. Hugh Allison. 41465.
9th Batt Cameronians.
Killed in action 9th April 1917.

Son of Maxwell and Elizabeth Allison of 3 Park Lane, Stranraer, Hugh was just 26 years old and he is named on the family headstone in the Glebe cemetery.

Hugh is buried at Bailleul Road West Cemetery, St Laurent-Blangy, grave reference B3.

Sapper Robert Auld, 177744.
Royal Engineers.
Died 24th January 1918.

Son of Robert Auld and Mrs Jane Morland. Before the war Robert was a house painter. For two years Robert was a widower, his 32 year old wife Elizabeth Martin had died at 4 Greenvale Street, in 1916.

When Robert was on leave he became seriously unwell with acute bronchitis and laryngitis. He died at 9 High Street, and is buried in the Glebe Cemetery, Stranraer, in the plot beside my great grandparents.

Pte. Charles Baird, 40984.
1st Battalion, Royal Scots Fusiliers.
Killed in action 26th September 1917.

Charles Baird was the son of George and Jane Baird of 65 then later 38 Lochryan Street Stranraer.

Before the war he had been a dairyman at Craigcaffie. He enlisted in June 1916 and was 33 when he was killed. With no known grave, he is commemorated on panel 60 to 61 of Tyne Cot Memorial.

Rifleman Thomas Baird B/200173.
10th Battalion, Rifle Brigade.
Died from wounds 28th October 1916.

Born in Stranraer, Thomas was the son of James and Jane Gilmour Baird. Thomas and his wife Elizabeth McKie had lost one of their daughters in 1913 when she was almost 9 months old. Tragedy struck again when Thomas died from wounds in Bellahouston Hospital in Glasgow, he was 30. His body was returned home, and many people attended his funeral. He is named on the family headstone in Sheuchan Cemetery, where he is buried.

His widow and two little girls lived in 20 Clenoch Street, Stranraer and they inserted the following words into the local paper on his death.

Oh, daddy, dear we miss you
And daddy we often call;
But there is nothing left to answer us
But your photo on the wall.

Pte. John Ballantyne, 16268.
1st Battalion Royal Scots Fusiliers.
Killed in action 26th September 1916.

Killed on the same day as the above named Charles Baird, and below named William Morrison, John had enlisted early in 1915 and had been wounded twice while fighting at the Front.

In October 1915 he was being treated for wounds in the Second General Hospital, Harve, Normandy. Wounded that same week was Pte. T. Lowe whose address was also given as 21 Dalrymple Street. Mr Lowe recovered and survived the war.

John was the youngest son of Mrs Ballantyne of 21 Dalrymple Street, Stranraer. He had a close family, his cousins Maggie and Annie Forsyth from Greenvale Street were devastated at his loss and they alongside his sister all inserted poems in the local newspaper on hearing of his death at the age of 27.His mother inserted the following poem:

He marched away so bravely,
His young head proudly held,
His footsteps never faltered,
His courage never failed.

Peaceful be thy rest, dear John,
'Tis sweet to breathe thy name;
In life we loved you very well,
In death we do the same.

With no known grave John is commemorated on Tyne Cot Memorial panel 60 to 61.

Pte. Robert Bodle S/18403.
5th Battalion, Cameron Highlanders.
Killed in action 12th October 1917.

Robert was a farmer's son from Low Mye, Stoneykirk. He was married to Elizabeth Rennie and they had moved to live in Glasgow.

He was 23 when he was killed and he has no known grave. Robert is commemorated on Tyne Cot memorial panel 136 to 138.

Lance Corp. James Boe, 1916.
1st Light Australian Battery, Australian Infantry.
Killed in action 20th July 1916.

James Boe was the son of John and Elizabeth Boe, Clenoch Street, Stranraer. James had a reputation of being a very good footballer and he had captained the YMCA junior team in Stranraer for a few seasons. Playing in the position of centre forward, he was a prolific goal scorer which made him very popular with the team supporters.

A plumber to trade, he had served his plumbers apprenticeship with Henry McLauchlan and Sons in Stranraer, and had been employed by them for some time after that. In 1913 James emigrated to Australia but on the outbreak of war he enlisted into the Australian Imperial Expeditionary Force.

He was wounded when arriving at the Dardanelles in 1915, but it was on the Somme battlefield he was to meet his fate. With no known grave, James is commemorated on Villers-Bretonneux memorial, Somme.

Pte. James Dally Bradford, 16234.
7th Battalion Royal Scots Fusiliers.
Killed in action 26th September 1915.

James was a builder and hewer to trade and was married to Sarah McCartney of 16 later 26 Hanover Square, Stranraer. He was the eldest son of Mr and Mrs Bradford of 33 Sun Street, Stranraer. James served his apprenticeship with Mr David Purdie the builder in Stranraer.

He was first reported missing during the battle of Loos, but he was later confirmed as having been killed on that date.

James left a widow and four children. With no known grave he is commemorated on panel 46 to 49 of Loos memorial.

Corp. James Brown, 240454.
1st/5th Battalion, Royal Scots Fusiliers.
Killed in action 24th November 1917.

Another man whose family address at the time of his death was given as 21 Dalrymple Street Stranraer. He was reported as having been killed in the same week as Samuel and William Caldwell listed below. With no known grave James is commemorated on panel 18 of the Jerusalem Memorial, Israel.

Pte. Thomas Bryden, 20917.
2nd Battalion Royal Scots Fusiliers.
Died from wounds 2nd August 1917.

Son of Thomas and Mary Bryden, Clenoch Street, Stranraer. Thomas was serving at the same time as his brother who was in the West Yorkshire Regiment. A sister was also reported to be serving in the nursing service in France.

Before the war Thomas had worked in Craig and Kyle the drapers in George Street, Stranraer.

Thomas was wounded first on the 11th June 1916 at the taking of Trons Wood. He made a speedy recovery and was returned to the Front. On the 31st July he was injured a second time and it was from those wounds that he did not recover.

Thomas is buried in Brandhoek New Military Cemetery, Ieper, Belgium, grave reference II.A.6.

Pte. Richard Cairney, 131526. 50th Battalion Machine Gun Corps. Killed in action 23rd October 1918.

Son of Mr and Mrs Patrick Cairney whose address at the time of gathering information for the CWGC was given as 59 Risk Street Glasgow.

Richard was not born in Stranraer and must have been in the area for some reason before the war, and perhaps descendants or future researchers will be able to clearly establish the local connection. There were then, and still are people with the name Cairney who have been living in the area for generations.

Richard is buried at Quietiste Military Cemetery, Le Cateau, grave reference C.9.

A further intimation appeared in the local newspaper for Pte. Francis Cairney of the Highland Light Infantry, late of Stranraer. He may have been related to Richard but it would be difficult then to establish why only Richard's name appears on the war memorial.

Able Seaman Roland Caldwell, ClydeZ/5045, R.N.V.R, Nelson Battalion, R.N.Division. Killed in action 13th November 1916.

Born is Stranraer as were his parents before him, Roland was the son of William and Agnes Caldwell of 34 Fisher Street. His father was an upholsterer to trade. His siblings were George, Mary, Jessie, Elizabeth and James.

Commemorated on Thiepval Memorial, pier and face 1A.

2nd Mate Samuel Caldwell, SS Teelin Head. Died from wounds 21st January 1918.

Nephew to the below named William Henderson Caldwell, Samuel was the youngest son of the late Hugh Caldwell of 11 Hanover Street Stranraer.

The cargo ship was transporting potatoes from Belfast with an unrecorded intended destination when it was torpedoed by a U-boat with the loss of thirteen men on board.

Samuel was rescued from the water, but he had died when he was brought back to Portsmouth. The story of his death was reported in the local Free Press. He was buried in Portsmouth Kingston Cemetery grave reference - Benjamin's 13.5. There is a man of the same name on Leswalt memorial and they were likely related.

2nd Engineer William Henderson Caldwell, SS Adela. Lost at sea 27th December 1917.

Uncle to the above named Samuel, 33 year old William was killed a month before his relative, and their deaths were announced in the same edition of the local newspaper.

William was married to Jane Baxter nee Forrester and they had lived in Kirkdale, Lancashire.

The Adela had a general cargo and was sailing between Dublin and Liverpool when she was sunk by torpedo from a U-boat off the coast of Anglesey with the loss of 24 men.

William is commemorated on Tower Hill Memorial, London.

Pte. Samuel Campbell, 285379. 6th Battalion formerly 7021 Argyl and Sutherland Highlanders, The Seaforth Highlanders. Killed in Action 20th November 1917.

Born at 26 Sheuchan Street, Stranraer, on 20th January 1882, Samuel was a different man from his namesake on Glenluce memorial. His parents were Samuel and Mary Campbell (nee McWhirter). Samuel did have a brother named William and it is more than likely that he is the man whose name appears below.

Samuel worked in Wigtownshire Creamery Stranraer before he enlisted in October 1916. He was married to Flora Findlay Irvine and lived at 48 Sheuchan Street, Stranraer. His father was a seaman and both his parents and his in-laws lived close-by each other in Sheuchan Street.

Sadly two months after he enlisted, the couple lost their daughter. The baby, also Flora, was premature but lived for 18 days. She died on Christmas Eve 1916 at 5 Seabank Road, Stranraer.

Less than a year later, Samuel's wife received word that he had been killed by a machine gun bullet. It was the first day of the battle of Cambrai. Samuel was 39 years old and he is buried in Orival Wood Cemetery, Flesquieres, grave reference I.D.31.

Corp. William Campbell, 12808.
5th Battalion Canadian Infantry.
Killed in action 24th May 1915.

Having checked through all death intimation notices during the war there is only one local William Campbell named and I believe the same man is also named on Glenluce Memorial. William was the third son of Jane and the late Walter Campbell, Main Street Glenluce. His parents had previously run the Caledonian Hotel in Stranraer.

In his death notification in the local paper he was listed as being in the 1st Canadian Western Cavalry when he was killed at Festubert. Aged 28 when he was killed he is commemorated on Vimy memorial.

Gunner John Caughie, 61086.
139th Seige Battery Royal Garrison Artillery.
Killed in action 16th May 1917.

John was the son of Mr Alex Caughie the joiner from Agnew Crescent, Stranraer. He had been employed by Mr MrCorkell a carting contractor before the war started.

John enlisted shortly after the outbreak of war and had been on active service for about a year when he was killed. He was 35 years old.

John is buried in St Nicolas British Cemetery, Pas de Calais, grave reference I.K.4.

Pte. Peter Collins, 43410.
12th Battalion Highland Light Infantry.
Killed in action 12th January 1917.

Son of Charles Collins, grocer, who lived at Allanbank, London Road, Stranraer. Peter was just 21.

With no known grave, Peter is commemorated on Thiepval Memorial, pier and face 15C.

Pte. Robert Nelson Collins, S/16593.
2nd Battalion Argyll and Sutherland Highlanders.
Killed in action 12th January 1917.

Born on the 14th April 1894 at Robert was the son of Peter and Agnes Collins (nee Nelson). His mother later became Mrs Agnes Russell, although she still lived in the house where Robert had been born at 53 Dalrymple Street, Stranraer.

Robert was buried at Hooge Crater Cemetery, Ieper, grave reference VIII.J.II.

Lance Corp. Matthew Cook, 7862
1st/5th Batt Royal Scots Fusiliers.
Killed in action 12th July 1915.

Matthew was married to Katie (Catherine) McGeoch on the 19th February 1901 when they were both 20 years old. They went on to have seven children. At the time they listed their address as 39 Fisher Street Stranraer. As was the usual case at that time those who lived in Fisher Street were involved in the fishing industry, Matthew worked for Mr Dan McDavitt, a fish merchant. He was mentioned in a letter home from the front written by James McCormack the local coal merchant's son. Matthew is likely to have known James very well because of the deliveries of coal to and from the West Pier in the town.

The loss of Matthew was not the only tragedy in the family, in 1922 one of his children, Terence, aged only 9 failed to come round from a general anaesthetic whilst undergoing surgery in Dumfries infirmary.

There was a further loss in the family when his son Leonard Cook was killed in the Second World War in Burma. Both men are named on the family headstone in the Glebe Cemetery Stranraer and their names are on the same side of Stranraer War Memorial. Matthew is commemorated on Helles Memorial.

A cold morning at the West Pier, fishermen and traders with the catch for sale.

Ordinary Seaman Edward Caldwell Crawford, J/42735.
HMS Harpy.
Accidentally drowned 5th October 1918.

Youngest son of John Crawford of Larne-Stranraer Steamers, and Garden House, Stranraer, Edward was accidentally drowned whilst on service aged only 19.

HMS Harpy was a Beagle class destroyer and had seen service in the Gallipoli campaign.

Edwards body was never recovered and he is commemorated on Chatham Naval Memorial, reference 28.

Lance Corporal Alexander Swainson Cuthbertson, 10660.
2nd Battalion Scots Guards.
Died from wounds 16th May 1915.

In a letter to the Rev. Hislop of St Ninian's Church, Stranraer, Pte. James McCormack wrote that his friend whom he named as Alick

Cuthbertson had been badly injured and had died from his wounds. No official word was received until some weeks later and this confirmed the detail of James McCormack's letter.

Alick was native to Newton Stewart; his father was a tanner to trade. Alick went to school at Stronord, and then was apprenticed to a Mrs McAuley's drapers in Victoria Street, Newton Stewart. He went on to work in Kirkcudbright, and then Glasgow before taking up a position with Swanson & Williamson the drapers in Castle Street, Stranraer in 1908.

A keen musical talent he sang in the church choir at St Ninians. He was also reputed to be a very good golfer and was a member of Stranraer Golf Club.

Though he died of his wounds, he was perhaps buried hurriedly as he has no known grave. Alick is commemorated on Le Touret Memorial, Pas de Calais, panel 3 and 4.

Deck Hand Adair Douglas Davidson, 1601/SD, HMS Northolt. Accidentally drowned 11th May 1919.

Adair from Fisher Street, Stranraer was a merchant seaman before the outbreak of the war, and he soon afterwards joined the navy serving on a number of ships. Most of the vessels were employed on minesweeping duties and he continued in this work after the armistice was signed.

Although the newspaper reports him as lost at sea, his body must have been recovered reasonably quickly as he was returned home and buried in Sheuchan Cemetery.

Pte. Alexander Davidson, 23012. 10th Battalion Cameronians. Killed in action 18th August 1916.

Alexander was born in Stranraer, and enlisted in Glasgow. His parents had moved to 200 Clarkston Road, Cathcart, Glasgow, but their connections with Stranraer were still strong as his death notice, and an 'In Memoriam' notice two years later, was inserted in the local Free Press.

With no known grave, Alexander is commemorated on Thiepval Memorial, pier and face 4D.

Pte. John Davidson, 51769.
1st Battalion Royal Scots Fusiliers.
Killed in action 12th April 1918.

The only information I could find out about John was that he was the husband of Daisy Mawhinney, of 58 Dalrymple Street, Stranraer, and the eldest son of the late Mrs Davidson Fernlea, Stranraer.

With no known grave, John is commemorated on Ploegsteert Memorial, panel 1.

Pte. Thomas Dewar, S/12259.
7th Battalion Black Watch.
Killed in action 21st March 1918.

With no known grave, Thomas is commemorated on Arras Memorial, bay 6. There is a John Dewar named on the memorial as having been killed in the Second World War, and it is more than likely a relative of the above Thomas.

Sergeant William Diamond, 16366.
10th Battalion Cameronians.
Killed in action 15th September 1916.

William was the second youngest son of Mr J, Diamond, mason, South Glenstocksdale, Leswalt. Like his father before him, William was in the building trade. He had served his apprenticeship as a hewer and builder with the late Mr David Purdie. Before the war he had been working in Glasgow.

William left a widow and six children behind. With no known grave he is commemorated on Thiepval Memorial, pier and face 4D.

Pte. John Dougan, 10782.
1st Battalion Highland Light Infantry.
Killed in action 18th January 1916.

John was the son of John and Helen Dougan of Foundry Lane, Stranraer. He had for many years been in the Territorial forces and had served seven years in India before war broke out.

With no known grave, John is commemorated on panel 35 and 64 of Basra War Memorial, Iraq.

Lieutent Herbert Dunn.
8th Battalion Cameronians.
Died 25th October 1915.

The shock of the death of Herbert Dunn was felt across Stranraer. Although he was a native of Glasgow in the five years he spent as minister of Sheuchan Church he had become a familiar and friendly face to many.

Herbert was said to have a frank and buoyant character, able to appeal to people of all ages. To some he seemed a lonely figure. Herbert was the member of a prominent Glasgow banking family and had studied for his ministry at Glasgow University.

Herbert Dunn and his final resting place.

Despite his education he enlisted as a private and earned his commission by proving his worth. Herbert was at the Gallipoli landings in July 1915. Having come through heavy fighting he became ill and was transferred to hospital at Alexandria where he died of gastroenteritis.

He is buried in Alexandria Military and War Memorial Cemetery, Egypt, grave reference Q.535.

A memorial tablet was dedicated to Herbert in Sheuchan Church which bears the inscription:

> *"In memory of Rev. Herbert Dunn, B.D., minister of this church 1909-1915. Lieutenant in Scottish Rifles, 8th Batt., who died on active service at Alexandria, Egypt. 25th October 1915, aged 22 years. Faithful unto death."*

A number of Herbert's relatives attended the unveiling ceremony in Sheuchan Church where the plaque was dedicated by the Rev. W.J. Service B.D.

Pte. James Emerson, 235129.
1st/4th Battalion Seaforth Highlanders.
Killed in action 26th October 1918.

James had previously been reported as missing between 26th and 29th October, but he was later reported as having been killed around those dates. He was 23.

The records show his grandmother was a Mrs Emerson and his aunt a Mrs McGaw of 13 Station Place, Stranraer.

James is buried in Aulnoy Communal Cemetery, Nord. The village had been a scene of very heavy fighting involving the Seaforth Highlanders in October and November 1918. Of the 150 graves at this site only a few are identified, James lies in grave reference C.2.10.

Pte. Robert Espie, 240730.
1st/5th Battalion Royal Scots Fusiliers.
Died of wounds 14th November 1917.

Another man whose address was given as 21 Dalrymple Street Stranraer,

Robert enlisted on the outbreak of war in 1914 and was soon drafted to Egypt.

In the same week two other local men from the Royal Scots Fusiliers were reported as wounded, Serg. William Agnew from High Auchneil, and Lance Corp. Robert Shaw from St. Andrews Street.

Ramleh war cemetery, was the site of a casualty clearing station during the war. Over 3000 men are buried there, his grave reference is R.6.

Corporal John Fagan, 34093.
16th Battalion Royal Scots.
Killed in action 22 October 1917.

John was the son of Edward and Annie Fagan of 6 George Street, Stranraer. Before the war he had been the manager of a grocery shop in Liverpool.

He was awarded a Military Medal for conspicuous bravery in the field and his parents must have been very proud of him, as was the town.

Aged 22 when he was killed, and with no known grave, John is commemorated on Tyne Cot Memorial, panel 11 to 14 and 162. John is also on Inch War Memorial.

Pte. Alexander Findlay, 22524.
15th Battalion Highland Light Infantry.
Died from wounds 11th September 1916.

The Findlay family men, like so many families locally were all serving at the same time. Their patriotism was credited with a feature about their good service in the local newspaper.

Charles Findlay, the father of the men in the centre had served with the Stranraer and Larne Steamship Company for almost 40 years. Alongside his son James Findlay (top left) they were serving on the Princess Victoria when she was taken to the Dover to Boulogne route to transport troops. The men would have been working with William Gibson and Neil Thom who are both on the war memorial.

Charles jnr (top right) served in the Boer War and held a South Africa medal for that service. He joined the A.S.C. on the outbreak of war. George bottom right was a Sergeant in the Royal Scots Fusiliers and Alexander (bottom left) was in the Highland Light Infantry.

JAMES FINDLAY.

CHARLES FINDLAY, Jnr.

CHARLES FINDLAY, Sen.

ALEX. FINDLAY.

GEORGE FINDLAY.

Alexander was married and his wife lived in Glasgow at 116 Watt Street. Prior to the war he had been a shoemaker to trade and he was employed by Mr R. Smith of Hanover Street Stranraer for many years before he moved to Glasgow. His mother lived in Agnew Terrace, Stranraer. He was injured on the 21st August by shrapnel which had struck him in the head. He was sent to St Omer Hospital, a large casualty clearing station in France, where he later died from his wounds. Alexander was buried at Longuenesse Souvenir Cemetery, grave reference IV. A. 53.

Pte. William Flanagan, 17688.
1st Battalion Kings Own Scottish Borderers.
Killed in Action 4th June 1915.

William was married to Bessie McCartney on the 10th December 1912. His occupation then was described as lunatic ward attendant, in the Wigtownshire poor house. He was the eldest son of David and Agnes Flanagan from Bishopburn who was a shoemaker to trade. With his wife and child he lived in Dalrymple Street, first at number 95 and later at 31. The couple had one child.

In a letter from Major G.B. Storey of the KOSB to William's wife the circumstances surrounding his death were described. After the Turkish trenches had been bombarded William was in the first line of troops told to advance towards the enemy and take the trench. The line was caught in very heavy crossfire and almost all the men in the line were killed or wounded.

> *"Your husband went forward most gallantly when called upon to do so, and he fell nobly doing his duty, and no doubt anxious to prove himself worthy. I sympathise greatly with you in the great loss you have sustained."*

With no known grave, William is commemorated on Helles Memorial 84-92 or 220-222. He was 34.

William's wife inserted the following poem on behalf of herself and his 'wee son' in the local newspaper on his death:

I never shall forget the day
My husband went away;
His thoughts were all of those he loved.
Yet we could not make him stay.

In a lonely grave across the sea,
In a far-off distant land,
Lies the one who was so dear to me-
A soldier and a man.
A loving husband and father dear
You proved to us while you were here.
And though the circle has been broken,
Your loving ways are not forgotten,
And though we are now left behind,
A better friend we ne'er will find

Pte. William Forsyth, 267612.
6th Battalion Seaforth Highlanders.
Killed in action 31st July 1917.

William was the youngest son of Mr and Mrs William Forsyth of 15 Greenvale Street Stranraer. Before the war he had been employed by a Mrs McWilliam from Little Lochans. He enlisted in July 1916 and was sent almost immediately to the Western Front.

William was invalided back home to Stobhill Hospital, Glasgow in January 1917 with a serious case of trench foot. Having recovered he was sent back to fight. With no known grave he is commemorated on panel 38 of the Menin Gate Memorial.

When he died his family inserted the following poem into the local newspaper:

Somewhere in France, in a lonely grave,
Beside his comrades he is laid;
A loving son, a brother dear,
None at his grave to shed a tear.

Your guardian-angel task is done.
Farewell! My brave, my noble son!
You young life gone ere yet begun-
Alas! You're the one who won't return.

We sit and think of days gone by,
When we were all together;
A shadow o'er our lives is cast,
Our dear brother gone forever.

We think of him in silence,
No eyes can see us weep;
And many a bitter tear we shed
When others are asleep.

Inserted by his loving Father, Mother, Sisters and Brothers. August 22nd 1917.

Pte. Duncan Moir Fraser, 135365.
19th Battalion Canadian Infantry.
Killed in action 2nd June 1916.

Born on the 14th July 1887 in Stranraer, Duncan was the second son of George Fraser, Cross Keys Hotel, Stranraer.

Duncan enlisted on 26th July 1915 in Toronto, Canada where he had emigrated to some time before. On his attestation papers he was described as 5ft 4 ¼ inches, with a fair complexion, grey eyes and brown hair.

While the CWGC records his death as 2nd June 1916 his death notice in the local newspaper states 2nd July of that year. Duncan is buried in Bedford House Cemetery, Ieper, enclosure number 4.1.R.4.

Pte. William Fraser, 277154.
10th Battalion Argyll and Sutherland Highlanders.
Died of wounds 15th March 1918.

William was the elder son of William and Mary Fraser of 17 Victoria Place Stranraer.

He was a very able and keen member of the Boy Scouts having risen through from Tenderfoot to Assistant Scoutmaster. He was said to hold the true spirit of a scout as he was always cheerful and ready to help others. The Scout troop felt he was a born leader and they held him in high esteem.

In his working life he was employed at the Stranraer branch of the Union Bank, where he was said to be professional and reliable with a keen sense of duty.

He enlisted in 1916 and was wounded by the November of that year. When he was wounded again in March 1918 he was taken to the 4th Casualty Clearing station where he died from his wounds. He was 22.

William is buried at Dozinghem Military Cemetery, Poperinge, grave reference XIV.I.5.

Pte. William Galloway, 7408.
1st/5th Battalion Royal Scots Fusiliers.
Killed in action 30th December 1915.

William was the son of Mr and Mrs James Galloway from 8 Rose Street in Stranraer. He was one of the five men reported killed at the Dardanelles in the same issue of the local newspaper. William had seen heavy fighting at Gallipoli and came through the 12th and 13th July 1915 unhurt. He was a bomb thrower and had been slightly wounded on 6th November and was allowed only two days recovery. He wrote home to his father on the 3rd December whilst resting off duty in a dug out.

Mrs Godfrey who also lived at 8 Rose Street, received the following letter from Lieut, J. M Kerr, 5th Royal Scots Fusiliers:

"On behalf of my company officer, self, and the men, it is my sad duty to write asking you to accept our sympathy in the bereavement you have suffered through the death in action of your brother, Private W. Galloway (No.7108), official intimation of which you will no doubt have received ere this reaches you. He was killed on the 30th of December, and was one of a fearless band of our grenadiers who did great work in helping to drive off the Turks that night when they made a desperate effort to regain trenches which we had wrenched from them on the previous day. He was much esteemed by both officers and men as a brave soldier, and the places of him and his comrades who fell will be very difficult to fill. The Chaplain conducted the burial service, and he now rests in the West Nullah about a mile south of Krithia, along with other comrades, including three good fellows from Stranraer, viz., Ptes. Gibb, McClumpha and Small. A tablet with all their names on it marks the spot and scene of the action."

Lieut. Kerr also lost his life in the war and is named on Portpatrick War Memorial.

Before the war William was employed by Mr Coulter, the aerated water manufacturer, in Stranraer. He was only 18 years old when he was killed. He is buried at Twelve Tree Copse Cemetery, Turkey, grave reference II.B.15. There is only one grave between him and Adam Gibb.

Pte. Adam Gibb. 6714. 5th Battalion Royal Scots Fusiliers. Killed in action 30th December 1915.

Adam was one of the five men all reported killed in action at the Dardanelles in the same newspaper. Like the others Adam had served in the Stranraer Company of the Territorials and had enlisted on the outbreak of war.

He was the son of David Gibb of 41 Fisher Street Stranraer and prior to the war he had been working as a carting contractor for Messrs. R. Johnstone and Sons in the town.

He was the second soldier killed who was on the Roll of Honour in the O.S. Church, Stranraer and sympathies were offered to his family and friends from the Rev. John Heggie the following Sunday.

On his death his father and sister inserted the following poem in the local newspaper:

Who could have dealt that horrid blow
On one we loved so well?
We never knew the pain he bore,
No mortal tongue can tell.

Oh this world is full of sorrow,
Now his pains and trials are o'er;
But some day we hope to meet him
On that bright, eternal shore.

No matter how we think of him,
His name we oft recall
There is nothing left to answer
But his photo on the wall.

For country's sake his life he gave,
And died, beloved by all.

Adam is buried in Twelve Tree Copse Cemetery, grave reference II.B.17. Only one grave lies between him and William Galloway named above. His brother David is listed below.

Pte. David Gibb, 40031.
7th/8th Battalion Kings Own Scottish Borderers.
Died from wounds 16th September 1916.

Brother to the above named Adam Gibb, David had worked for some time for the Larne and Stranraer Steamers. He had been serving on the Princess Victoria which was commissioned by the admiralty to run between Dover and Boulogne as a troop and supply ship during the war.

For whatever reason David enlisted in the KOSB rather than remain in the merchant navy. There were three brothers in the Gibb family all serving at the same time and when David died from his wounds, his father only had one son remaining.

Once again Rev. Heggie from the O.S.Church in Stranraer offered sympathies to the family from the pulpit.

David is buried at Dartmoor Cemetery, Becordel-Becourt which was close to a main dressing station on the Somme. His grave reference there is II.A.18.

Fireman & Trimmer William Gibson, SS Sycamore.
Lost at sea 25th August 1917.

Until his death, William Gibson was the youngest surviving son of William and Elizabeth Gibson. His father was an ostler in Stranraer. William, who was born in the town, was a tinsmith to trade though he later listed his occupation as a creamery worker. His sister Jessie was a dressmaker and he had a brother James who had died in 1916.

He was married to Mary Gordon Harrison in 1907 at her family home in 29 Queen Street, Stranraer. They rented their own home after they were married at 7 Lewis Street; the landlords also owned the pub the Stair Arms which stood beside their house on the corner of Bridge Street and Lewis Street.

The couple had two children who died, both were named Alexander. One died in 1915 from whooping cough aged only nine months and the other the other died in 1919 from measles aged almost four. William and Mary had another three children, William, Ellen, and Margaret.

In what must have been dreadful times for Mary, she lost her husband, two sons, her father, and her sister died in childbirth. Mary raised one of her sister's children despite seeing so much loss in the family.

William's family had been led to believe that he was ferrying troops back and forward to France, and indeed a letter from a neighbour in Stranraer confirms this. The neighbour, Edward Caldwell in fact addressed his letter to William aboard the SS Princess Victoria which had been commissioned by the admiralty to leave Stranraer and serve as a troop ship on the Dover to Boulogne route.

> "My *Dear Friend*
>
> *I thank you very much for your remembrance in sending a p.c. I intended to write to you sooner but I have not had very much time. I hope you are keeping in good health and cheerful. No doubt you are exposed at present to danger........I hope the time is not too far distant when peace will be declared and all those brave fellows on board HMS Princess Victoria will get back safely home. I saw your wife today and she informed me that all the family are in good health and that she is also well......with kind regards from Mrs Caldwell and myself and hoping to have a p.c. from you at your convenience. I am your sincere friend well wishing.*
>
> *Edward Caldwell."*

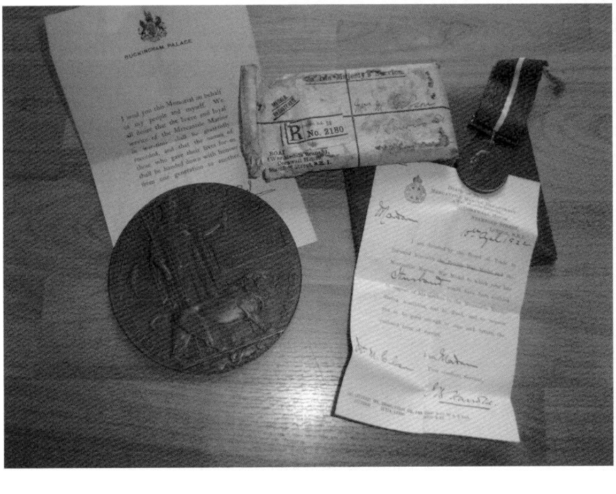

Death plaque, medal in original box, scroll and letter sent to William Gibson's wife after the war. William served in the Galloway Rifle Volunteers.

For whatever reason, William was serving aboard the Sycamore when it was struck by a U-boat north west of Portstewart, Northern Ireland. The steamer was unlucky to be one of the only two ships sunk by UB-61. She had been travelling from Baltimore to Liverpool with a general cargo when the torpedo hit. Eleven of the crewmen were killed including William who was 34. UB-61 struck a sea mine less than two months later and all 34 hands were killed.

His granddaughter Marybelle Buchanan has kept all his memorabilia including his postcards home, and many family photographs. Her grandmother, William's wife found it hard to look at the memorial which must have been difficult as she lived just across the road from it.

Pte. John Gillespie, 10322.
1st Battalion Seaforth Highlanders.
Killed in action 20th December 1914.

John was the 24 year old son of Mr and Mrs Gillespie of Foreland Place, Stranraer. His sister, Mrs Menzies of Queen Street received notice from the company chaplain to inform the family of his death.

The chaplain expressed regret that since the regiment was still very heavily engaged in battle he could offer no details or addresses. The company had then been marching and there had been a delay in offering the sympathies of his regiment.

John had been in the army for seven years and was serving in India when war broke out. He had served alongside Robert Rennie, named below, who was killed the following day. The two men had enlisted at the same time since their serial numbers are sequential. Robert is recorded as having been killed the following day. Another local man, William Pirrie was serving alongside John Gillespie and Robert Rennie, he wrote home to say that John had been injured and Robert killed, but both men died.

With no known grave John is commemorated on Le Touret Memorial, panel 38 and 39.

Pte. David Govan, 3/6977.
1st Battalion Black Watch.
Killed in action 9th May 1915.

David was the son of Robert and Jean Govan (nee Garrett) who lived in 12 High Street then 14 Queen Street Stranraer. The Garrett family had very strong fishing connections both in Stranraer and Kirkcolm. One area of Kirkcolm being known locally as Garrett Corner where the family used to string up their fishing nets for maintenance and repair.

David had worked for a time in the Wigtownshire Creamery, and then he had been working in the locomotive department of Stranraer Railway Station. He had been another of the young men who had been an enthusiastic footballer playing in the Junior League at Stair Park.

When war broke out David and his brother William enlisted in the Balck Watch. They had four siblings who had all died very young. David was reported as missing since 9th May 1915 and despite the best efforts to trace him after the battle of Festubert, he was never found. He is named on the family headstone in Kirkcolm and is commemorated on Le Touret Memorial, panel 24-26.

Able Seaman David Hall, Clyde Z/5057.
Howe Bn. Royal Naval Division.
Died of wounds 8th June 1917.

David was the son of Mr and Mrs James Hall of 33 Dalrymple Street, Stranraer. He had worked for a short time for Mr Montgomery the grocer in Stranraer, but had decided instead to serve his apprenticeship in the painting trade with his father.

He enlisted in June 1915, and took part in the Gallipoli campaign, he was then sent to France. He was badly injured and taken to a casualty clearing station where he died from his wounds. David is buried in Duisans British Cemetery, Etrun, grave reference IV.F.48.

Pte. James Harris Hall, 33259.
1st Battalion Kings Own Scottish Borderers.
Killed in action 11th April 1918.

James was the eledest son of David and Maggie Hall who lived at 71 Dalrymple Street, Stranraer. He had a sister named Elizabeth and he is likely to have been related to John Costley Hall listed below. James was first reported missing and later reported killed on that date.

With no known grave, he is commemorated on panel 5 of Ploegsteert Memorial.

Pte. John Costley Hall, 36651.
15th Battalion Highland Light Infantry.
Killed in action 4th October 1918.

John was the son of James and Hannah Hall of 33 Dalrymple Street and it is likely he was related to James Harris Hall listed above. His father was a house painter and he was one of six brothers, David, Robert, James, William and Adam.

John is another one of a few men listed who had worked in the employment of Mr John Clement the grocer for over four years in Castle Douglas.

He is buried in Sequehart British Cemetery No.2, grave reference A.13.

Pte. James Halliday, 4562.
1st/3rd Royal Scots Fusiliers.
Killed in action 11th November 1914.

James had been a reservist and had been called up on the outbreak of war. He had at least two brothers, John, who lived in St Andrew Steet, and Robert who was in the 1st/6th Royal Scots Fusiliers. James was well known about Stranraer harbour where he was employed in discharging steamers. His brother Robert had been injured at Neuve Chapelle, but he recovered from his wounds and was returned to the Front. James had also previously been injured but had also recovered from his wounds.

James was amongst the heavy fighting at Ypres. With no known grave, he is one of over 54,000 names on the Menin Gate. His name can be found amongst those on panel 19 and 33.

Pte. Alexander Hamilton, 17537.
1st Battalion Kings Own Scottish Borderers.
Killed in action 6th June 1915.

Alexander was born in Stranraer and he worked for many years as a coach painter for Mr W. McColm, Harbour Street, Stranraer. He lived with his wife and a large family of children in Sheuchan Street, Stranraer.

He was amongst the thousands of men killed at the Dardanelles who have no known grave. He is commemorated on Helles Memorial panels 80-92 or 220 to 222.

Corporal John Hamilton, 10324.
Seaforth Highlanders.
Died 14th May 1918.

Son of Hugh and Susan McKie Hamilton, of 9, Greenvale St., Stranraer.

He became increasingly ill and for 9 months suffered from breathing difficulties. In those days it would be called consumption – it was pulmonary tuberculosis from which there would have been no cure or effective treatment.

John was discharged from service due to his illness and he died at home aged 29. He is buried in the Glebe Cemetery, Stranraer.

First Engineer Thomas Hamilton, SS Don Arturo. Killed in action 17th June 1917.

Not the same man as his namesake on Inch Memorial, this Thomas Hamilton was in the Mercantile Marine and is also named on the plaque inside the High Kirk, Stranraer along with his rank, and the service he served in.

Born in Stranraer, Thomas was the son of John and Nicolas Hamilton. He was married to Christina Hamilton (nee McWhinnie) and they lived at 17 London Road, Stranraer.

The date of his death recorded with the CWGC as above does not match with other records of the vessel being sunk. Under the command of Max Schmitz, UC-62 torpedoed the vessel. The CWGC records of the date are almost certainly correct since other men who were killed when Don Arturo was sunk all have their date of death recorded as 17th June 1917.

His body was never recovered and Thomas is commemorated on Tower Hill Memorial.

Pte. James Hannah, 37407. 8th Battalion Scottish Rifles (Cameronians). Killed in action 29th July 1918

James had served for a time in the Navy at the beginning of the war, but he opted to transfer into the army. Before his company were drafted to France, James had been serving in Egypt.

He was the son of Robert and Elizabeth Hannah, 9 St Andrews Street, Stranraer. His mother, Elizabeth, had died in 1917. Aged 22 when he was killed, James is named on his parent's gravestone in the Glebe, broken sandstone cross against the hedge on the right hand side of the cemetery.

In 1918 at Soissons the 15,000 Allied forces were killed, and many more injured. James is named on the Soissons Memorial, Aisne which commemorates almost four thousand men with no known grave

Pte Henry (Harry) Harvey.
31st Seaforth Highlanders.
Killed in action 26th January 1919.

Born in Stevenston, Ayrshire, Harry was the only son of Henry and Elizabeth McKean Harvey, of 19, Harvey Terrace, Lochwinnock, Renfrewshire. Harry was 28 when he was killed.

Harry's death notice in the local paper was requested to be copied to the American newspapers. He is buried in Beirut war cemetery grave reference 246.

Pte. John Higgins, 53211.
1st Battalion Royal Scots Fusiliers.
Killed in action 3rd October 1918.

John was the son of John and Marion Higgins of 19 Glen Street, Stranraer. The family lived just along the street from the family of Alexander (Sandy) Brown who had won a Military Medal for bravery in the field. Sandy was hospitalised with trench foot, and the Germans had poisoned a well the British were drinking from.

It must have been difficult when one son returned home from the war yet a few doors down another family would not see their son again. With no known grave, John is commemorated on Vis-en Artois-Memorial, panel 6.

Pte. Charles R. Hollis, 13166.
15th Battalion Highland Light Infantry.
Killed in action 28th August 1916.

Charles was the son of Robert Hollis and had lived with his parents, brothers and sisters in Stranraer at their home in 52 Sun Street. Before the war he had gone to work on the Glasgow Corporation Tramways, he enlisted into the army two weeks after the outbreak of war, whilst two of his brothers were in the navy.

Charles was killed by a German sniper and is buried in Cambrin Churchyard Extension, Pas-de-Calais, grave reference Q.55.

Pte. George L S Hood, 47606. 6th/7th Battalion Royal Scots Fusiliers. Killed in action 12th March.

George was the grandson of the late John Hood, merchant, Stranraer. His mother was Mrs Janet Hood of 6 Rose Street, Stranraer. Whilst the war memorial lists his middle initials around the opposite way, his records and death notice in the local newspaper record them as above.

His cousin Samuel Lindsay inserted the following poem in the local newspaper on hearing of his death:

In dreams I see his dear, kind face,
And kiss his still cold brow,
But in my aching heart I know
I have no cousin now.

George is buried in Mory Abbey Military Cemetery, Mory, Pas de Calais, grave reference III.H.3.

Able Seaman and Lamps John Houston, SS Polandia. Killed in action 10th March 1917.

John was one of three local men all to lose their lives when the SS Polandia sunk. Hugh McKay and Thomas Robinson were also killed and are named on the Stranraer War Memorial. The troopship was sailing from Birkenhead to Cherbourg on 10th March 1917, and it was supposed that she struck a mine since no U-boat claimed responsibility.

John was born in Portwilliam, and with no known grave he is commemorated on Tower Hill Memorial, London.

Pte. John Preston Hughan, 42445. 16th Battalion Royal Scots. Killed in action 10th April 1918.

John was the younger son of Mrs John Hughan of 40 Sun Street, Stranraer, his brother served in the Signal Section of the Royal Engineers.

A joiner to trade, John had been working in Glasgow before he joined the army. He was married to Violet Hughan and the couple had one son. At the time of his death his wife and child were living at 37 Garngad Avenue in Townhead. They were in the same street as Maggie Williamson, mother of John Williamson, named below.

John was killed in action and has a special memorial in Le Grand Beaumart British Cemetery, Steenwreck, reference B7. The special memorials were to those known to have been amongst those killed when the Germans advanced on Steenwreck, or to the men whose graves were destroyed by shellfire or whose graves could not be found.

Driver David H. Johnston, T4/214792.
Royal Army Service Corps.
Killed in action 28th March 1917.

Born in Kirkcolm, David was the fourth son of R. Johnston, contractor, Thistle Street, Stranraer. Adam Gibb named above worked for David's father.

David is buried in Sarigol Military Cemetery, Kriston, Greece, grave reference C.41.

Pte. James Johnston, 41497.
7th/8th Battalion King's Own Scottish Borderers.
Killed in action 27th June 1918.

Before joining the colours James had worked for Mr John Ewing, butcher in Stranraer. His father was Robert Johnston of 54 then later 4 Sheuchan Street. Stranraer.

He was 19 when he was killed and he is buried in Aubigny Communal Cemetery Extension, grave reference IV.J.9.

Lance-Corporal Samuel Johnston, T4/092129.
16th Army Aux. Horse Coy. Army Service Corps.
Killed in action 4th November 1918.

Samuel was the son of Janet and the late Malcolm Johnston of Stranraer.

Aged 40 when he was killed. He is buried in Premount British Cemetery, Aisne, grave reference II.A.24.

Pte. Tom Sillars Keenan. 23078.
1st Battalion Cameronians.
Killed in action 21st September 1918.

Son of John and Agnes Keenan whose address at the time of his death was given as 55 Henderson Street, Glasgow. Tom was a Lewis Gunner in the Cameronians. Tom was aged 22 years when he was killed.

He is named on the family headstone in the Glebe. Tom appears to be missed from CWGC records.

Soldiers from the 1st Cameronians - somewhere in France.

Sapper David Kelly, WR/276954. 53rd Broad Gauge Operating Coy. Royal Engineers. Died 17th December 1918.

David Kelly was married and had one child. His family lived at 5 North Strand Street, Stranraer, but his wife moved to Drumdoch, Stranraer when he was killed. His father was Mr James Kelly from Minnigaff who had died some years beforehand. David had worked as a signalman at Stranraer Harbour Station before the war. He had served in his regiment for four years and was 34 years old.

David became unwell and was taken to No.55 Casualty Clearing Station, France. He died there as a result of the influenza virus which was claiming many lives amongst the troops and medical staff.

David is buried in Charleroi Communal Cemetery, Belgium, grave reference P.6.

The same issue of the Free Press lists a few military honours, one name in particular is still well known in the town of Stranraer, Gunner Hugh Aitken, A/102 Royal Field Artillery was awarded the Meritorious Service Medal. He was assisting his father in the jewellery business before enlisting in the army.

Pte. James Kelly, 7404.
1st/5th Battalion Royal Scots Fusiliers.
Killed in action 10th June 1915.

James Kelly had been in the Territorials, but his time had expired in their service. He had been born and raised in Leswalt. Later he worked for Mr Harper of Sheuchan Parks before the war and was married and living in St.John Street, Stranraer. He re-enlisted on the outbreak of war and was killed in action at the Dardanelles,

His wife received the following letter on his death:

> *"You will, I have no doubt, receive official intimation from the War Office of the death of your husband, but I feel sure you would desire details from one able to furnish them. I am an officer in B Company and it was our job last night to occupy the post of honour, the firing line trenches. To get there entailed a long march and we had just left the shelter of a small valley and were rushing to the protection of a breastwork of sandbags. Your husband had just reached the shelter, and was shot in the head at that precise moment. I at once went to his assistance, but he was beyond human aid. I left him in the hands of kindly friends and our regimental doctor, who saw him passing, pronounced life extinct. So passes a brave life. He died on the field of duty, with his face to the enemy. I hope you will accept my sincere sympathy in your great loss, and will be sustained by the knowledge that he died doing his duty to King and country, and that his behaviour in his hour of trial was worthy in every way of the fine regiment of which he and I have the honour to be considered members."*

Although from the Machars, Kirkcowan soldier, Tom Hyslop from Wellhouse, Kirkcowan, and great uncle of the author, wrote home and told of James Kelly's death. Tom had worked for the Earl of Stair as head gamekeeper of Stair Estates before the war.

> *I am writing this in a Soldiers' Home in Alexandria. I am keeping better. We left Liverpool just two days before the railway smash. The soldiers were in the same division as we are, but we never heard how many were killed. We got a wireless on the boat two days after we had sailed. There were between four and five thousand on board...We never stopped till we went to the island of Lemnos, 60 miles from the Dardanelles...We never got going ashore...It was on a Sunday when we got orders to get ready... We got to within about ten miles of the Dardanelles we could hear the*

big guns...We got landed, and moved right up till about 2 ½ miles from the firing line, and by this time the noise was deafening. We got orders to dig ourselves in, as the whole place is shelled from morning till night, but the Turks, so far, have not fired their big guns at night, as they are afraid of giving their position away. It was night when we landed, and when the morning came, some of us had not a very deep trench made- some had not worked very hard; but when daylight came, I guarantee some of us never worked as hard before. We were sitting some of us very near sleeping, when thud! Thud! And we heard a roar coming through the air, and the shells burst in among us. So, between the shells, we got our trench deepened. You ought to have seen us getting down when we heard a shell coming. There is no place you can get clear of the shells, as we have only driven the enemy back about six miles, so that they can shell right up to where we have our landing base. I am putting in a piece of map to give you an idea of the thing, but in the meantime all the fighting is for a hill they call Achi Baba. It is terribly strongly fortified, and the trenches are concreted. We are about 500 yards from the top. I think if we had that hill we would soon give them the shunt back. We got orders on Wednesday that we were to relieve the Royal Scots, and as we had been only two days landed, it was pretty hard on us. Some only got prepared when we were about half a mile from the firing line. I will never forget it. The dead were lying all around. They were mostly Turks, but one could see an odd khaki among them. It was that night poor Kelly, from Stranraer, got knocked out. You will think it funny when I tell you it's safer in the firing line than any other place. I will explain the reason. Our trenches and those of the Turks are so close in some places that they can't get their guns sighted on us for fear of dropping the shells in on their own trenches, but, of course, if there is a bayonet charge, it is quite different. There is every nationality out here and they are a fierce lot the Ghurkas, but there is nothing to beat the Australians. They don't care for their officers. They go off on a bayonet charge of their own. The Turks call them "the hopping kangaroos." We had lost a few men when I left and I have not heard how they are getting on since then. I met Sandy McMeekin on the boat, coming back to the hospital. Poor Kelly was the first to fall. I was picked out for a sniper the first day I was in the trenches. I fired about 150 rounds, but, of course, you could only get a pop at them now and again. The Stranraer boys are doing their whack. I think I will be able to rejoin my regiment in a few days.

Tom's brother, Jock Hyslop, was one of the Australians. The railway crash mentioned at the start of the letter was the Quintinshill disaster of 22nd

May 1915, where 227 men, mostly troops, were killed in the worst train disaster in Britain. The disaster was kept secret from the wider public until after the war.

James Kelly, who had travelled to the Dardanelles with Tom Hyslop and their battalion, is buried at Redoubt Cemetery, Helles, grave reference XII.B.10.

Hugh Kirkwood, 21339.
11th Battalion Highland Light Infantry.
Killed in action 25th September 1915.

Hugh was the son of Hugh and Jean Kirkwood, Commercial Hotel, Stranraer and it was there they received word of their son's death. The couple later moved to Ayrshire. Before the war young Hugh had been employed in the Hyde Park Locomotive Works, Glasgow.

Hugh had been killed at the battle of Loos. His photograph appeared in the local newspaper and listed his regiment as the 5th Dragoon Guards. He has no known grave and is commemorated on Loos Memorial, panel 108 to 112.

Lieut. John S Kyle, 174931.
253 Seige Battery, Royal Garrison Artillery.
Killed in action 3rd November 1918.

John was the fourth son of Alex and Lizzie Kyle, Drumdow, Kirkcolm. Aged 21 John died in the clearing of the forest at Nord. He was buried by 17th, 33rd and 38th Welsh Divisions at Forest Communal Cemetery Nord, grave reference D.9.

John died very close to Armistice and his death notice was not in the local newspaper until 28th November. It is likely his family were not informed of his death until after Armistice was declared. John is also named on Kirkcolm war memorial.

Pte. John Laidlaw, 15805.
2nd Battalion Royal Scots Fusiliers.
Killed in action 30th September 1915.

John lived with his wife Agnes at 7 Greenvale Street, Stranraer. Before the war he was working for Mr Andrew White, St. Andrew Street, Stranraer.

With no known grave John is commemorated on panel 46 to 49 of Loos Memorial.

Pte. James Lawrie, 20785.
6th/7th Battalion Royal Scots Fusiliers.
Died of wounds 28th April 1917.

Before the war James was working for Mr Coulter, in Hanover Square, Stranraer. When war broke out he enlisted and whilst in France he received an early injury. His right arm had been badly wounded and he was taken to a London hospital. His parents, Mr and Mrs Robert Lawrie, who lived at Thorney Cottage, Auchtrelure had been informed of his injury on that occasion.

James was to be fatally injured on 27th April, and he was taken to No.19 Casualty Clearing Station, where he died the following day from his wounds. He is buried in Duisans British Cemetery, Etrun, grave reference IV.H.22. His surname is spelt Laurie on Stranraer War Memorial.

Pte. John Skimming Lees, 7030.
1st/5th Battalion Royal Scots Fusiliers.
Killed in action 14th July 1915.

John was born in Leswalt. His parents were Mr and Mrs David Lees of Burgess Cottage, Leswalt. He is on Larbrax School Roll of Honour as being in the Gordon Highlanders, but must have transferred to the R.S.F.

He was 18 when he took part in horrendous fighting at Gallipoli. He is commemorated on Helles memorial, panel 72 to 75. John is also on Leswalt Memorial.

Pte. Robert Hugh Little, 4152.
17th Battalion Australian Infantry.
Killed in action 3rd May 1917.

Robert was born in Stranraer; he was the son of Nathan and Margaret Jane Little. When his father died, his mother moved to Motherwell and in 1913 Robert emigrated to Australia. Robert became a tram conductor there. His brother Nathan ensured that Robert was remembered on Stranraer and the Australian War Memorials.

According to the records, Robert was killed at Bullicourt. He has no known grave and is commemorated on the Villers-Bretonneux Memorial.

Pte. Alexander Carrick Lock, 645605.
54th Battalion Canadian Infantry.
Killed in action 9th April 1917.

Alexander was the son of Mr and Mrs Horace Lock, County Buildings, Lewis Street, Stranraer. Before he emigrated to Canada in 1913, he had been a booking clerk at Stranraer Town Station. In Canada he worked for the B.C. Electric Railway, Vancouver.

Alexander's brother had written a long letter home which was published in the local newspaper and it is printed under John Wyllie's name.

When he enlisted on 27th January 1916 in Canada, he was described as 5ft 7 ¼ inches tall, with sallow complexion, brown eyes and dark brown hair. Aged 31 when he was killed, Alexander is buried in La Chaudiere Military Cemetery, Vimy, grave reference VIII.D.14.

Pte. William Logie, M2/148911.
956th Mechanical Transport Coy. Army Service Corps.
Killed in action 19th August 1917.

William Logie had been employed for more than 17 years by Dr Monro of Lewis Street, Stranraer, as a coachman. He had the reputation of being a very quiet man who had a large circle of friends.

He was married to Jane Agnew and the couple had two children by the 1901 census when they were living in Greenvale Street. His sister Mrs Agnew, from Lochryan Street was informed of his death first.

When he enlisted he was attached to the Headquarters Staff as a motor driver. He was around 42 when he was badly injured and transported to 43rd Stationary Hospital Egypt. He died of his injuries and was buried at Kantara War Memorial Cemetery grave reference E.433.

William's widow, son and daughter all moved to 44 Robert Street, Govan after his death. They inserted the following poem in the Free Press:

His Country's call he answered,
The dear old flag to save;
But now he lies in a far-off land,
And fills a hero's grave.

Engineer Commander John Mann, Royal Naval Reserve. Died around April or May 1919.

John Mann was native to Stranraer; he went to Sheuchan School and then went on to serve an apprenticeship locally in engineering. After completing his apprenticeship he was employed by the British India Steamship Company in Glasgow where through good work he received regular promotion. By the time war broke out in 1914 John was the company's representative in Colombo, Ceylon. However his wife and sons were living in his house at Windsor Terrace, Academy Street, Stranraer, and when home on leave he attended St. Mark's church and had a small circle of friends he socialised with.

On the outbreak of war he immediately returned home to enlist in the R.N.R. and was given an appointment as engineer commander of one unit of the Grand Fleet. His ship saw much service in the Eastern Mediterranean and the North Sea.

His good service was once again recognised, this time with a Distinguished Service Order which was presented to him at Buckingham Palace.

A few months before the end of the war he fell ill. Whatever the illness, it restricted him physically to a stage where he was released from duty and was taken to hospital in Bombay where he died from pneumonia. John is not listed with the CWGC or SNWM presumably because he had been discharged from service.

Pte. John William Marshall, M318303.
39th Motor Amb. Coy. Army Service Corp. Died 6th December 1917.

Younger son of Matthew and Jessie Marshall, of Bridgebank, later Fairview House Stranraer.

He is named on the family headstone at Inch, which stands not far from the Gothic arch which contains the war memorial there though he is not on that war memorial. John became very ill and died of dysentery in the 31 Stationary General Hospital Baghdad.

He was buried in Baghdad North Gate War Cemetery, grave reference XII.G.8.

Pte. William Monteith. 240990.
1st /5th Royal Scots Fusiliers.
Killed in action 1st October 1918

Son of William and Annabella Monteith of 12 North Strand Street, Stranraer. William was first posted as missing, he had already served 2 ½ years in Egypt and was at the front in France from April 1918.

Aged 20 when he was killed, William is named on family headstone at the Glebe cemetery. He is buried at Proville British Cemetery, Nord, grave reference I.C.7.

Lance Cpl. James Morgan, S/4255.
9th Battalion Black Watch.
Killed in action 25th September 1915.

James was born in 1886 at Bo'ness and was employed there as a miner. He was the son of Mary Morgan and his mother married and became Mrs McIntyre who lived at 2 Greenvale Street, Stranraer.

James was reported missing after the Battle of Hill 70, in the Pas-de-Calais area of the Western Front in France. His death was not confirmed to his family until 1917. With no known grave he is commemorated on panel 78-83 of Loos Memorial.

Sergeant William Morrison, 5071.
4th Regiment South African Infantry.
Killed in action 24th March 1918.

William was first reported as missing to his parents who lived at 12 Edinburgh Road, Stranraer. The German authorities however quickly reported that he had died a prisoner of war on the same day. He was 28.

William had worked in the grocery trade, having served his apprenticeship with Messrs. Hamilton & Sons, Bridge Street, Stranraer. He had emigrated to South Africa around 1915 where he enlisted following Kitchener's appeal for men.

With no known grave William is commemorated on Pozieres Memorial, panel 95-98.

Pte. William Morrison
Ayrshire Yeomanry att. Royal Scots Fusiliers.
Killed in action 26th September 1917.

Prior to joining the army in May, 1916, William had been working for Mr James Robertson for 14 years. He acted as church officer in Sheuchan United Free Church for Some time and Rev. Thomas Russell spoke of him in a service after his death:

"Today our church is a house of morning. During the week there was laid away one who was full of years. During the week also there came the sad news of the death of one who was in the full bloom of his manhood. I think it is fitting that I should say a word or two about William Morrison, who in a sense belonged to us all.

He was our church officer for a year or two, before he had to go, and in that connection I am sure that there is no one who knew him who is not able to bear witness to his hearty and obliging ways. It is not so easy a matter to be a beadle. He has about as many duties as a minister, and yet because his whole heart was in the church, and its well-being his great concern, he had come to have a very sure corner in every heart. I feel the pain of a personal loss, in the fact that he will never be back amongst us anymore. Yet I am glad that I can speak of him as I am now speaking.

There was a certain diffidence about him which was very likeable. He was never self-assertive. If you spoke to him about anything he always said, "I'll do my best," and what was more, in the most whole hearted way he did it. This was not only true of his work in the church; it was true of him also in his daily work as well.

The great agony of the war fell upon the world and it was a very hard thing for him to go. He had his home which was very dear to him.

Aged 28 when he was killed, William was married to Sara McCulloch of Park Lane, Stranraer. He is commemorated on panel 60-61 of Tyne Cot Memorial.

Pte. Robert Murchie, 9094.
2nd Battalion Highland Light Infantry.
Died of wounds 3rd August 1916.

Robert was the son of Mr W. Murchie, Balgreen, Stranraer and before the war he had been working as a grocer in Glasgow. He had been in the regular army and had served seven years in India and thee in Egypt.

Since the beginning of the Great War, Robert had been wounded twice previously but recovered from those wounds. He died from his wounds on the third occasion of being injured and is buried in Corbie Communal Cemetery Extension, Somme, Plot 2, row A, grave 37.

Pte. David Murdoch, 8755.
2nd Battalion Seaforth Highlanders.
Died of wounds 25th May 1916.

Son of David and Elizabeth Gray Murdoch of Stranraer, David was married and lived at 2 Trade Street, with his wife Margaret (nee Kennedy).

David was injured and taken to a Field Ambulance Station at the village of Englebelmer. There he died of his wounds and was buried at Englebelmer Communal Cemetery Extension, grave reference F.30.

Pte. George Murray. 55486. 15th Bn. Highland Light Infantry. Killed in action 1st October 1918.

James and Mary Murray of 34 Station Street, Stranraer, had already suffered loss when their oldest son died in 1900 aged just four. Before the war, George had worked as an assistant draper with Messrs' Craig & Kyle, George Street, Stranraer.

George is commemorated on Vis-en-Artois memorial panel 9 and 10. He is also named on the family headstone in the Glebe cemetery.

Pte. John Baillie Murray, 202200. 1st Battalion Gordon Highlanders. Killed in action 16th June 1917.

John was the son of Mr and Mrs Murray of 48 Fisher Street, Stranraer. Before the war he had worked for Mr A. Jack the butcher in Stranraer. The couple had four of their sons serving at the same time. When he was killed the Chaplain of his Battalion wrote to his parents:

> *"He fell at the foot of Infantry Hill. He was killed by a shell and death was instantaneous. He was bearing himself gallantly at the time, and his loss is much regretted by officers and men alike."*

With no known grave, John is commemorated on bay 8 and 9 of Arras Memorial.

His parents inserted the following poem in the local newspaper; it is all the more poignant since John had no known grave:

And he sleeps in a grave in a far-off land,
That his comrades kindly made him;
May he rest in peace in his narrow bed,
Where friendly hands have laid him.

Sapper Joseph McCabe, 96749.
175th Tunnelling Coy. Royal Engineers.
Killed in action 11th September 1915.

Joseph was one of the oldest men killed in the war from the Rhins area. Either he lied about his age to enlist or he genuinely did not know his exact age. He was born at Backrampart Stranraer on 29th July 1864, and although the CWGC records his age as 44 at the time of his death, he would have been 51 years old.

Joseph was married, his wife Mary, later listed her address as Garngad Road, Glasgow, which was the same street as the family of the above named John Hughan, and one wonders if the families knew each other through the Stranraer connection.

With no known grave, Joseph is commemorated on the Menin Gate, panel 9.

Pte. Samuel McCandlish, 22162.
1st Garrison Battalion, Royal Scots Fusiliers.
Killed in action 12th January 1918.

Having already served in the Boer War and received medals for his efforts there, and although he was still a reservist, Samuel again volunteered to go to the front on the outbreak of war. He had been working in Greenock with Messrs. Caird & Co. Shipbuilders. He was a widower and his little girl lived with his mother in Stranraer.

He and his two brothers were all serving at the same time. Robert was a gunner with the 1st Australian Division and was wounded in the arm in 1917 and was sent to a hospital in Gloucester to recover. Another brother was fighting at Salonika. Sam had fought at Neuve Chapelle, Auber's Ridge, Festubert, Givenchy and Loos. Those at home in Stranraer were very proud of him as he had won the D.C.M. for conspicuous bravery in the field, on 16th June 1915 at Givenchy, the citation read:

> *"For conspicuous gallantry in leading his section, nearly half of whom were casualties before getting over our own parapet. He nearly reached the enemy's wire alone. His bravery and devotion were very marked."*

Samuel wrote home to a friend speaking of the day he had earned the medal, at that time he had no idea he would be commended for his bravery:

> *"I am just down from the trenches. We put in three awful days. It was terrible. I never encountered anything like it before...we lost very heavily. I am thankful to be here today. All of my comrades were killed or wounded two days ago. I asked God to guide and protect me, and I am glad today my prayer was heard. I went over the parapet with twelve of a section, and only two of us returned. It was an awful afternoon. The roars of the shells were frightful and it is wonderful that any of us are left...When you send the Free Press put a packet of writing paper in it weekly. In the attack, I threw my pack off and lost all."*

Samuel was wounded at Loos and he must have received mail from home offering their sympathy and wishes for him to return to fitness. He wrote home to Rev. J.Heggie:

> *"Just a note to say I received your very welcome letter. I thank you and the others referred to for their sympathy. I had many wounds all over my body – fortunately, none of them serious... I think about ten days will make me prepared for leaving here. I went right through the battle of Loos without injury, and was beginning to think I was safely through that great battle. We had dug ourselves in, and settling down to hold the position when the enemy counter-attacked on our left. He was forcing his way through a communication trench. I went down to assist the bomb-throwers in holding the enemy in check. On searching there I commenced with another to try and force them from this part of the trench. We held them in check in the trench, but others in the rear of me failed to keep a look-out on my left (it was very wet and dark - 11p.m.). The enemy crawled round on my left, I saw three heads, and a German bomb dropped at my side. If I had run to my rear I could have escaped it. It was a time fuse, and from the time they are ignited they take, roughly, five seconds before exploding, but I was determined to drop one of my souvenirs among those I had seen. I lighted mine and at the same time it left my hand the one lying at my side exploded. I don't know whether I was blown up or down, or what, but I felt pains all over."*

Sam was a regular writer to the Free Press and his published lengthy letters were very popular.

"Your letter was twenty-two days on the way before I received it. I have seen a great deal of fighting lately, especially during the last three weeks. Many days during that period I thought would be my last. On Sunday 16th we were in the reserve trenches as support to the firing lines. It was an awkward day for all of us, the shells sweeping our trenches from daylight to dark. We had many casualties. We got a few hours rest during the night, and moved off at 2am to German trenches taken on the Sunday by our troops. The sights were terrible. The enemy's dead lay in piles, some of them unrecognisable- cut to pieces by our artillery. We got many relics in their trenches. We were still being heavily shelled and losing men. At 1pm we moved from their trenches and attacked them in the open. We moved forward by short rushes at intervals and gained about 200 yards. Then word was passed along every second man to keep up fire, while his right-hand man got out his entrenchment tools and commenced digging ourselves in. I never wrought harder in my life. To tie on your flag and dig a trench for two, and bullets whizzing in every direction, is anything but a comfortable position, and before I could get sufficient cover both my right and left hand men were hit. My right hand man through the temple, my left hand man through the leg. I bandaged both to the best of my ability, then commenced digging again, thankful I was not like my comrades I refer to. I managed however to finish my part of the trench. I then turned my attention to my rifle and the enemy in front, and I peppered at them until darkness hid their whereabouts from us. We then posted sentries and commenced digging under cover of darkness thankful that those who were left were fit to do so. Shortly after this the Guards Brigade advanced and relieved us, many of them being hit in doing so. We retired after handing over our position the Guards, all tired and done up after several hard and trying days. We remained in reserve for two days away from rifle fire, but still exposed to shell fire. We are now ten miles in rear of the firing line, and billeted in farmhouses. We are down for a fortnight's rest. On my way through the trench for attack, I shook hands with James McCormack (son of Mr McCormack, coal merchant Stranraer). It was a miserable wet day, and he was taking the shelter of his waterproof sheet, and like myself suffering the hardships of the campaign. He said he hoped we would meet again soon in Stranraer. I said I hoped to get through this day safe. We had no time for conversation. I am writing in a straw shed, but it seems comfortable after lying in the open for nearly three weeks, never getting a good meal or a fresh drink of water, as all the water is more or less filthy about the trenches. We often drink from a hole made by a he country here is splendidly in bloom and it reminds one of home. Everything seems peaceful, but in the distance we hear the continual boom of the guns like distant thunder. This is Sunday.

The Presbyterians are at an open-air service, and duty has prevented me from getting to it. I like to get to service. Scenes and deeds done here make one repent on their past life, and when one is carried safely through many dangers, one feels thankful to Providence for His protection. There is another Stranraer man in my platoon – Ballantyne, who is thankful he pulled through safely in our last engagement."

He was an Acting Sergeant at the time of his death and in comparison to many other men, at 42 years old he was considerably older than many of the others.

Samuel had written home to his mother in Sheuchan Street, Stranraer two weeks before he was killed and told her not to be surprised if he was injured as there were a great number of casualties in the trenches.

In a service the Rev. John Heggie remembered Sam:

"He was a good man of natural abilities and shrewd intelligence, and always faithful as a friend. He was a born soldier, tactful as he was courageous. He was a veteran soldier; for he had fought in the South African War...they would miss him for he had always come to that church. He went out to India on draught after coming home on furlough and had died there of a fractured skull."

The Rev. Heggie went on to say that when he was awarded the D.C.M., Sam was the first Stranraer man to be awarded such a distinction locally and how he hoped that in time Stranraer would honour Sam and his exploits in a suitable way.

Samuel must have received a head injury whilst on garrison duty. He died of a fractured skull. He is buried in Jhansi Cantonment Cemetery, but the graveyard is in a state of complete disrepair and has not been transcribed or plotted. His name is also on Face 13 of the Madras War Memorial, Chennai.

Shortly before he died he wrote home to his mother words to the effect that he would like nothing better than to be sitting under the tree at the top of the Dam Road (Seabank Road), looking out to the loch and watching the world go by.

Sergt. William McCandlish, 684010. 87th Battalion Canadian Infantry. Killed in action 14th August 1917.

William was the youngest son of Robert McCandlish of 45 Hanover Street, Stranraer, the family had originally lived around Ibrox in Glasgow. He was a draughtsman to trade and before moving to Canada he had served in the 5th Battalion of the Scottish Rifles. He was 23 when he enlisted and according to his attestation papers, he had a light complexion, grey eyes and auburn hair. William won a D.C.M. for his bravery and received the following letter from the Brigadier-General commanding the Canadian Infantry Brigade:

> *"I have very much pleasure in congratulating you on the award of the Distinguished Conduct Medal to you. It is reported to me that during the night of June 8-9 you showed conspicuous gallantry and high qualities of leadership in leading your platoon to the attack of a machine gun emplacement. Also that you were able to capture and bring back the machine gun. This is exceedingly good work, and is highly appreciated. With best wishes for your future success."*

William had gone over to France with the Canadians in December 1916.

His Commanding Officer wrote to his parents:

> *"I wanted to write to you personally to tell you how I sympathise with your loss, and also how proud you should be of a son who did such noble work for the great cause, even to the final sacrifice. He was everything that a soldier should be, and a fine example to the men."*

The letter is scant on detail and it is likely because he was killed alongside many of his comrades. William has no known grave and is commemorated on Vimy Memorial.

Pte. Alexander McCarlie, 241436.
1st/4th Seaforth Highlanders.
Killed in action 20th July 1918.

Alexander was married to Helen King from Kirkland Cottage, Lochnaw, they had four young children and he worked for Sir Andrew Agnew. His parents lived at 5 Queen Street, Stranraer. He had a brother on active service and sisters at home.

Alexander had been on active service for fourteen months. He had previously been admitted to No.22 General Hospital France suffering from trench fever. He was 31 when he was killed. His parents inserted the following poem in the local newspaper when he died:

We cannot forget him, we loved him too dearly
For his memory to fade from our lives like a dream
But our lips need not speak when our hearts mourn sincerely,
For grief often dwells where it seldom is seen.

Alexander is buried in Marfaux British Cemetery, Marne, grave reference VIII.D.5. He is also named on Leswalt War Memorial.

Serg. William Hendry McCash, 27482.
28th Coy. Machine Gun Corps.
Killed in action 7th May 1917.

Mr and Mrs Thomas McCash of Castle Street, Stranraer, later 'Arranview', Royal Crescent, received a letter from William's Company offering their sympathies. William enlisted in 1915 and had been on active service in the field from April 1916. He had come through some very heavy fighting, including the Somme since his arrival at the front.

"It is with great regret that I have to report that your son. Sergt. W.H.McCash has been killed in action. He was in the front line trench in charge of a gun team, when the enemy started shelling. A shell exploded near him, killing him instantaneously, together with two other men of his gun team. I know words are of little use in a case like this, but it is of some consolation to know that he died doing his duty nobly and well. We feel his loss tremendously in the Company, as he was well liked by both officers and men."

With no known grave, William is commemorated on Arras Memorial, bay 10.

Pte. Matthew Nelson McClumpha, 8112.
1st/5th Battalion Royal Scots Fusiliers.
Killed in action 30th December 1915.

Matthew was the youngest son of William and Annie McClumpha of Auchabrick, Portlogan; they had previously lived at Killumpha and are likely to have known Edward Morland very well, who is named on the war memorial in Drummore, because of the Killumpha connection. By the time of his death they lived Glebe Cottage, Stoneykirk.

Matthew married Isabella Fleming in 1914 and their baby daughter was born in 1915 in Stranraer where they lived at 12 Millhill Street, Stranraer.

Matthew was killed in action aged 22, at the Dardanelles on 30th December 1915 having taken part in very heavy fighting in Helles. He is buried at Twelve Tree Cops Cemetery, Turkey, grave reference II.A 1. Matthew is also named on the Kirkmaiden (Drummore) War Memorial.

Pte. William McCluskie, 16439
8th Battalion Royal Scots Fusiliers.
Killed in action 19th September 1918.

William was the only son of Jean McCluskie, Agnew Crescent, Stranraer. He was first reported as missing then officially reported killed on that date.

William's body was recovered and buried at Doiran Military Cemetery, Greece, grave reference III.D.1.

Deck Hand John McClymont, 3856/DA.
H.M.M.L. 151. Royal Naval Reserve.
Died 10th December 1918.

John was the son of Mr and Mrs William McClymont of Foundry Cottage, Sheuchan Street, Stranraer. He had lived there with his parents and siblings.

Aged 22 he became ill and was taken to Haslar Hospital, Gosport, where his condition deteriorated. John died in the naval hospital and his body was returned home. He is interred in Inch Parish Churchyard.

Another McClymont man, likely to be related, Pte. Andrew McClymont, 1st/5th R.S.F., wrote home to his mother about the action he had seen at the Dardanelles:

> *There was a big fight here on 12th July ... There were a lot of the Stranraer boys wounded, but I am not sure if there were any killed. I got a bullet through my chin, just at the start of the fight, and I can tell you I wasn't sorry for the trenches were full of dead Turks, and the smell was terrible. The Turkish trenches were battered to pieces by the British artillery. The big guns bombarded the Turkish trenches for three hours. The noise of them was terrible. Each gun fired two hundred shells, and it was a terrible thing to see. I am at present in hospital in Cairo. You need not annoy yourself, for I am quite happy and glad to get into hospital for a rest. I don't expect the fighting to last long. Sam was all right. He wasn't in the fight. He was the Brigade orderly and along with the General, Sam is as lucky as a black cat. Mrs Snodgrass's husband got his arm hurt with a shell bursting...I was passing up the trench at the time...when I heard the crack of a rifle and just then the bullet struck my chin....I could see him all right. He was just about a hundred yards off, so I struck my rifle up and popped him. I got him all right, I think."*

From the 1901 census there is a John, Andrew and Samuel McClymont all living at Sun Street, Stranraer. Although Andrew is only slightly younger, he would have been a nephew of John and Sam.

Pte. William McClymont, S/18516. 5th Battalion Cameron Highlanders. Killed in action 18th October 1916.

Before the war William was the chief clerk at Stranraer Railway Station in the goods department. He had been home to visit his family in St. John Street, Stranraer on furlough six weeks before he was killed. It was the last time his wife and two young children were to see him.

He had come through some of the worst fighting of the war unscathed but his fortune was brief. With no known grave, William is commemorated on Thiepval War Memorial, pier and face 15B.

Pte. Robert McCracken, 273113.
12th Battalion Royal Scots.
Killed in action 1st May 1917.

Robert was married to Edith Lawrie and the couple lived at 5 High Street, Stranraer. Robert Worked with Mr McCormack the coal merchant from Hanover Square up until he enlisted. He spent some considerable time amongst Stranraer pals in the trenches and is mentioned in several letters home from James McCormack which is included at the end of the section here. James was one of the sons of the coal merchant that Robert had worked for before the war.

Robert had returned home earlier in the war to carry the coffin of his comrade Robert Gunion Reid, who is interred at Inch and named on the memorial there.

With no known grave, Robert is commemorated on Arras Memorial, bay 1 and 2.

Petty Officer Robert L McCrae,
H.M. Minesweeper.
Killed in action 15th July 1919.

Robert had been serving on minesweepers throughout the war and it was a very hazardous job. His good work had earned him a Distinguished Service Medal.

Just a short time before he was killed, Stranraer Town Council had met to agree the names of the men who were to be awarded the freedom of the burgh, and it had been unanimously agreed that Robert was to be one of those men to receive the honour.

The ship Robert was serving on, HMS Gentian, struck a mine and he lost his life. Robert is commemorated on Chatham naval memorial.

2nd Lieutenant John Forrest McCredie, 235th Coy.
Machine Gun Corps.
Killed in action 30th November 1917.

John was the elder son of Mrs Agnes Aitken McCredie and the late Thomas McCredie of 18 Academy Street, Stranraer. He had been a first year medical student at Edinburgh University on the outbreak of war, but enlisted and received officers training at Inns of Court Officers' Training Corps., London, and was gazetted in November 1916.

John was sent to France in July 1917, and when he went missing on St. Andrew's day that year, his commanding officer wrote:

> *"On the morning of the 30th November, during an attack of the enemy, your son was with his machine guns in the front line. None of the men from this position or near it have returned, and I can, therefore, obtain no news whatever of him, but we only hope that he has been taken prisoner as the enemy came through is position. His Company Commander is also missing, so I am writing for him, being the Divisional Machine Gun Officer. Though I have only known your son in the last month, I know what a good, capable and fearless officer he was, and it is characteristic of him, that he evidently remained at his post till the enemy gor round it. The whole Company will very much miss him, and it is a great loss to us. We can only send you our sincerest sympathy in your anxiety, and hope that you may shortly hear news of him."*

In a letter that seems to come more from the heart than the official ones Pte. Matthias, signaller later wrote:

> *"His death took place at a place we called Turner Quarry, and that is where he is buried. I thought a lot of Mr McCredie. He stood by me when I was in trouble, and I only wish to God he were living. He was both an officer and a gentleman. You can rest assured that he died doing his duty, and that you have m deepest sympathy. I must say that I never served under a kinder and better officer all the while I was in the Army.*

Mr Hugh Miller, lecturer in zoology, Edinburgh University wrote:

> *"Your boy was a fine type, and he had a brilliant career in front of him."*

With no known grave, John is commemorated on Cambrai Memorial, Louveral, panels 12 and 13.

Able Seaman Harry Walter McDowall, Clyde Z/5050.
Howe Battalion, Royal Naval Division, R.N.V.R.
Killed in action 14th August 1917.

Harry was the second son of Harry and Mary Ann McDowall of 16 Station Street, Stranraer. He was born in Maryhill, Glasgow. His father had been a grocer, but had died some time earlier. He was an apprentice to the butcher trade with Councillor Waddell.

Harry had attempted to join the army early but was rejected because of his age. In June 1915 he joined the R.N.D. and was sent to the fighting in the Dardanelles, before being sent to France. He had been invalided home from there in 1916 as he had pneumonia. As soon as he recovered he was sent to France again.

His mother was sent a letter from the chaplain of the Battalion letting her know that death was instantaneous and the result of a trench mortar which had chiefly wounded his legs. Harry was buried the following morning in a garden at the end of the front trench, he was 20.

Harry is buried in Orchard Dump Cemetery, Arleux-en-Gohelle, Pas de Calais, grave reference IX.J.5.

Pte. Terence McGeoch, 557.
9th Battalion Australian Expeditionary Force.
Killed in action 24th April 1915.

I could find very little detail on Terence, other than he had once lived in Stranraer and had emigrated to Australia. On the outbreak of war he enlisted and was one of the Australians who fought amongst the fierce battles at Gallipoli.

Buried at Lone Pine Memorial, Turkey, grave reference 31. Terence is also on the Australian War Memorial.

Pte. John McGivern, S/7388.
1st/2nd Battalion Gordon Highlanders.
Died from wounds 1st July 1916.

John worked alongside his father at the dairy at Airyhemming before the war. His parents were James and Jane (nee Paisley) McGivern, and during the war his parents moved to Glebe Street in Stranraer, though they later moved to 4 Birnam Place, Stranraer. His sister lived in Pinwherry. At some stage the family must have been living in (the) Lochans as the newspaper reported the story of 'Three Lochans Soldiers'.

John was serving at the same time as his two brothers, he had been previously injured in the right shoulder and spine whilst fighting at the second battle of Ypres. Aged almost 31, John was killed on the first day of the Battle of the Somme and is commemorated on Thiepval Memorial. Pier and Face 15B and 15C. John is named on the family Headstone in the Glebe Cemetery.

Brothers of John McGivern;
Pte. D. McGivern Motor Transport, and Trooper T. McGivern Scottish Horse.

Captain Robert McHarrie. 5th attd. 1st Battalion Royal Scots Fusiliers. Killed in action 9th June 1918.

Robert was the son of Mr James McHarrie of Ann House, Stranraer. He had been a member of the local Territorials and when war broke out he immediately volunteered to go abroad.

During training at Cambusbarron he became ill with pneumonia and was invalided to hospital. This prevented him from Foreign Service for a time. Aged just Robert then received a promotion on his return to health and at that time was the youngest Captain in the British army.

On arrival in France he was given command of his Battalion and immediately ordered to the trenches. After only three weeks at the front he was killed by a shell. The Chaplain wrote to his father that Robert had been buried with full military honours in the English cemetery a few miles behind the firing line. Amongst those who attended his funeral was Pte. James O'Connor R.S.F. from Stranraer.

Robert is buried at Sandpits British Cemetery, Fouquereuil, grave reference II.D.12. Robert is also on Cairnryan War Memorial.

Gunner John McIntyre, 129593. 346th Seige Bty. Royal Garrison Artillery. Died of wounds 15th August 1917.

John was the twin son of Mr and Mrs McIntyre of Dally Bay. He was married to Elizabeth Geddes who later lived in Foundry Lane, Stranraer, and the couple had four children. Before the outbreak of war John McIntyre worked for Mr Clement the baker for 12 years as a van driver.

John was 42 when he was badly injured and died at No.7 Casualty Clearing Station, France. His parents, brothers and sisters inserted the following poem in the local newspaper when he was killed:

No mother's care did him attend,
Nor o'er him did a father bend;
No sister by to shed a tear,
No brother by his words to hear.
Sick, dying in a foreign land,
No father by to take his hand;
No mother near to close his eyes-
Far from his native land he lies.

John is buried at Noex-Les-Mines Communal Cemetery, France, grave reference II.H.34. He is on Kirkcolm and Stranraer Memorials, his photograph is beside his Kirkcolm entry.

Bosun Hugh John McKay, Mercantile Marine, SS Polandia. Killed in action 10th March 1917.

Born at Islandmagee, Hugh was married to Jeanie K. Robinson and they lived at 37 Agnew Crescent with their family. It seems more than likely that Hugh was the brother-in-law of Thomas Robinson also named on Stranraer War Memorial as they both served on the Polandia. Three local men were killed when the ship sunk.

The troopship was sailing from Birkenhead to Cherbourg on 10th March 1917, and it was supposed that she struck a mine since no U-boat claimed responsibility.

Hugh's intimation of death appears in the local newspaper as having been lost at sea on the 10th March and this matches up with the date the ship went down. However the date Hugh is recorded with the CWGC to have been killed is not the date the Polandia sunk, so it is possible he either survived that, or was not aboard. Interestingly the CWGC lists two Hugh McKay's as having been killed on 24th November 1917 serving in the Merchant Navy. It is my belief that this is an error of recording and that

Hugh has been recorded on the wrong date. The only other possiblilty is that Hugh was not serving on the Polandia when it was sunk but was serving on the Sabia when it was struck without warning by torpedo from U-96 in November of the same year.

His wife inserted the following poem in the local newspaper on his death notice in March 1917:

No green grass grows above his head,
Nor o'er his grave a tear we'll shed;
In a sailor's grave he lies asleep.
Far out on the ocean, dark and deep.

He was a father truly fond,
A friend both kind and true;
A better father never lived
His equals were few.

Hugh McKay and Thomas Robinson are both commemorated on Tower Hill Memorial. Hugh was 41.

Pte. Robert McKenzie, 8092. 4th Regiment South African Scottish. Killed in action 9th April 1917.

Born in Kirkcowan, Robert was the youngest surviving son of the late A.W. McKenzie, and of Mrs McKenzie, Bowling Green Road, later 3 Station Street, Stranraer. Aged 33 years, Robert is buried at Cabaret-Rouge British Cemetery, Souchez, grave reference XV.N.10.

Pte. David McKie, 13102. 2nd/3rd London Field Ambulance attd. Royal Scots Fusiliers. Died 18th April 1919.

David was the third son of the late David McKie and Mrs M. McKie of 33 High Street, Stranraer.

Mrs Katherine MacRobert, hotel keeper of the King's Arms Hotel in Stranraer appealed for exemption for David from conscription as he had worked at the hotel for some time as a hearse and motor driver. Her appeal was refused and David was conscripted into the Royal Scots Fusiliers. As his job had been driving in civilian life, he was given the job of driving field ambulances.

David died of pneumonia as a result of the influenza virus at University War Hospital, Southampton. David is not listed on the CWGC or SNWM.

Stranraer men line up for a photograph.

Pte. James McKie 7206.
5th Batt Royal Scots Fusiliers.
Died 14th August 1915

James was born in Stranraer, the second son of Mr and Mrs David McKie of the King's Arms Hotel and he was employed as a driver at the hotel for some time. Immediately before joining the Colours, he had been working for the Larne and Stranraer Steamship Joint Committee. James was also a keen footballer. He was married and lived at 33 Harbour Street, Stranraer with his wife and young son.

After enlisting, James left with his Company for the Dardanelles in May 1915. He served a short time at there before he was injured in the left hand. The wound infected and he became very weak. He was taken to hospital but became very debilitated and succumbed to enteric fever, a typhoid infection.

James was said to be a popular, kind and cheery man during his life, he is commemorated in Alexandria (Chatby) Military and War Memorial cemetery, grave reference K29.

Pte. John McKillops. Gordon Highlanders. Killed in action 9th April 1918.

Born on the 6th March 1892 in Glenluce to John and Agnes McKillop (nee Cronie). John McKillops was the second son of the couple and one of three brothers all serving at the same time, including the below named William. His birth entry in the register is immediately below John Parker who was serving the Colours at the same time and whose brother James is on Glenluce Memorial. His mother Agnes was later living at 33 Harbour Street, Stranraer, and the family must have moved to the town at some stage. Before the war John was employed by Messrs. Smith, Dundee Equitable, Inverurie.

John had enlisted early in 1915 and was on his third trip to the front in France when he was reported missing. He was later to be reported killed on or around the date he went missing. John is not listed with the CWGC or SNWM, and has no known grave. His death is listed amongst the service and war returns, he was 26 years old.

Bombadier William McKillops, 548. C Battery, 89th Brigade, Royal Field Artillery. Killed in action 25th July 1916.

Before the war William had served his apprenticeship as a grocer with Mr John Clement in Stranraer. He then moved to working in the wholesale Glasgow grocers Messrs. Brown, Laurie and Sloan.

William and his two brothers enlisted on the outbreak of war and all three sons who had lived at 33 Harbour Steet with their mother Agnes, were on active service at the same time.

Aged 22 when he was killed, William is buried in Gordon Dump Cemetery, Ovillers-La Boisselle, Somme, grave reference VII.C.3.

There is another man with the same name on Leswalt memorial and it is likely that the two were related.

Pte. Kenneth McLennan, 79536. 31st Battalion Canadian Infantry. Died of wounds 4th April 1916.

Kenneth was born in Stranraer on 8th May 1890. Although his father lived in Glasgow, Kenneth had been raised by his aunt, Mrs Thompson, Charlotte Street, Stranraer. He was educated at the Academy and High School in Stranraer and afterwards was apprenticed to the ironmongery trade with Mr David McGeoch. He had also served 2 ½ years in the Royal Scots Fusiliers before emigrating to Canada around 1911 where he worked in farming.

On enlisting he was described as having light hair, blue eyes and a light complexion. He was 5ft 4 ½ inches tall.

James was reported to have died of his wounds received in action however he has no known grave and is commemorated on panels 24-28-30 of the Menin Gate. He was 26.

Able Seaman Donald Jones McMillan, ClydeZ/2063. RNVR. Hood Battalion RND.

Donald is commorated on the Pozieres memorial, Somme, alongside over 14000 other British forces with no known grave. He was almost 23.

His father had died in Liverpool, but he was the nephew of Mr and Mrs John Gracie of Taylor's Parks, Lewis Street, Stranraer.

A successful recruiting campaign was run in Stranraer for the RNVR, where twenty young men were recruited in one day. Before leaving for training at the Crystal Palace, London, they were treated to lunch in the town hall amongst local dignitaries. After the lunch and speeches they marched through the town led by a band and boarded the 11.30 am train to Glasgow. A large crowd gathered on the town station platform to give them a good send-off. As the train was leaving the station, fog-signals were exploded to announce their departure to the town.

RNVR recruits at Stranraer town station where they were given a good send-off.

After training at the Crystal Palace. From the back: J. McDowall, R. McWillliam, -Thomson, W.Holmes. Middle Row: Peter McCulloch, J. Raeside and James Ross. Front George Heggie.

James McWhinnie, 51010.
1st/4th Battalion Royal Scots Fusiliers.
Killed in action 24th September 1917.

James was the elder son of Mr James McWhinnie, Lochryan Street, Stranraer. He was aged 37 when he was killed.

James is buried in Port Said War Memorial Cemetery, Egypt, grave reference F.11.

Pte. William James McWhirter, 41398.
1st Battalion Cameronians.
Killed in action 20th May 1917.

The second son of Mr McWhirter of Birnam Place, Station Street, Stranraer to be killed in the war, less than a month after the first. William was the brother of David Blain McLellan McWhirter. Before enlisting William had worked in the stables of the Buck's Head Hotel in the employment of Mr Dan Wilson. He had been on active service for about five months.

William is buried at Croisilles British Cemetery, grave reference III.E.18.

Pte. David Blain McLellan McWhirter, 183699.
10th Battalion Canadian Infantry.
Killed in action 28th April 1917.

David was the first of the McWhirter brothers to be killed, less than a month later his brother William fell. David enlisted in Canada in December 1917, he was described as 5ft 6 ½ inches tall with a dark complexion, grey eyes and black hair.

David is commemorated on Vimy Memorial. He was 27.

William McWilliam, unknown service or date of death.

A difficult name to trace locally since there were a number of McWilliam families born in the Rhins. What was recorded in various military sources did not give any direct links to Stranraer, although there were possibilities with three men listing their addresses as being in Belfast, Ayr and Dundrennan, but none of these meant I could discount other men from further afield, or those whose addresses were not recorded.

There is an Alexander McWilliam named on the family headstone in the Glebe Cemetery. I could not find any trace of him on the CWGC or SNWM with the date of death that is recorded. Nor is that Alexander on any local memorial. I may speculate that he is the same man, perhaps known by a different first name which is fairly commonplace in this area. Perhaps more will be known if a relative comes forward or after the 1911 census is published.

Sapper Gilbert Bingham Neil, 93258. 218th Field Coy. Royal Engineers. Killed in action 9th July 1917.

Gilbert was the youngest son of the late Hugh Neil and Mrs Ellen Neil of 11 Sheuchan Street, Stranraer. Before the war he had been employed with Mr John Forsyth, plumber, Stranraer. He had been serving for nineteen months in the army and was aged 22 when he was killed. His brother is named below and he died six months after Gilbert.

Gilbert was buried at Coxyde Military Cemetery, Belgium, grave reference I.D.7. He is also named on the family headston in Sheuchan Cemetery Extension.

Pte. Hugh Neil, Army Service Corps. Died December 20th 1917.

Hugh was the elder brother of the above named Gilbert, there was almost 10 years between the two men. A tinsmith to trade, Hugh had worked for the Scottish Co-operative Society at Bladnoch before he enlisted.

He became ill in 1916 whilst serving abroad and was invalided home to his mother's house where he died around a year later from tuberculosis. His cousin Philip Torrance registered his death.

Hugh is buried in Sheuchan Cemetery extension in the family plot, his brother Gilbert is named on the headstone. Hugh was 32.

Pte. Charles McDowall Nelson, 240192.
1st/5th Battalion Royal Scots Fusiliers.
Died of wounds 11th May 1917.

Born on the 1st December 1895, Charles was the eldest of the four sons of Alexander and Maggie Ann Nelson. The family were not well off and they lived in poor circumstances in Sloss's Close off Dalrymple Street.

Prior to the outbreak of war Charles, like his father before him was a fisherman. Charles was also in the Territorial Army stationed at Falkirk and it was while he was there he married Mary Colvin a 21 year old widow, in Blythswood, Glasgow on 27th May 1916.

The three older boys seemed glad of the opportunity to serve their country. Alex and Willie had joined the navy. Alex was known as Chat as he was a Chatham rating, whilst Willie, who had lied about his age to be able to join the navy, was known as Pompey as he had completed his initial training in Portsmouth. By the time of their brothers' death, Alex was in Trinidad and Willie was stationed in Portsmouth. Robert the youngest brother was not old enough to go to serve in the war.

Charles came through some of the heaviest fighting at Gallipoli on the 12th July 1915, but he had then written home to his mother to say he was recovering from sunstroke.

Charles was aboard the SS Invernia on 1st January 1917 when that ship was torpedoed without warning by the submarine UB47. The vessel was operating as a troopship and had been off the coast of Greece at Cape Matapan. The vessel sunk with the loss of 125 men, and Charles was some considerable time in the water before being picked up. He wrote home to his mother that he had been "none the worse of his exciting experience."

Again he was fighting at Gallipoli where he was severely injured. He was taken to Alexandria Hospital, Egypt but died as a result of paralysis. The report in the local newspaper gave the date of his death as 15th May, but CWGC and SNWM record it as 11th. Charles is buried in Kantara War Memorial Cemetery, grave reference F246. Charles was the uncle of local historian and author Donnie Nelson.

Pte. Robert Nish, 14090.
6th/7th Battalion Royal Scots Fusiliers.
Died of Wounds 23rd August 1917.

Robert was the youngest son of Mr John and Mrs Sarah Nish from Hanover Square in Stranraer. His father had been a well known local builder.

Lisjssenthoek was the site of a number of casualty clearing stations during the First World War, it was behind the front lines and out of reach of most of the German artillery.

Robert is buried in Lijssenthoek Military Cemetery, Poperinge, grave reference XVIII.B.11.

Rifleman Charles O'Keefe, R/15731.
9th Battalion Kings Royal Rifles.
Killed in action 9th April 1917.

Charles was the youngest son of a well known local hairdresser, Michael O'Keefe who had died in 1896. More of the O'Keefe family were involved in hairdressing business in the town, and perhaps more will be known about them when the 1911 census is made public.

Charles' name is listed as Keefe with the CWGC. He was 38 years old and with no known grave is commemorated on bay 7 of Arras Memorial.

Second Lieutent Robert William Ormiston.
6th Battalion King's Shropshire Light Infantry.
Killed in action 25th March 1918.

Brother to the below named Uri, Robert was the son of John Baptie Ormiston of Waverley House Stranraer. Robert was rejected six times before enlisting in the Royal Engineers. He was then given his commission in November 1917.

Aged 22 When he was killed, Robert is buried in Roye New British Cemetery, Somme, grave reference SP.Mem.B.5.

Robert had a cousin called Robert Kennedy Ormiston who had joined forces in Canada. He was killed on 8th August 1918. The family had already lost Uri named below.

Pte. Uri John Baptie Ormiston, 302957.
1st/8th Battalion Argyll and Sutherland Highlanders.
Killed in action 23rd November 1917.

Uri's father was the governor of the Wigtownshire Combination Poorhouse, Stranraer. Before the war Uri had completed his grocer's apprenticeship with Messrs. Hugh Hamilton and Sons, Stranraer.

His father was told that his eldest son, aged 26, had been injured on the 20th November, the first day of the Battle of Cambrai, but that Uri had refused to go back to a casualty station as he had wanted to remain with his fellow soldiers. He was killed by a shell while attacking a village.

With no known grave, Uri is commemorated on the addenda panel of Cambrai Memorial, Louverval.

Deck Hand John Palmer,
HMS Vivid, Royal Naval Reserve.
Died 16th December 1915.

John was the son of Samuel and Annie Palmer (nee Cunningham). His parents lived at 30 Sheuchan Street, Stranraer. He died at Haslar Naval Hospital, Gosport, aged just 37. His two brothers, William and James had both died in infancy.

In what must have been a dreadful time for his mother, John's father died around ten weeks after him. John's body was returned home and he is buried in the family plot in Kirkcolm Parish Churchyard. John is also on the war memorial in Kirkcolm.

Pte. William Paterson, 270334.
12th Battalion Royal Scots.
Killed in action 23rd March 1918.

William was the youngest son of Mrs D. McCaw, Trade Street, Stranraer. When he was killed, his mother inserted the following into the local newspaper:

"Loved by all. He saved others, himself he could not save."

With no known grave he is commemorated on Pozieres Memorial, Somme, panel 13 and 14.

Able Seaman William Wright Patrick, Z/5051.
Nelson Battalion, Royal Naval Division, Royal Naval Volunteer Reserve.
Died from wounds 13th November 1916.

William was the son of Mr D. Patrick, Hanover Street, Stranraer. Before the war he had worked for Mr R. Smith, shoemaker, also in Hanover Street, Stranraer.

After he enlisted, William was posted to Gallipoli and remained there until the evacuation. He was then drafted to France, and was amongst very severe fighting on the Somme. It was there he was injured and his father received notification that he had died from his wounds. William is buried at Martinsart British Cemetery, Somme, grave reference I.H.29.

Pte. John Pirrie, 27418. Machine Gun Corps. Died 21st October 1918.

Son of the late Margaret Pirrie, of 5 Backrampart, Stranraer. Aged 23, John died of pneumonia at home and he is buried in Sheuchan Cemetery.

Margaret may have had three sons all on active service. It is likely that John's brother was a Lance Corporal William Pirrie who was badly injured at Mesopotamia on 11th September 1918.

John was 24 when he died at home from pneumonia. He is buried in Sheuchan Cemetery, Stranraer.

Pte. John Pirrie. 8079.
1st/5th Battalion Royal Scots Fusiliers.
Killed in action 13th July 1915.

Only son of William and Mary Pirrie of 21 Dalrymple Street Stranraer. John was employed by Mr Hugh Caldwell of Culhorn Parks before the war.

Aged 24, John was one of the thousands killed at Gallipoli. Many local names appeared in the newspaper, and Johns photograph appeared on the same page as Matthew Cook and Alexander Rennie, all three men were in the same battalion. Many more names from the same battalion were to appear over the next few weeks. The fighting had been so heavy and the losses so great that letters notifying the families were delayed.

John is named on the family headstone in the Glebe cemetery, Stranraer. His father, William died in December the same year. John is commemorated on panel 72 to 75 of Helles Memorial, Turkey.

Pte. Colin Porteous, 25936.
1st Battalion Highland Light Infantry.
Killed in action 11th January 1917.

Colin was the son of Mrs Porteous of 9 Greenvale Street, Stranraer. Before the war Colin had been employed as a barman in Glasgow.

Colin was first reported as missing to his mother before official confirmation came through that he had been killed on that date. With no known grave, Colin is commemorated on Basra Memorial, Iraq, panel 35 and 64.

Lance Corporal Alexander Rennie, 6859.
1st/5th Royal Scots Fusiliers.
Killed in action 12th July 1915.

Alexander was a brother of Robert Rennie listed below. Alex's mother lived at Backrampart, Stranraer, and received the following letter from Sgt. Lock:

"I daresay by the time you receive this note the sad news of your son's death will have reached you, he and I being companions at home I have taken it upon myself to sent the enclosed post cards and postal order for 3s that were taken from his pockets before he was buried. He died in action and death was instantaneous, so it will be a little comfort to you to know that he did not suffer. In case you have not had any official word he died on 12th July a day that will be remembered by all who took part in the greatest fight that has taken place here since the landing. Alex was well respected by all of us here and his loss is much regretted. I cannot express in words the sincere sympathy I feel for you in your second sad bereavement. Alex was a brave fellow and has given his life for a great cause in the defence of King and country and those at home and may God comford you in your sad bereavement.

We lost heavily on the 12th and 13th but you will likely read about it all in the papers and if I am spared to get back home I will call upon you and tell you as much as I know."

Alexander Rennie was one of at least 17000 British casualties killed between June and July 1917. Hundreds were lost from the local King's Own Scottish Borderers regiment and more still were lost from the Royal Scots Fusiliers. In some parts of the trenches men were refusing to attempt the advance since they had seen many of their colleagues cut down instantaneously on going over the top. The noise from the bombardment was deafening and the Turkish response was very strong.

The list of names in the local Free Press of the dead, missing and injured meant the newspaper had to add additional pages, and the long list of casualties brought shock and fear into the local community

The Turkish losses were more than double the Allies, but it was far too great a price to pay for an advance by the British of less than 500 yards. The smell from the unburied dead was reported to be horrendous, and flies helped spread disease.

Alex had been a postman at Drummore before the war. He had also served in the Stranraer Company of the Territorials and he had known of his brother's death a few short months beforehand.

Alex, who was 25, has no known grave and is commemorated on panel 72 to 75 of Helles Memorial, Turkey.

5th Battalion Royal Scots Fusiliers Football Team. Alexander Rennie standing centrally in the striped shirt. The men were locals.
Top row: Corpl. J. Paterson, Pte. Sweetin, Lance-Corpl. Findlay, Corpl. Riddell, Lance-Corpl. Rennie, Pte. Irving, Pte. McKie, Lance-Corpl. Train, Pte. Cruickshanks.
Second row: Sergeant Liddell, Sergeant Campbell, Captain Crawford, Major Russell, Pte. Hay, Lance-Corporal Thorne.

Sergeant Liddell in the above photograph wrote to the Free Press telling of the death of his friend Alex Rennie:

> *Thank you very much for sending on the Stranraer paper. I have had my right thumb blown off by an explosive bullet, and expect I shall be here for a while yet. We had a heavy list of casualties in our Company, and my platoon (Stranraer men) suffered greatly. Lance Corporal Rennie, one of my section commanders, was killed by a high explosive shell instantaneously, the same shell killing Lieutenant Maxwell. Lance Corporal Rennie was a favourite with the men, and very efficient. No doubt he will be missed by his Stranraer chums. Private Claude Forsyth, while coming across the open (under heavy fire) to join us, was struck on the chest, the bullet penetrating right through his identity disc. No doubt he'll be keeping it for a curio. I saw him on the boat. He was looking all right after his trying ordeal. I heard there were other men wounded after I left, but I haven't heard any details. Sergeant Horace lock, also a Stranraer man, in another platoon, gave a good account of himself that day (12th July). Being one of the best shots in the battalion, he played great havoc with the Turks, accounting for one every time, at the same time giving great encouragement to his platoon. He proved himself to be a very efficient leader and his men greatly respect him. Taking it all through, the men of Stranraer have thoroughly proved themselves heroes every one – fearless, and worthy of mention. No doubt more will be heard of the 'Stranraer Huns' fighting abilities.*

A letter home from Claud Forsyth to his parents is included amongst a collection of letters home at the end of the Stranraer section.

Corp. Robert Rennie, 10323. 1st Battalion Seaforth Highlanders. Killed in Action 21st December 1914.

Robert was in the same battalion as John Gillespie named above and they must have enlisted together since their regimental numbers are sequential. They had served seven years together in India before the war. He had also been in the Galloway Rifles before that. Robert was a brother of the above named Alexander.

The same chaplain who had written to John

Gillespie's sister also wrote to Robert's mother, and once again the chaplain apologised for the delay in informing her of her son's death.

> *"The regiment has had some very hard fighting during the month of December, and I am sorry to say that among those who fell was your son, who was killed in action on 21st December. A long time has elapsed since that, but while the regiment has been engaged, it has been difficult to get particulars, or to get the addresses of friends at home. It will be some comfort to you to know that he has been buried beside the trenches, where he fell, by his comrades. The whole regiment has done splendidly in these operations, and everyone is proud of them. I am sure we have much reason to be proud of those who have given their lives for their country, and in keeping the name of the regiment so bright and high. It is sad that, instead of his homecoming, it should be this news that has to reach you. We all sympathise with you in your loss, but know that, mingled with your sorrow, there will be pride in the memory of one who died a soldier's death. I believe your son would have been recommended in the "Gazette" had he lived.Trusting that comfort and help will be given you in this time of your loss."*

When Robert's mother received the letter from the chaplain at her home at 3 Backrampart, she had not received any notice from the war office. Despite the letter from the Chaplain stating that they had buried Robert close to the trenches with comrades, just like his friend John Gillespie, Robert has no known grave. He is commemorated on Le Touret Memorial panel 38 and 39.

Another local man, William Pirrie, who was serving in the Seaforth Highlanders alongside Robert, wrote home:

> *"We are all lying back from the firing line for a well deserved rest, getting re-clothed for action in another week. We were up to our waist in water in the trenches before but are still cheery...Bob Rennie was killed by a 'Jack Johnston', and J. Gillespie was wounded....Hamilton who was wounded some time ago is all right again... I am returning Princess Mary's gift box and card home by post along with a card from the ladies of Stranraer Parish Church....I hope to be home by May or June."*

A Jack Johnston was the name British troops gave to shells. John Gillespie is recorded to have been killed the day before Robert. William Pirrie who wrote the letter survived.

Another local Rennie man, Samuel Rennie, possibly related to Robert, wrote home to the local minister saying:

> *"The weather is awful and I feel like a mudlark. I want a nice spring bed with a hot water bottle at my feet."*

Lance Corporal William Rennie 7860. 1st/5th Royal Scots Fusiliers. Killed in action 12th July 1915.

William was for many years a member of the Stranraer Company of the Galloway Rifle Volunteers. In the 1899 Boer war he served in South Africa alongside other local men and as well as earning a South African medal he was given the freedom of the burgh on his return home.

Although he was a painter to trade, William had spent the past few winters earning a living herring fishing in Lochryan. He was married and lived with his wife Susan, and five young children in Sheuchan Street. His parents also lived in Sheuchan Street and he had two brothers serving in the forces at the same time as him. Tom was on HMS Ballerophon, and Duncan was in the Cameron Highlanders. He may well have been related to the other Rennie men named on Stranraer and Leswalt War Memorials.

There were a number of local men who did not survive the heavy bombardment and fierce fighting at the Dardanelles. The local newspaper editions for that time had to have more pages in order to report those who were missing, injured or killed. With no known grave, William is commemorated on Helles Memorial panel 72 to 75.

A letter home from an Australian forces man, who landed at the Dardanelles was Pte. William Burns from Stranraer and he wrote a graphic account of his experience at the Dardanelles to relatives in Stranraer:

> *"I have been wounded in the knee by a bullet, and had four hits in the back with shrapnel. The shrapnel struck my haversack causing wounds about half an inch deep, but I think I am lucky. When we reached the Dardanelles it was an awful job getting landed in the small boats. The Turks had barbed wire all along the shore and big stones about twenty yards from the beach. We left the ships about two o'clock in the morning, and made a rush for the shore. The firing was awful as soon as we reached the shore. We jumped into the water up to the chest and got it from machine guns and rifles all the time – just like hailstones dropping around you. A lot of us fell over the stones and went over the head in the water, rifle and all; but we got up and rushed the hill, fixing bayonets on the run and giving a cheer. You should have seen the way they did it. It was a great charge, bullets flying, and the wounded lying in every direction. But we got the Turks out of the trenches and captured a mile of ground in quick time. We had been running a good bit and the rest*

we got afterwards was badly needed. We lost heavily in the charge but it had to be done to get the troops ashore. About half an hour after that the Turks opened fire on us and we had to take cover, but we did not get much as there were only a few small bushes about. Our orders were not to retire one inch as the Turks were entrenched all around us, and giving us shrapnel. Every kind of gun was against us and all we had was our rifles and machine guns because our artillery had not got ashore. British battleships then engaged the forts, and the air was thick with fire. Everywhere we went there were dead and wounded. It was an awful night and all you could do was rush at a Turk now and again. The whole place was mined in that section. I got hit about thirty yards from the Turks by a bullet in the inside of the knee coming out the other side. My comrades had to fall back and I knew I had to also as the Turks were bayoneting all the wounded lying about, then stripping the dead of their clothes. I crept along on my stomach for about 300 yards and the wounded were moaning all over the place. At the time the shrapnel was flying about and I got struck again as I was creeping along. The Red Cross stretcher bearers could not get working for the danger. Then the Indian Battery and some of the guns were got ashore and what a glad sight it was. They could have no idea how important it was to hold the position. The artillery got into action, and being reinforced the day was won. Two chaps got me and carried me down to the beach and I was taken aboard the hospital ship for Alexandria. The General came on board and told us they were entrenched in a strong position and they had taken a thousand prisoners."

A B. TOM RENNIE, H.M.S. Bellerophon.

Pte. DUNCAN RENNIE, Cameron Highlanders.

Lance-Corporal WILLIAM RENNIE, R.S.F.

The Rennie brothers from Sheuchan Street.

Pte. James Richardson, 9477. (Royal Highlanders) Black Watch. Latterly under service number 72168 Machine Gun Corps. Killed in action 2 August 1917.

Son of James and Agnes Richardson from Sheuchan Street, Stranraer. James' father was a marine stoker. During the war he married Martha Garrett from 11 Fisher Street on 6th January 1917. Both James and Martha were 27 when they married, but it was to last only a few months since he was killed in the August of that year.

Prior to the war he had served his apprenticeship as a grocer with Mr R.Murray, Sheuchan Street, but he had left the town for work in Clydebank.

His transfer to the Machine Gun Corps probably lessened his chances of survival in the war. There is a birth entry for a James Richardson in Stranraer in 1918 and it would seem very likely to be James' son although there is another James Richardson on the war memorial at Leswalt.

With no known grave, James is commemorated on the Menin Gate memorial panel 56.

Pte. John Charles Robertson, 14676. Right Flank Coy. Scots Guards. Killed in action 23rd August 1918.

John was the eldest son of John and Janet Robertson of Jessamine Cottage, Glebe Street.

John was just 21 when he was killed. He may have died from wounds since the site he was buried at was close to several casualty clearing stations. He is buried at Bucquoy Road Cemetery, Ficheux, grave reference IV.K.15.

Guardsman Joseph Robinson, 11976. 1st Battalion Scots Guards. Killed in action 27th September 1915.

Joseph, who was born in Stranraer, had been a painter for Portpatrick and Wigtownshire Joint Railway before the war. He was an enthusiastic pigeon fancier and was involved in Stranraer Homing Society and the Bird Show.

His birds had won in both races and at the shows.

When he was first posted as missing, his parents from 37 Lochryan Street, placed a plea in the local newspaper asking for any news of their 23 year old son.

With no known grave Joseph is commemorated on panel 8 and 9 of Loos Memorial.

Donkeyman Thomas Robinson
SS Polandia.
Lost at sea 10th March 1917.

Husband of Mary Thomson, of 16, St. John St., Thomas was born in Stranraer. His name is on the Family grave in the Glebe, alongside his daughter Elizabeth and sons Thomas and James.

It seems most likely that he was a relative, possibly brother-in-law of Hugh McKay who is also named on the memorial Robinson was the maiden name of Hugh's wife. The troopship was on sailing from Birkenhead to Cherbourg when it was thought to be struck by a mine, since no U-boat claimed responsibility. Both men are commemorated on Tower Hill Memorial.

Sergt. John Parker Ross. 1863.
9th Btt Highland Light Infantry.
Killed in action 27th December 1916.

John was the elder son of James and Elizabeth Ross, 1 Clifton Terrace Stranraer. His father was the Inspector of Poor, whilst John had become an engineer with the Post Office in Glasgow. John had a brother named James and sisters named Jane and Mary.

Another officer of the same battalion sent a letter home to convey the news of John's death. The letter stated that a shell had exploded in the midst of the platoon and that John had died almost immediately. He assured them that John had been given a Christian burial.

As well as being commemorated on the family headstone in the Glebe, John as a military headstone where he was buried at Hem Farm Military

Cemetery, I.D. 1. About a third of the graves in this cemetery are unidentified and there is a memorial to the British soldiers within the cemetery.

I believe this is the same man who is named on the memorial plaque inside Glenluce Public Hall, although he is not named on Glenluce War Memorial.

Pte. James Rowden, 282550.
7th Battalion Highland Light Infantry.
Died 2nd September 1917.

James Rowden was born in 1894 at 15 Agnew Crescent. His father was a seaman and by the time of the war his parents were living at 51 Lochryan Street.

James had been taken as a prisoner of war, and according to his death notice in the local newspaper died of malaria whilst in captivity at Dorak, Turkey. With no known grave he is commemorated on panel 35 and 64 of the Basra Memorial.

Gunner Thomas Russell, 125799.
332nd Siege Battery Royal Garrison Artillery.
Killed in action 21st March 1918.

Thomas Russell Enlisted in October 1916, before that he had been working for Messrs. Hugh Hamilton & Sons, provision merchants, Stranraer for over thirteen years. Although the newspaper announces that Thomas was the husband of Mrs Russell 53 Dalrymple Street, Stranraer, it also states that Mrs Russell's second son, Robert was killed on 25th September 1917, and her eldest son Peter had been wounded in January the same year. This could mean that Thomas was actually the son of Mrs Russell, or that he was old enough that he was serving the Colours at the same time as two of his sons. Whatever their relationship, it seems unusual that Robert Russell's name does not appear on the memorial. There are three Robert Russell names killed on the 25th September 1917 listed with the SNWM.

With no known grave, Thomas is commemorated on bay 1 of Arras Memorial.

Pte. Alexander Saul, 5799. No2. Machine Gun Section, 7th Battalion Seaforth Highlanders. Died of wounds 25th September 1915.

Alexander was the son of John and Mary Saul of 42 Sheuchan Street in Stranraer. He enlisted in November 1914 but had served his apprenticeship as a tailor with Messrs. Craig & Kyle in Stranraer.

Alexander was an excellent swimmer and had won a gold championship swimming medal in 1911 which had been presented to him by Viscount Dalrymple.

The Battle of Loos began on the day Alexander was killed and Douglas Haig had given the command for the push forward and commanded the army to attack the German machine gun position with poison chlorine gas. Because of the wind direction much of the chlorine gas blew back into the British trenches. By the end of the battle around fifty thousand British troops were lost. William Chalmers on Kirkmaiden war memorial and Robert McWhirter on Leswalt war memorial were killed on the same day.

He was originally buried at Vendin-le-vieil Communal Cemetery but at the end of the war his body was moved to Arras Road Cemetery, Roclincourt, grave reference III.O.34.

Pte. Edwin Small. 4567. 2nd Battalion Royal Scots Fusiliers. Killed in action 14th March 1915.

Edwin was born in Stranraer. Immediately before the war he had been employed at the Great Western Auction Market in Stranraer. He married Rachel Polland in Stranraer in 1902, and the couple lived in St. John Street in the town.

A letter home from Samuel McCandlish who is listed above, tells of how Sergeant Small from the same regiment had been killed in the trenches. He was shot in the head by a single sniper bullet. Whilst CWGC and SNWM record Edwin's rank as Private, some of the local newspaper cuttings and announcements refer to him as Sergeant.

With no known grave, Edwin is commemorated on Le-Touret Memorial, Pas de Calais, panel 12 and 13.

Pte. Hugh Small, 6715. A Company, 1st/5th Battalion Royal Scots Fusiliers. Killed in action 29th December 1915.

Hugh, the son of Agnes Wilson from Glebe Street, had been a very popular figure in the town He had been a keen Territorial in the local company and enlisted immediately on the outbreak of war. Early in August 1914 he was sent to guard Portpatrick Wireless Station, but was soon sent for training at Cambusbarron.

His trade was as a compositor for the Free Press where he had served his apprenticeship. After working for a short time in Glasgow he returned to Stranraer and was employed by Mr James Moodie of Hanover Street. He was also a keen footballer and had often played in Junior League games.

Hugh wrote the following letter home to Mr John McRobert, a spirit merchant of 80 George Street, Stranraer:

> *"Here we are again! Are we down-hearted? Thousands, if no millions of no's! We had, as you will have seen from the newspapers, a great day on the 12th July. It should be a bit quieter in Scotland and Ireland this year. Lock and I are all right. Claud Forsyth is wounded...I should like to play you a game of dominoes for "Aldouran". Are we downhearted? – No! I hope to see you again soon, and we will have a game."*

When he was killed his mother received the following letter from Lieutenant J.M. Kerr who was later to lose his own life:

> *"It is my sad duty to write expressing the sympathy of my company officer, self, and men, with you the loss of your son, Private H. Small (no.6715), who fell in action on the 29th December in a successful advance made by this battalion on the enemy's trenches. Duty always came first with him. He was a brave soldier, and we will all miss him from the company, and mourn his loss. His last resting place is in the West Nullah, a little south of the village of Krithia, where he was buried along with other comrades, the chaplain conducting the service. A tablet with all their names upon it, marks the spot."*

Hugh was 28 and was married, his widow and child lived in St John Street, Stranraer. He is buried at Twelve Tree Cops Cemetery, Turkey, grave reference II.C 15.

Gunner Andrew Kennedy Smellie, 25328.
1st Battalion Otago Regiment, N.Z.E.F.
Killed in action 5th April 1917.

Spelt Smillie on the New Zealand records, Andrew was the eldest son of John Charles and Mary Waddell Smellie, of 21 Princes Street, Stranraer. He had emigrated around 1913, and had been working on a ranch since he arrived in New Zealand.

When he enlisted he boarded a troopship in Wellington and sailed to Devonport on the 26th June 1916. From England he was then transported to the front. He came back to Stranraer for a brief furlough around Christmas 1916 and was aware that his name was on the O.S. Church Roll of Honour for those from the parish serving in the war. He was said to be a devoted and considerate son, manly and kindly in nature and generous spirited to all who knew him.

Killed on his 19th birthday, Andrew is buried at St Quentin Cabaret Military Cemetery, Heuvelland, Belgium, grave reference II.C.14.

Lance-Corporal Hugh Snodgrass, 7852.
1st/5th Battalion Royal Scots Fusiliers.
Killed in action 12th July 1915.

Hugh was married and he lived at Backrampart, Stranraer with his wife. Before the outbreak of war he was a seedsman with Mr S. Harper.

Hugh was posted as missing then later assumed to have been killed. With no known grave he is commemorated on Helles Memorial, Turkey panel 72 t0 75.

Able Seaman/Bombadier Hugh Stewart, Z/5055. Howe Battalion Royal Naval Volunteer Reserve. Killed in action 13th November 1916.

A different man to his namesake on Kirkcolm Memorial, but they may have been related. Hugh was the son of Mr A. Stewart, 5 Rose Street, Stranraer. Before the war Hugh had been working as a barber in Stranraer. He was a member of the O.S. Church there and his name was the fifth on their Roll of Honour who had been killed in the war.

Like William Patrick also named above, Hugh saw service at Gallipoli and remained there until the evacuation of the peninsula. Hugh was then drafted to France and it was while he was attached to a regiment there that he was killed. He had been recommended for a D.C.M. for his gallantry whilst serving in France.

With no known grave, Hugh is commemorated on Thiepval Memorial, pier and face 1A.

2nd Engineer Neil Thom. SS Princess Victoria. Lost at sea 27th October 1918.

Neil was born on the 4th April 1890 at 7 Victoria Place, Stranraer. His father David Thom was a tailor, and his mother was called Helen. He was one of four brothers all in service at the same time, John, David and Gordon Thom all gave up good positions in employment to enlist on the outbreak of war. Younger brother, Andrew, was working at G.R. Smith the ironmongers, Stranraer and he was exempted from conscription for a short time. Generations of their family have lived at Victoria Place in Stranraer.

Neil had been 2nd Engineer aboard the SS Princess Victoria for a number of years and continued to crew the vessel when she was commissioned by the admiralty. The ship spent much of the war on the Dover - Boulogne route, and had at least one near miss from an enemy torpedo

Neil is not listed with the CWGC or SNWM and I could find no listing for his death through marine deaths records or government websites; however his sister, Jean worked for a time in the Bacon Factory in the 1950s which was on the corner of Bellevilla Road and Thistle Street, Stranraer. In one of her conversations she spoke of her brother who was lost when his ship had been torpedoed or mined during the Great War, at the time she was showing off a beautiful china tea service which it was thought Neil had brought back from his previous travels before the war. Though this remembered conversation was more than fifty years ago.

Since the Princess Victoria was never mined or torpedoed, he must have been serving aboard another vessel. One British ship was sunk by a mine on the date of Neil's death. The Calceolaria was sunk with the loss of five men. It is likely that Neil was on that ship.

The Thom brothers from left to right, John, 9th Royal Highlanders, David, Scottish Horse, Gordon, RAMC, and Neil who is on Stranraer War Memorial.

David Thom was promoted to 2nd Lieutenant in the Highland Light Infantry having been wounded on service in Gallipoli and invalided home for a time. The family's good service record in the war was featured in the local Free Press.

In a letter home to a friend in Stranraer, Neil wrote that they had "stirring times" at Dunkirk:

> *"The Germans have been shelling the town, and made a terrible hand of it. We saw it after the first bombardment, and it was awful to see some of the sights – streets of houses laid low, and many people killed. One of the big shells we saw dropped at one of the cranes and smashed it to atoms, and also the shed close by, making a hole in it about 12 feet square. We have played four football matches, and came out on top every time. The first match was against a team from HMS Excellent, the latter being by two goals to nil, and in the match against HMS Bustard, our team won but four goals to two. We are known as the champions of Dunkirk."*

Local officers, engineers and crewmen on board the Princess Victoria at Dunkirk. The steamer was taken over by the Admiralty to act as a supply and troop ship and she served on the Dover Boulogne route for most of the war.

In the centre of the lifebelt is a copy of "The Galloway Advertiser"

Pte. Alexander Thompson, 302897.
1st/8th Battalion Argyll and Sutherland Highlanders.
Died of wounds 12th April 1917.

The local newspaper records Alec's rank as Lance-Corporal and he may have had promotion before his death or it could be an error in recording.

Alec was born in Kirkcolm, his parents were Sergeant and Mrs Thompson.

When he was fatally wounded Alec is likely to have been taken to the 42nd Casualty Clearing Station. He was buried in Aubigny Communal Cemetery Extension, grave reference II.C.13.

Pte. Alexander F. Thomson, 42096.
Highland Light Infantry. Formerly 23678, Scottish Rifles.
Killed in action 26th June 1917.

Mrs Thomson of 61 Dalrymple Street had four sons all on active service at the same time. In reading the death notices in the local paper and the names of those on the war memorial it seems that Mrs Thomson lost three of her four sons. Alexander had enlisted in the Scottish Rifles but was later transferred to the Highland Light Infantry.

One of a number of men who had served their grocers apprenticeship with Mr John Clements, and he had been employed there until he enlisted.

Mrs Thomson received two letters from of sympathy from officers of his Company. Alexander is buried at Ramscappelle Road Military Cemetery, grave reference Nieuport, Mem. 1.

Pte. James Thomson, 20938.
1st Battalion Royal Scots Fusiliers.
Killed in action 18th September 1918.

In the 1901 census James was the eldest son living with his parents James and Elizabeth at 10 South Strand Street. At that time his siblings were listed as William, Alexander, Bessie, Sarah, Maggie, David and Walter. He later married Helen (Nellie) Williamson.

James had seen very heavy fighting and he was wounded on three occasions before he was killed. He is buried at Sanders Keep Military Cemetery, Pas-de-Calais, grave reference I.E.10.

Pte. William Thomson, 203701.
2nd Battalion Royal Scots Fusiliers.
Killed in action 27th March 1918.

Isabella Thomson (nee Robinson) of 19 Princes Street, Stranraer received word that her husband William was missing since 27th March, and presumed dead. He had been born in the parish of Inch and had enlisted in Stranraer.

William has no known grave and is commemorated on Pozieres Memorial, Somme, panel 34 and 35. I believe this is the man who is named on the plaque inside Glenluce Public Hall, although he is not on Glenluce War Memorial.

Pte. Daniel Torrance, CH/2420(S).
1st Royal Marine Battalion Royal Naval Division.
Killed in action 2nd September 1918.

Eldest son of Mr and Mrs Daniel Torrance of Innermessan. Daniel was described as a promising young student at Stranraer High School and was attending university in Edinburgh when he reached the age for enlisting.

He was 19 years old when he was lost in the period leading up to armistice. Daniel has no known grave and is commemorated on panel 1 of Vis-En-Artois Memorial, France. He is also named on Inch War Memorial.

Pte. James Wither Tully, 21382.
1st Battalion Scots Guards.
Killed in action 27th March 1916.

James Wither Tully was the son of William and Agnes Jane Tully of Colfin. He had a brother who had died aged just four and a half years. His niece would have been Barbarah Hannay who ran a very well known shop in Castle Steet, Stranraer for many years. Before the war James was serving an apprenticeship at the Union Bank in Stranraer. He enlisted in November 1914 and undertook training before being sent to France. He had written home to friends and family at Colfin asking them not to worry about him.

> *"Don't fret too much about me. I am going out to do my duty, and I shall do it. I won't shrink from anything that's got to be done, and if I am killed it will be while doing my duty."*

His parents were told he was mortally wounded when he had been on guard duty. He had died within five minutes of being shot by a sniper.

A service which gave thanks for his life was held in Ivy Place Church, Stranraer by the Rev. James Salmond and his name alongside many others is on a brass plaque inside the church which is currently known as the Town Kirk.

John is buried in Potijze Chateau Wood Cemetery, Belgium. He is named on the family headstone in Portpatrick Cemetery. A photograph of James is beside his entry under Portpatrick War Memorial.

Pte. David Tunnock, 41282. 13th Battalion Royal Scots. Killed in action 23rd April 1917.

David was the son of Matthew and Agnes Tunnock and he was employed by James McLauchlin the joiner in Dalrymple Street.

His widow and children lived at 11 Greenvale Street Stranraer. He was first reported missing and later confirmation came through that he had been killed on that date. When he was killed the following poem was inserted into the local newspaper:

There is a link death cannot sever-
Love and remembrance last for ever
When days are dark and friends are few,
Dear daddy how we long for you.

With no known grave, David is commemorated on bay 1 and 2 of Arras Memorial.

Pte. Thomas Wallace, 7398. 1st/5th Battalion Royal Scots Fusiliers. Died of wounds 1st January 1916.

Thomas was the son of Mr and Mrs Hugh Wallace of 36 High Street, Stranraer. He was born on 20th December 1891 at 28 Agnew Crescent, Stranraer. He was one of five local men reported killed at the Dardanelles in one week in the same newspaper.

Just like Hugh Small, Thomas had also been in the Territorials and enlisted immediately on the outbreak of war. He was also very well known in local football circles and he played in the Junior League. Thomas was a grocer to trade and had served his apprenticeship with Mr Thomas Dyer of Church Street. He was also a member of the local Lodge of Good Templars.

A letter was received by his parents from Lieut. J.M. Kerr of the same battalion.

"I was very much grieved when I learned that your son, Thomas had died

of the wounds he received on 30th December, and I now write to ask you and Mrs Wallace to accept the sincere sympathy of his Company Officer and myself in your loss of a son who was such a credit to you. He was wounded by a shell on that date, during a severe artillery bombardment, to which were subjected by the Turks after having taken their trench on 29th December, and from inquiries I made from those who took him to the dressing station, I had great hope that he would recover, as he took even his wounds in his characteristic cheery, manful way. Though he has not been spared to us, you will no doubt feel – as we do – some consolation from this fact. As he was in my platoon I was always in constant touch with him, and I may say that for no man could I have formed a higher regard. He was a great help in the work of the platoon, always cheerful and willing for any duty, whether by night or by day and was a favourite with all. I have written at some length, but have not said too much for him, and I thought you would like to know what I have been able to tell. Your other son, who came out to join us recently, is, I am glad to say, in good health and spirits."

He was injured during the evacuation of the peninsula at Gallipoli, but he died from his wounds and is buried at Lancashire Landing Cemetery, Turkey, grave reference J.89.

On his death his parents inserted the following poem to the local paper:

The grave may hide a loved one dear
Upon that foreign shore
But we will always cherish thee
For ever and evermore.

He little thought, when leaving home,
That he would ne'er return;
Now he lies in a soldier's grave,
And we are left to mourn.

On 18th January 1916 Lieutenant Colonel Agnew, M.V.O., D.S.O. sent the following letter to the Free Press. In reading it so many years after the war has passed, one wonders if it brought any comfort to friends and relatives of the men who were lost. It somehow seems distant, and though he would have an important role to play in the war, he would rarely, if ever be fighting alongside the men:

"Sir, - I feel sure you will be glad of news of the 5th Battalion Royal Scots Fusiliers, who have done so well in Gallipoli. I came across them first at Helles shortly after the big fight of 12th July, and was glad to hear from their Commanding Officer (Colonel Pollok McCall) as also from

Brigadier-General Erskine (the Brigade Commander) that they had behaved splendidly. As you know the Wigtownshire Company suffered heavy casualties in that fight, but they were quite undaunted. Since then they have had continuous work in the trenches, and last week again distinguished themselves in a dashing and successful attack immediately preceding the evacuation of the peninsula. Unfortunately, there were a number of casualties. The regiment is now resting, preparatory to proceeding to a new field of operations. Yesterday I saw Brigadier-General Pollock McCall (now commanding the Brigade), also their new Commanding Officer (Lieut.-Colonel Leggett), and both spoke highly of the manner in which the Wigtownshire men had conducted themselves throughout the campaign, which has been one of the great hardships. The Colonel paraded the Wigtownshire men for my inspection, and I had a word with them, and found them in excellent trim and spirits, and ready for any work. It was with pride and pleasure that I heard this good account of the regiment, which I know will be shared by all in the county. As regards myself I have commanded two battalions and two brigades out here, and at present am Commandant of Mudros, and expect to be fighting in another part of the world shortly. It has been most interesting work and a great experience, and so far I have kept wonderfully well and gone through without a scratch – Quentin Agnew."

Second Lieut. Alan Hill Whyte, 11th Battalion Argyll and Sutherland Highlanders. Killed in action 9th April 1917.

Alan Whyte was educated at Stranraer High School and Merchiston Castle. When he left the school he started working for the Clydesdale Bank and passed a number of exams until he was promoted to an Edinburgh branch. He completed some basic training and received his commission in September 1916. He was immediately posted to France and did not have the opportunity to return to his parent's home at The Park, Stranraer.

He had a wide circle of friends who seemed to have thought of him as a true gentleman. Sympathies were expressed to his parents John and Isabella and to his older brother who was still on active service.

Alan is buried at Caberet-Rouge British Cemetery, Souchez, grave reference XVII.J.45.

Engineer John Wilson.
Royal Naval Reserve.
Died 3rd November 1918.

John was very difficult to trace, but for a very hard to read notice of his death. He was the younger and only living son of William Wilson who had been the headmaster of Sheuchan School.

He became very ill whilst on active service and was discharged home to Alhambra, California, where he died of the illness. He is not listed with the CWGC or SNWM records.

Brigadier William Allan Wilson, 87334.
200th Siege Battery Royal Garrison Artillery.
Died of wounds 31st May 1917.

William lived in Girvan with his wife Agnes whose address is recorded as Orchardlea, Girvan. Although he was born in Kilwinning and lived in Girvan, he enlisted in Stranraer, and must have had another local connection – probably his employment.

William was injured and taken to a Casualty Clearing Station where he died of his wounds. He is buried in the largest Commonwealth cemetery in Belgium, Lijssenthoek, grave reference XII.C.2A.

Pte. John Williamson, 43968.
12th Battalion Royal Scots.
Killed in action 20th September 1918.

According to his next of kin details, John was the son of Daniel and Margaret Allison of 22 Backrampart, Stranraer. However in the 1901 census he is listed as the only son with four sisters who were all children of Alexander and Maggie Williamson. Both the Williamsons and the Allisons were listed as living at the same address. Later Maggie Williamson moved to 78 Garngad Hill, Townhead, Glasgow.

John enlisted in 1916 and had been on active service for about five months when he was posted as missing. With no known grave he is commemorated on Tyne Cot memorial panel 11 to 14 and 162. Although the CWGC lists his age as 20, his parents list his age as 22 in his intimation in the local newspaper.

Guardsman Fred Maxwell Wood, 5467. 2nd Battalion Scots Guards. Killed in action 18th December 1914.

Whilst official military records would have it that Fred was born in Hew Lace, he was in fact born in New Luce in 1888. His parents had already lost a child of the same name from bronchitis in 1884. His father was a police constable and his parents had been married in Mochrum. For about three years before the war, Fred had worked in the offices of the Free Press. He had two brothers, Sam, named below, and Malcolm. At the time of receiving the news of Fred's death, Sam was at home recovering from wounds received at Kemmel, Flanders. Fred had completed seven years in the Scots Guards, and was a reservist who was called up early in the war in Stranraer.

With no known grave, Fred is commemorated at Ploegsteert Memorial, Belgium, panel 1.

Pte. Sam Wood, 3/7069. 8th/10th Battalion Gordon Highlanders. Killed in action 31st May 1916.

Sam was the brother of Fred Wood, named above. He was born in Wigtown, and had served some years in the Stranraer Volunteers; he later joined the Royal Garrison Artillery and had served his full time. Although his time as a reservist had expired, he joined the Gordon Highlanders on the outbreak of war. He listed his next of kin as his sister, Mrs M. Gibson of Whitecairn, Barrhill.

When Sam went to the front, the weather was very warm, but it had more recently been raining, snowing or freezing and on a number of occasions they had been up to their knees in water in the trenches. Sam had been fighting at Ypres, and La Bassee, then Kemmel and it was there he was injured when a shrapnel shell burst amongst them, and he was wounded on the right leg and left side of his face. His comrades had fought on and captured the German trench. The push had begun in the afternoon and Sam had lain wounded in the open until dark before he could be picked up by stretcher bearers. Sam's wounds took time to heal and he was sent home to recover. He was at home when news of his brother's death was sent.

Sam recovered and was sent back to join the regiment. Having taken part in further heavy fighting over the next year he was killed. He is buried at Noeux-les-mines Communal Cemetery, Pas de Calais, grave reference I.N.30.

Corp. John Wyllie, 7409. 1st/5th Battalion Royal Scots Fusiliers. Killed in action 12th July 1915.

Prior to enlisting John had helped out his father who was in the Army Veterinary Corps training horses. His mother lived in Greenvale Street Stranraer.

On enlisting shortly after the outbreak of war, John was sent to Cambusbarron, Stirling, where he spent some months training before being posted to the Dardanelles.

With no known grave, John is commemorated on panel 72-75 of Helles War Memorial. His name is spelled Wylle on the CWGC website.

A letter from Sergt. Horace Lock of the same battalion was sent to a Mr and Mrs Cruickshanks in Castle Kennedy, in it he described the horrendous fighting that the battalion had endured, in which John had lost his life.

> *"Just a note to let you know I received the tin of "fags" you sent me, and I thank you very much for them. We have been out of the trenches for over a week, and have been in our dug-outs doing fatigues, digging, etc. The last time we were in the firing line we had a very hot time of it. The biggest bombardment that has yet been here took place on 12th July, and we were in the thick of it. It started at 4am., and the thunder of the guns from the sea and land, and those of the Turks, was deafening. It was terrible advancing over the open in the face of shell and machine gun. The bullets ripped my haversack and mess tin that was strapped on to my back. A bullet also found its way into my iron ration that was hanging from my left breast. It stuck inside the tin of corned meat. These were narrow shaves, but I am thankful I am here today, for when one looks back on the Monday and Tuesday one wonders how we lived through such a murderous fire. I cannot give you the number of casualties; we are not allowed to do so; but you will see the list in the papers....The Turks got an awful cutting up. When we got into their trenches we had to walk over the mangled bodies, which spoke of the good work done by our artillery fire. The French artillery is magnificent, and cannot be beaten. Yesterday the Turks made an advance, two battalions of them. They were completely mowed down, and the few that were left got back on their hands and knees. Just now the Turks are shelling our dugouts, but so far they have killed only a mule. They have started to shell us through the night now, a thing they never did before. Today we are to be inoculated*

against cholera as the season is now on, and the troops fighting against the dirty Turk are always in danger of that loathsome disease. Willie Colman is all right, and got through the last big fight without a scratch."

Horace lost his brother in the war and he is named on Stranraer War Memorial.

A group of local men 'somewhere in England' reading their Free Press

Sons of Stranraer remembered

The following men all had local connections. Some of the men should perhaps have been named on Stranraer War Memorial, for others the connection is that Stranraer provided their last resting place. However in this section there are also some short stories of those who survived the war.

Pte. David Russell Baxter, 12067.
1st Battalion Scots Guards.
Killed in action 16th September 1916.

David's parents lived in Gartsherrie, Coatbridge. He enlisted in October 1914 and after a brief period of training he was sent to France in May 1915. He had taken part in some very severe fighting at the front.

Before the war David was a policeman and member of the Wigtownshire Constabulary, he had been stationed in Stranraer for some time prior to enlisting and had become a familiar local face.

With no known grave, David is commemorated on Thiepval Memorial, pier and face 7d.

Pte. Alexander (Sandy) Brown.
1st/7th Black Watch. Survived.

Alexander had worked for the Dundee Equitable Boot Department in George Street, Stranraer and had then moved to Inverkeithing to become branch manager there before the outbreak of war. Born on 24th March 1893 at 26, Agnew Crescent, Stranraer, he was the second son of Alexander and Helen Brown (nee Loch) who had a grocers shop in George Street. His parents later lived in Glen Street, Stranraer. He was admitted to hospital on at least two occasions during the war; the first time after drinking from a well which had been poisoned by the Germans and the second time because of trench foot. He won a Military Medal for conspicuous gallantry and was one of a number of men who received the Freedom of the Burgh of Stranraer when he returned from the war.

Sandy married and had three children. He served in the Home Guard during the Second World War. His younger brother was a pupil of George Gunn Campbell who is named below. Sandy was the great Uncle of the Author.

Sandy Brown during the First and Second World Wars.

Able Seaman Harry Bryceland. SS/4503.
Royal Navy HMS Victory.
Died 25th January 1918.

Harry died at 17 St John Street Stranraer aged 22. Harry was single and had made a career for himself in the navy. Harry had tuberculosis, and he is buried in Stranraer Glebe Cemetery.

Leading Trimmer Edward Burns, 2371/ST.
Royal Naval Reserve . HMS Victory.
Died 13th July 1918.

Edward was the son of Edward Burns and Agnes McDonald Burns. He was married to Catherine McCrorie and the couple lived at 16 Glen Street, Stranraer.

Edward returned home when he became ill early in 1915. Aged 35, he died of a brain tumour within eighteen months. Edward is buried in the Glebe Cemetery, Stranraer.

Pte. Francis Cairney, 4730. 14th Battalion Highland Light Infantry. Killed in action 15th August 1917.

Francis may have been related to Richard Cairney whose name is on Stranraer War Memorial. His death intimation was in the local Free Press and although it gave few details it did say that he was 'late of Stranraer', and he must have had a fairly strong connection to Stranraer for his family to have reported his death in the paper.

Francis was buried in Fins New British Cemetery, Sorel le Grand, Somme, grave reference I.B.5.

Corporal George Gunn Campbell, 17345.
King's Own Scottish Borderers.
Died 2nd February 1916.

George Gunn Campbell was a manual instructor and assistant of the higher classes in Stranraer Academy. His parents were William and Elizabeth Campbell of Cairnroich, Caithness. George was very popular with the pupils who knew him as a typical Highlander.

George was badly injured in the battle of Loos and he was sent to recover in Dublin. Although he seemed to be progressing well at first, he succumbed to his wounds and died. He is buried in Grangegorman Military Cemetery, Dublin, grave reference Pres.85.

The Academy (which later became Dalrymple School) stood on the site of the current college on the corner of Academy Street and Lewis Street. Staff and pupils placed a brass plaque in his memory there which was unveiled in a school ceremony. The school was demolished to make way for the college building around 1989, I could not establish if the plaque was removed or preserved in any way.

Teacher George Gunn Campbell with a class of boys at Stranraer Academy. Back Row: C.Hay, J.Berry, D.Elliot, J. Caldwell. Middle row: B.Holmes, J.Galloway, D. Brown, A.Ross, R.Gemmel. Front Row: J.Clement, J.Campbell, G.Morrison, J.McMeikan, A.McKinnon, A.Hannah, H.Murray.

Pte. Hugh Campbell, 1044.
1st/5th Battalion King's Own Scottish Borderers.
Killed in action 12th July 1915.

Another one of the many men killed in action around the same date at the Dardanelles. Hugh was the son of the late Peter Campbell and grandson of the late George Campbell, High Street, Stranraer.

Aged just 19, and with no known grave he is commemorated on Helles Memorial, Turkey, panel 84 to 92 or 220 to 222.

Corporal Stewart Dill, 87156.
5th Brigade Canadian Field Artillery.
Died of wounds 29th October 1917.

Stewart Dill was born in Stranraer in 1880. He was the son of John and Jane Dill and had two sisters, Jane who was married to James Wallace, Jessie and a brother John. The family all lived at 19 Queen Street Stranraer.

When his father died in 1900 aged just 50, the family moved to Glasgow. Stewart was married to Margaret Douglas Lamb and the couple lived there at 122 Holland Street.

Although the CWGC records his date of death as 29th October the local paper records him as having been seriously injured on the 27th and having died on the same day of his wounds.

Stewart is buried in Nine Elms British Cemetery, Poperinge, grave reference VII.F.7.

Sergeant Major Frederick Ferris, 16488.
Royal Horse and Field Artillery.
Died 28th January 1915. (Reservist)

Frederick was a drill sergeant. He had been married first to Margaret Griffen then later to Mary Brownlie or Murray. He lived with his second wife at 44 Station Street, Stranraer.

At 60 years old, Frederick was a reservist, having served in the Soudan Campaign. He had already received his Long Service and Good Conduct

Medal, when he died of broncho-pneumonia. Frederick is buried in the Glebe Cemetery, Stranraer. Although he did not die as a direct result of the war, he is listed with the CWGC.

Corp. Hugh Fitzimmons, M2/188230.
Royal Army Service Corps.
Died 1st May 1920.

Son of Hugh and Mary Fitzsimons, his father was a retired police constable; Hugh was married to Jean Davidson Campbell (nee Fitzsimons), of II, Millhill St., Stranraer.

Hugh died of peritonitis as a result of an ischial abscess, and since he has a war grave then perhaps the abscess was as a result of some sort of wound he received when in the war. Hugh is buried in the Glebe Cemetery, Stranraer.

Mr H.G. Fletcher,
Hon. Secretary, Stranraer Welcome Club.

Mr Fletcher initiated the Stranraer Welcome Club, which looked after soldiers and sailors arriving at the railway stations during the war. It was a way of acknowledging the service the men were doing and welcoming them home, with a hearty meal or cup of tea. Each week a list of the men who were home was published in the Free Press, and it locals regularly checked to see which of the men were home on furlough. Local ladies voluntarily staffed the welcome club, and funds were raised through charitable events which always seem to have been well supported.

Pte. James Harvey. 41236. Royal Scots.
Died 8th December 1919.

After the war James Harvey had returned to his work as a dairyman at Dinduff Croft, Kirkcolm. He was 35 when he became ill and his cause of death was recorded as 'acute military tuberculosis.' James is buried in the Glebe Cemetery, Stranraer. If he was known by his middle name, and that middle name was James then I would further speculate that it is possible he could be the man listed as R.J.Harvey on Glenluce War Memorial as he is not the James Harvey listed on Leswalt Memorial. This particular James Harvey is not named on any local memorial unless he is indeed the man named at Glenluce.

Rifleman John (Jack) Heron, Rifle Brigade, Mistakenly reported killed in action 21st November 1917.

John was the husband of Maggie Hyslop, of 25 Sheuchan Street, Stranraer. He was the third son of Mr and Mrs Heron of 18 Agnew Crescent. Two of Maggie's brothers, Tom and Jock Hyslop, fought at the Dardanelles. Jock was wounded whilst serving with the Australian Forces and Tom was serving in the 1st/5th Royal Scots Fusiliers. Tom wrote a letter home talking of the death of one of his comrades and it is included alongside James Kelly's entry.

For many years Jack Heron worked as a postman before the war. His death notice was placed in the local newspaper and it was some three months later before his wife received a postcard to say he had been captured and was a prisoner of war. Though the full story is not known, somehow John escaped from his captivity. He continued in battle and came through some severe fighting. After the war he returned to his family and his job as a postman.

Jack Heron as a postman in 'the' Lochans, after the war.

Pte. John Douglas Kilpatrick. 46380. 3rd Batt. King's Own Scottish Borderers. Died 5th February 1919.

Aged 27 when he was killed, John was the son of Jane Kilpatrick (nee Douglas), of Valparaiso Villa, Stranraer, and the late James Kilpatrick. He was a teacher in Arbroath High School. Although John died in Arbroath, his body was returned to Stranraer and he is buried in Sheuchan Cemetery. John was one of the thousands who died from the influenza virus.

2nd Lieut. John Alexander King, 4th Battalion Gordon Highlanders. Killed in action 12th September 1916.

John Alexander King was not a native of Stranraer and the connection is not that strong, but I feel he should be included since I could find no trace of his name on the war memorials in his home town of Banff, or in Kirkcaldy where he was a school master.

John married Alice McCash whose father was a well known local upholsterer in Stranraer. Thomas McCash ran his business in Castle Street. Alice was also a school teacher and had moved to the same school as John King. When he came home for a brief furlough from the war they married in Edinburgh in June 1916. Three months later he was killed by a trench mortar. John is buried in Cite Bonjean Military Cemetery, Armentieres, grave reference II.F.28.

Pte. Ivie Grieg Lafferty, 7801. 1st/5th Royal Scots Fusiliers. Killed in action 12th July 1915.

Native to Stranraer, Ivie was the son of William and Agnes Lafferty. His wife, Susan, later gave her address as 6 Greenfield Street, Govan, although the couple were known to have been living in Ayrshire.

Serving in the same battalion as a number of local men, and killed on the same day as many of them, his name appears on the same panel as them on Helles Memorial, Turkey. He is further commemorated on Dalmellington War Memorial – which is a silver painted tin plaque attached to a monolith. The plaque also has signs that it has been used as target practice for someone with an air rifle.

Leading Stoker Charles H Living, K/6983(CH). Royal Navy HMS Pembroke. 21st August 1915.

While the CWGC records his ship as HMS Pembroke, the death register records his vessel as HMS Garry. Charles became ill and must have been taken to the nearest port which was Stranraer. He died of a renal calculus and abscess in the Garrick Hospital Stranraer. He either was a patient there for three months or he had known about the illness for three months before he died. He was 25 years old and is buried in the Glebe Cemetery, Stranraer.

Stoker 1st Class William John McConnell, 228579(PO). Royal Navy, HMS Ardent. Died 2nd February 1915.

William was found drowned at the slipway at 7.40am in the morning. He was on the east side of the breastwork near Stranraer Harbour. His usual residence was Belfast. William must have been in Stranraer as he was thought to have drowned only a short time before he was found.

William, who was 28, is buried in the Glebe Cemetery, Stranraer.

Lance Corp. John McCracken, 351615. 12th Batt Royal Scots. Killed in action 25th April 1918.

John's father Alexander had died in 1902 and his mother was Mary McCracken (nee Doran), of 17, St. John St., Stranraer. Aged 24 when he was killed, John is commemorated on the family headstone in the Glebe cemetery in the town. With no known grave he is also named on Tyne Cot memorial. Panel 11-14 and 162. He is not on any local war memorial

Alexander McWilliam. Killed in action 16th April 1918.

Alexander is named on the family headstone in the Glebe Cemetery Stranraer. His mother was Sarah McWilliam (nee McLean) and his father was William McWilliam. If his date of death is accurate on the headstone then I could find no trace of him through the SNWM or CWGC, nor could I find any local newspaper death announcement. However since I can find no real reference to the William McWilliam who is named on the war memorial he could in theory be the same man who was perhaps known by two different first names. This is purely speculation however, and without a relative coming forward, this man may well have been forgotten.

Pte. Edward Saunders Murray, 21061. 6th/7th Battalion Royal Scots Fusiliers. Killed in action 3rd September 1916.

Mr and Mrs Andrew Murray of Hanover Street, Stranraer had at least three sons. In the summer of 1916 their 22 year old son, also Andrew drowned at the Gill Pool in the River Cree, beyond the Coronation Bridge. He had been bathing with his friends James Herdsman and Peter White and initially all seemed well, but he disappeared beneath the water and did not resurface. Despite rescue attempts from his friends, they could only recover his body from the water. It is possible that Edward's friend James Herdsman is the same man who is named on Leswalt War Memorial, since it is an unusual name in the area.

A few short weeks after this first tragedy, the couple received a letter from Capt. A.W. Ferguson informing them that their 25 year old son Edward had been killed by a shell.

Edward had been employed by the well known drapers J.M. Caldow in Stranraer prior to the outbreak of war. A quietly spoken man, he had been a singer in the choir of Stranraer U.F. Church, and taught Sunday School there. It seems very sad that his name is not on the war memorial, and with such strong association with Stranraer his omission could perhaps be an oversight. He is buried at Flatiron Copse Cemetery, Mametz, grave reference VII.J.8.

Petty Officer 1st Class John Henry Pizzey, 161874. R.N., HMS Queen Mary. Killed in Action 31st May 1916.

Although not native to Stranraer, John had worked for very many years here with the Stranraer Oyster Company, and he was very well regarded by his workmates and employers.

There were very few survivors from the sinking of the ship and Stranraer friends of John had to wait quite some time to hear definite news of his fate. The Queen Mary was sunk on the first day of the Battle of Jutland.

Aged 41 when he was killed, John is commemorated on Chatham Naval Memorial.

Corp. George Quarrell, 240340. 1st/5th Battalion Royal Scots Fusiliers. Died of wounds 29th June 1917.

George was born in Stranraer. His parents, John and Margaret, had lived at East Challoch, Dunragit, where he had assisted his father with the dairy, but they later moved to Crossford, Fife. His sister, Mrs Wilson lived by the Creamery at Dunragit.

Aged 26, John received his wounds whilst fighting in Egypt. He did not recover and is buried at Cairo War Memorial Cemetery, grave reference F.269.

Serg. John Alexander Ross, 3/5094. 14th Battalion Hampshire Regiment. Killed in action 3rd September 1916.

Though not part of a local regiment, John had a local connection, his father was Superintendent Ross of Stranraer, and his death was announced in the local newspaper. He was 23.

John is commemorated on Thiepval Memorial pier and face 7C and 7B.

Chief Refrigerator Engineer Samuel Thorburn, SS Verdi, Mercantile Marine. Drowned 22nd August 1917.

Born in Glasgow, Samuel was the son of Mr Robert Thorburn and Mrs Mary Thorburn (nee McEwen), 30 Nithsdale Road. His grandfather, Mr Samuel Thorburn of Hanover Square, was native to Stranraer and placed the announcement of his death in the local newspaper.

Samuel is commemorated on Tower Hill Memorial, London.

Pte. Archibald Wright, 28703. 8th Battalion Royal Scots Fusiliers. Killed in action 28th February 1917.

Archibald was the son of George and Jane McGarva Wright of 79 Paisley Road West, Glasgow. His father had been a ship builder for a number of years in Stranraer and his death announcement was placed in the Free Press.

Archibald is buried in Karasouli Military Cemetery, Greece, grave reference F1230.

STRANRAER BURGH ROLL OF HONOUR MEMORIAL

At some time Stranraer Burgh Roll of Honour memorial was moved from its' original location in Lewis Street Town Hall, to the Old Town Hall (now museum), and for whatever reason, at a later stage it was moved from there into what seems like permanent storage. By spring 2011 there was no record of the memorial in the museum store computer, however a visit by a member of the Scottish War Memorial Project meant the memorial was rediscovered. It was in good condition and had been well protected by bubble wrap. The memorial has an ornate wooden surround, with central brass plaque. Each local man who enlisted in 1915 was named by regiment and a small circle was placed beside those who lost their lives. By 1916 the men were no longer listed by regiment, their names simply placed in alphabetical order and during that year the list must have stopped being added to, perhaps by that time the realisation was that a larger memorial was going to be needed. Not all the men who lost their lives had a circle placed beside them – perhaps because it had been decided not to update the ever increasing list. I have transcribed the names on the following pages as they are an important record for future historians. Those whose name has a circle beside it is transcribed in bold. It is far harder to find the records of men who fought and survived the Great War than those who were killed.

Stranraer Burgh Memorial

FOR KING AND COUNTRY. FOR GOD AND THE RIGHT.
IN HONOUR OF AND TO COMMEMORATE THE SELF SACFIF-
ICING SPIRIT OF THE MEN FROM THIS BURGH WHO JOINED
HIS MAJESTY'S FORCES DURING THE GREAT WAR.

-ROYAL NAVY-

WILLIAM M ADAIR
R M CRAWFORD
JAMES CRONIE
WILLIAM GIBSON
THOMAS GARRETT
ADAM GARRETT
SAMUEL GIBSON
JOHN HANNAH
WILLIAM HALL
ROBERT HOLLIS
WILLIAM HOLMES
GEORGE S HEGGIE
A S JOHNSTON
JOHN LOWRIE
JAMES LATTA
JOHN MAIR
KENNETH MUNRO
ROBERT MILLIGAN
JAMES MUIR
P MCCULLOCH
JOHN MCKEAND
ROBt MCWHIRTER
P MCCULLOCH
ALEX MCCULLOCH
JAS MCLELLAND
THOs MCLELLAND
WALT MCDOWALL
SAM G MCKINSTRY
JAS R MCKINSTRY
ALEXR PALMER
THOS PATERSON
THOMAS RICE
THOMAS RENNIE
THOMAS REID
JOSEPH TRAIN
JN SWEETING JR
WILLIAM WEIR
WILLIAM WRIGHT

-RNVR-

DAVID ALLISON
ALEXR ALLISON
VANS BROWN
JAMES BLAIN
JOHN COGIE
ROBERT CRAIG
R CALDWELL
MATT CAMPBELL
WILLIAM DUNBAR
DAVID DRYSDALE
DICK MAXWELL
ADAIR DAVIDSON
HUGH DUNN
WILLIAM GODFREY
JOHN GARRETT
JOHN GIBB
JOHN F HASTINGS
ROBERT HERON
JAMES MURDOCH
JOHN MURDOCH
THOMAS MUIR
JAMES MURDOCH
NORMAN MURRAY
HENRY MCDOWALL
TMCLELLAND
R MCLELLAND
ALEX D MCHAFFIE
HENRY MCKILLOPS
JOHN MCCLYMONT
JAS F MCCONNELL
ALEXR NELSON JR
WILLIAM NELSON
ALEXR NELSON
WILLIAM PATRICK
WILLIAM PATERSON
JOHN PALMER
ALEXR POLAND
THOMAS RICE
JAMES REID
THOMAS REID
JAMES W ROSS
JOHN RAESIDE
GEO RICHARDSON
JAMES ROSS
HUGH STEWART
HENRY SWEETING
WM SWEETING
JOHN SWEETING
ALEX WHORLOW
A WHORLOW
JOHN WHROLOW
WM WHORLOW
JOHN WILSON

-ROYAL FLYING CORPS-

THOMAS ADAIR
N MCC ANDERSON
CHAS ANDERSON
HERBT CUMMING
GEORGE DOWNIE
WILLIAM A GIBB
WILLIAM JEFFREY
A MCCULLOCH

R T MCHAFFIE
JAMES MIRREY
JAMES MCKIE
ALEXR MURRAY

-ARMY SERVICE CORPS-

THOMAS BOYD
THOMAS S BLAIR
GEORGE BRUNTON
EDWARD BIGGAM
TOM BOYD
WILLIAM CAIN
WILLIAM H CURRIE
JAMES COSTLEY
WILLIAM CAMPBELL
JOHN CARLE
DAVID CONNELL
GEO DAVIDSON
JOHN DIGNEY
ROBERT DALZIEL
DUNCAN ANTHONY
ROBT FERGUSON
CHAS FINDLAY
GEORGE FULTON
JAMES FERGUSON
CHAS FINDLAY
SAMUEL GIBSON
JOHN GARRETT
ANDW GALLOWAY
WM GIBSON
JAMES HOLMES
WILLIAM HALL
ADAM HALL
ALEXR HOLLIS
JOHN HILLAN
ROBERT HANNAY
JAMES HOLMES
WILLIAM HIGGINS
ROBT A HAINING
ANDW HAMILTON
HUGH HALLIDAY
HUGH IRVING
G H JOHNSTON
WILLIAM KEENAN
JOHN KEENAN
HUGH KYLE
DAVID KELLY
MICHAEL LYNCH
MICHAEL LYNDIE
ROBERT LAMB
WILLIM LOGIE
JOHN LAMB
JAMES MONEGLE
MICHAEL MURRAY
ALEXR MURRAY
M BARTHOLOMEW
WILLIAM MUIR
WM MCCULLOCH
W H MCCASH
JAS MCDONALD
JAS MCGUFFIE
JOHN MCGUFFIE
THOMAS MCCASH
STAIR MCCHLERY
A MCCALISTER
AND MCINTYRE
ROBERT NISH
H NEILL
JAMES PALMER
A PATTERSON
R H B PRENTICE
JOHN PRESTON
JOHN RAVEY
ARTHUR SWAN
FRED WHAW
WILLIAM SIMPSON
GEORGE SMITH
JAMES STEWART
W H THOMSON
JOHN THORBURN
DAVID THOMSON
ALEX THOMSON
JAMES WILSON
ANDREW WYLIE
DAVID WATSON
ANDREW YOUNG

-ASC-
MOTOR TRANSPORT

HENRY BURNS
T F BRADFORD
JOHN CRAIG JNR
R MCC DOUGLAS
H FITZSIMMONS
JAMES GRACIE
H GORDON
WILLIAM GIBSON
WILLIAM HERON
JOHN W LAMB
WM MONTEITH
JAS MCCULLOCH
ROBERT MCKIE
WILLIAM MCKIE
G MCCRACKEN
WM MCCULLOCH
A MCGREGOR
PETER MCGEOCH
THOS MCGEOCH
GEO W RANKIN
JOHN M RANKIN
THOMAS RANKIN
JACK SWANSON
JAS THORBURN
E THOMSON

-ARGYLL & SUTHERLAND HIGHLANDERS-
ANDREW CLEMENT
G CARSWELL
JAMES CRAIG
JAMES CAIRNS
ROBERT COLLINS
WILLIAM FRASER
EDW GALLOWAY
ALFRED KENNY
J W MCPEAK
URI ORMISTON
EDWARD O'NEIL
DANIEL RODGER
ALAN HILL WHITE

-ARMY ORDNANCE CORPS-
ALEXANDER COOK
JAMES HIGGINS
THOS W WALMER

-ARMY VETERINARY CORPS-
WILLIAM DOUGAN
ALEX G HILL
PETER HANNAH
THOMAS WYLIE
THOS WYLIE JNR

-AYRSHIRE YEOMANRY-
J S BRYSON
ROBT FERGUSSON
A M FINDLAY
JAMES GIBSON
GREGOR S KYLE
DAVID LEITH
JOHN LUNDY
WM LIGHTBODY
WILLIAM MURRAY
WILLLIAM MORRISON
ROBT MCCRACKEN
JOHN A MCREA
ALEXR PERIE
ALEXR PERRY
JOHN STEWARTT
A K STEWART
J B W THOMSON
ROBERT TOPPIN
ANDW T WALKER
THOMAS WILSON

-GLASGOW YEOMANRY-
JOHN K BOWIE

-AUSTRALIAN EXP FORCE –
JAMES BOE
ANDW JOHNSON
JOHN JOHNSON
HUGH KEENAN
THOS MORLAND
ROBT MCCANDLISH

-CANADIAN CONTINGENT-
ANDREW BIGGAM
WM CAMPBELL
DAVID CAMPBELL
JOHN CAMPBELL
THOMAS DOBBIE
DUNCAN FRASER
K MCLENNAN

-CAMERON HIGHLANDERS-
ROBERT BODLE
JAMES BATESON
HUGH BOYD
JAMES CAIN
JAMES GORDON
HENRY IRONS
ROBERT KELLY
HARRY KENNEDY
DAVID KELLY
ROBERT KELLY
DAVID KIDDIE
T MCDOUGALL
JN MCLACHLAN
WM MCCLYMONT
SYDNEY MCCOLM
DUNCAN RENNIE
WILLIAM RODGER
P J SMITH
J R THOMSON
ROBT C WITHER
THOMAS WILSON

-DRAGOON GUARDS-
HUGH KIRKWOOD

-GORDON HIGHLANDERS-
JAMES AGNEW
P BRANNEY
JA DAVIDSON
ALEXR GORDON
M GARRETT
JOHN W HANNAH
JOHN MCKILLOPS
PETER A WEIR

-HIGHLAND LIGHT INFANTRY-

PETER COLLINS
ARTHURN CAMERON
JOHN DOUGAN
D C FERGUSON
A KERR GARVEN
ROBERT HOLLIS
CHARLES HOLLIS
EDWARD HOLMES
DAVID KIRKWOOD
GEORGE M KYLE
GEORGE MARTIN
GEORGE MCINTOSH
WM MCCASH
JOS MCCLYMONT
JAMES NISH
ADAM Y RUSSELL
JAMES ROWDEN
JOHN P ROSS
JAMES THOMSON
JAMES THOMSON
JAMES TURNER
JOHN WEIR

-KINGS OWN SCOTTISH BORDERERS-

PETER AIRD
JAMES BALFOUR
JM BALLANTYNE
WM W BALFOUR
GEORGE B CAMPBELL
JOHN T CLARK
JOHN CAIN
THOMAS DUNLOP
WM FLANAGAN
T S GALLOWAY
DAVID GIBB
ALEXR HAMILTON
JAMES KANE
WILLIAM R LYALL
ANDW MURDOCH
JOHN MCCLOY
A MCLAUGHLIN
NORMAN MCLEOD

-LOVAT SCOUTS-

JOHN M RIDDELL

-MIDDLESEX REG-

WILLIAM AGNEW
DAVID KYLE
A KILPATRICK

-IRISH GUARD-

JOHN THOMSON
WM THOMSON

-MACHINE GUN CORPS-

JOHN HOLLIS
M KILSEY
THOS MCCASH
JN F MCCREDIE

-NORTHUMBERLAND FUSILIERS-

JOHN ROWDEN

-NEW ZEALAND EXPD FORCE-

JOHN PIRRIE
ANDW K SMELLIE

-P O RIFLES-

THOMAS BAIRD
PETER COLLINS
REVD H DUNN

-RAMC-

JOSEPH ALLISON
ERIC ANDERSON
ALEX G BIGGAM
THOMAS BIGGAM
THOMAS DUNBAR
JAMES A DOBIE
WILLIAM HALL
WILLIAM HUNTER
MALCM JOHNSTON
ALEXR MASON
J F MCCONCHIE
JAS PATERSON
WM THOMSON
GORDON THOM
ALF A WALKER

-ROYAL DEFENCE CORPS-

DAVID WATSON

-ROYAL ENGINEERS

ROBERT AULD
CHAS COLLINS
WILLIAM CASEY
JOHN A CLARKE
JOHN FORREST
H H D FERGUSON
JN HENDERSON
HUGH HENRY
GEO A S KYLE
ANDREW LAUDER
ANDW MURDOCH
RICHD MURDOCH
HUGH MCDAVITT
H N MCDOWALL
WM MCCUBBIN
WM MCKENZIE
THOMAS MCKAIL

G NEILL
WM ORMISTON
JAMES RENNIE
JAS ROBERTSON
JAMES RENNIE
A E THOMSON

-ROYAL FIELD ARTILLERY-
WM ALEXANDER
JOHN BRYDON
THOS CALDWELL
JAMES CAIN
W F CANNON
ALFRED CANBURN
JOHN DALLY
ALEXR R FINDLAY
JOHN GIBSON
JOHN GIBSON
JN HENDERSON
JN MCD MCKECHNIE
JOHN LOCKHART
JAMES MUIR
WM MCKILLOPS
DAVID MCGEOCH
JOHN MCCREDIE
WM MCKILLOPS
FRED PEARSON
GEORGE RANKIN
EDWIN A RUSSEL
JOHN G THOM
DAVID WARREN
JOHN WHITE
JOHN FERGUSSON

-ROYAL GARRISON ARTILLERY-
THOS H BRUNTON
JOHN CAUGHIE
DAVID CASEY
JAMES GIBSON
ROBERT GRANT
ALAN B HILL
JOHN HALLIDAY
FRED JOHNSON
JOHN M MAY
C MCTAGGART
WM STEWART
JOHN TORRANCE
JN M THORBIRN
W A WILSON

-ROYAL HORSE ARTILLERY-
DAVID BODDEN
JAMES LITHGOW

-ROYAL HORSE GUARDS- (THE BLUES)
DAVID THOMSON

-ROYAL HIGHLANDERS-
(BLACK WATCH)
ALEXR BROWN
ALEXR BROWN
ALEXR FAIRLIE
WILLIAM GOVAN
DAVID GOVAN
ALEXR HIGGINS
ANDREW IRVING
HARRY IRVING
ARCHIE KENNEDY
DAVID THOM

-ROYAL INNISKILLING FUSILIERS-
THOS MCCOLM

-ROYAL MARINE LIGHT INFANTRY-
GEORGE WITHER

-ROYAL SCOTS-
ROBT CAMPBELL
DAVID DOUGAN
ROBERT HIGGINS
KICHAEL KELLY
R R STEVENSON
JAMES THOMSON
ROBERT WRIGHT

-ROYAL SCOTS FUSILIERS-
JOHN C ANDREW
ROBT ALEXANDER
WILLIAM ADAMS
ROBERT ALLISON
WILLIAM ALLISON
JOHN ALLISON
THOMAS ALSTON
JAMES AIRD
JOHN AGNEW
EDWARD BURNS
ALEXR BERRY
JAMES BLAIN
JAMES BURNS
JOSEPH BRADLEY
JOHN BLAIN
FREDERICK BLAIN
SAMUEL BUCHAN
JOHN BROWN
THOMAS BERRY

JAS BROADFOOT
JAMES BROWN
DAVID CAMPBELL
MATTHEW COOK
ALEXR COOK
R CRUICKSHANKS
H CAMPBELL
THOMAS CAIN
DAVID CONNOR
ADNW COLTART
JAMES CAMPBELL
WM CAMBURN
TOM CALDWELL
JAMES DORRANS
WILLIAM DURHAM
R DAVIDSON
JOS DOWLING
EDWARD DORANS
WILLIAM DILL
R DAVIDSON
ROBERT ESPIE
GEORGE ESPIE
WILLIAM ESPIE
ALEXR EDGAR
JAMES EDGAR
CLAUDE FORSYTH
WM FORSYTH
A W FERGUSSON
GEORGE FINDLAY
THOS GALLACHER
W GARRETT
WM GALLACHER
JN GALLACHER
ROBERT GRIER
WM GARRETT
WM GALLOWAY
JAMES GOVANS
ADAM GIBB
GEO HENDERSON
CHAS HAMILTON
JOHN HIGGINS
P HALLIDAY
WM HAMILTON
ROBT HAMILTON
ALEXR HAMILTON
HUGH HALLIDAY
JAMES HALLIDAY
THOS HAMILTON
SAMUEL HERON
JOHN HAINING
SAMUEL HERON
WM IRVING
WM JOHNSTON
EDW JOHNSTON
ANGUS KELLOCH
ROBERT KING
JOHN KENNEDY
GEORGE KERR
ADAM KING
JAMES KELLY
JOHN KELLY
NATHANIEL LOWE
JOHN LAIDLAW
CHARLES LUNDY
HORACE LOCK
JOHN S LEES
WM LAIDLAW
A M LAFFERTY
ROBERT LEES
WM MILLIGAN
R B MARSHALL
DAVID MILLER
WALKER J MAY
HENRY MENZIES
JOHN MURRAY
DANIEL MALLOY
JOHN MURDOCH
WM MONTEITH
WILLIAM MURRAY
EDWARD MURRAY
WM MCMILLAN
JAS MCWHINNIE
JAS MCLELLAND
THOS MCNAUGHT
THOS MCMILLAN
JAS MCDAVITT
A MCCULLOCH
D MCDOUGALL
JOHN MCDONALD
S MCNAIRNEY
WM MCKINNON
JAS MCCREADIE
ROBT MCCREADIE
D MCCULLOCK
M MCCLUMPHA
ROBT MCCOLM
D MCDAVITT
JAS MCMILLAN
H MCMILLAN
D MCMILLAN
JAS MCCREADIE
DAVID MCKIE
JAS MCKIE
JAMES MCNAIR
S MCCANDLISH
ROBT MCHARRIE
H MCCURCHESON
A MCCLYMONT
S MCCLYMONT
JOHN MCEWAN
T MCWHIRTER
DAVID MCCALL
ALEXR NELSON
ROBERT NISH
CHAS NELSON
JOHN PURKISS
WM J PETTIGREW

WM PATERSON
JOHN PERRIE
P PATERSON
ALEXR PATERSON
JOHN PATERSON
ARCHIE PIRRIE
WILLIAM RENNIE
ALEXR REID
ALEX RENNIE
JOHN RICE
WM A REID
ANDREW RENNIE
H SNODGRASS
PETER STEWART
EDWIN SMALL
JAMES SPROULE
GEO SWEETING
GEO SWITTING JR
ROBERT SHAW
JAMES SHAW
JOHN SPROULE
HUGH SMALL
SOHN SWEETING
ANDW THORBURN
ALBT TOWNSEND
JAMES TRAIN
JOHN THOMSON
EDWARD THOMS
ALEX TURNER
THOS WALLACE
JOHN WYLIE
JOHN WALLACE
JAMES WATSON
WILLIAM WALLACE
J WEATHERSTONE
D WHITEHOUSE
J WILLIAMSON

-SOUTH AFRICAN HORSE-
ROBT MCKENZIE
WM DAVIDSON
P DAVIDSON
JAS DAVIDSON
WM MORRISON
-SCOTTISH RIFLES-
WM DIAMOND
WILLIAM LEITH
WILLIAM LEEK
THOMAS MUIR
JOHN PIRRIE
JOHN THORBURN
WILLIAM CALDER
R MC TURNER

-SCOTTISH HORSE-
JAS JAMIESON
W MCC WILSON

-SEAFORTH HIGHLANDERS-
JAMES AGNEW
JAMES CONNELL
WM FORSYTH
JOHN GILLESPIE
JOHN HAMILTON
HENRY HARVIE
THOMAS HIGGINS
ANDREW HANNAH
DAVID MURDOCH
JOHN MERCER
WM MCCLUSKIE
WM MCKINNON
JOHN NORRIS
WILLIAM PIRRIE
S ROBERTSON
DANIEL RODGER
DANIEL RODGERS
JAMES ROSS
ALEXR SAUL
PHILIP TOMAN JR

-TRENCH MORTAR BATTERY-
EDWARD NISH

-SCOTS GUARDS-
JOHN ARNOTT
H S ANDERSON
JAS D BRADFORD
WILLIAM CAIRNS
A S CUTHBERTSON
WILLIAM CARRUTH
WM CALDWELL
JOHN CALDWELL
JAMES DAVIDSON
WILLIAM GIBSON
JAS HAMILTON
JOSEPH IRONS
WILLIAM MCCOLM
ROBT MCCRACKEN
R S G MCKINSTRY
G MCFADYEAN
JAS MCCORMACK
R ROBINSON
JOS ROBINSON
J C ROBERTSON JR
JOHN SMITH
ALEXR THOMSON
JAMES TULLY
ALEXR WRIGHT

-WELSH REGIMENT-
GEORGE KING
H KING
JAS W LEWIS

A B THOMSON
WM J WHYTE JR

-BRITISH WEST INDIAN REGIMENT-
JOHN B THOMSON

-ENLISTED SINCE 1916-
THOMAS BRYDEN
ROBERT BLACK
EDWARD BURNS
D CRAWFORD
JOHN CAMPBELL
ROBERT DORANS
JAMES DONALD
ROBERT GOVAN
JAS C D HALL
REV D H HISLOP
JOHN HERON
ARCHD IRVING
DANIEL IRVING
THOMAS KELLY
JOHN KYLE
HENRY KAY
ROBERT KING
JOHN KERR
JOHN MURRAY
JAMES MURRAY MC-CANDLISH
THOS MCGRIGGAN
THOS MCLACHLAN
ALEX MCCHLERY
WM MCCARLIE
JAS MCDOWALL
GEO MCDOWALL
JOHN MCGAW
WM MCGARVA
A MCCUTCHEON
D MCKINNON
JAS MCWILLIAM
THOS MCLACHLAN
JOHN O'KEEFE
CHAS O'KEEFE
JOHN ROBB
JAMES RODGERS
GEO ROBINSON
R RICHARDSON
PHILIP G SAAD
WILLIAM SHAW
DOUGLAS TAIT
ALEXR TOMAIN
WM THOMSON
JAMES WILSON
WILSON
ANDREW WATSON
DAVID WILSON
D DILL
ERNEST SISSON

LETTERS FROM THE FRONT

1915

Pte. James McCormack, son of coal merchant William McCormack, wrote a number of letters home during the course of the war to his many friends, some of the contents of his letters have already been included earlier in the book. The following letter seems particularly moving and demonstrates that the men longed for home:

> *"Come on, Jock; get the fire on an' make us a drap o' tea." Thus Joe Irons to his bosom pal Jock Smith. Bill Peebles jumps up to give Jock a hand; the rest of us carry on the conversation till we hear the welcome shout. "Come on, boys, gaither roon."' It has been our custom, while in billets, always to gather together on Sabbath evenings. On this occasion, picture us in a small field adjoining a farm just off the main road. Two sides of the field are bounded by two rows of tall trees, the other side by a deep stream. Dotted here and there are bivouacs of various shapes and sizes, each the temporary residence of two or three men, as the case may be. As usual, till Jock and Bill get the tea on, our conversation has chiefly been relating to our various experiences during our last spell in the trenches; but now, as we gather round the fire, war, and all the hardships associated with it, are forgotten, and for "a wee short 'oor" we are back in the dear old homeland. Supper over, pipes and cigarettes are set a-going. It is nearly dark now for darkness falls early in France, and most of the boys have turned in long since. And there, round our fire of dry twigs, we, in conversation and imagination, are home once more. One after another relates some incident that brings before our minds some particular street or place, and as we gaze into the fire we see that place as vividly as if we stood in it. It is nearly time for us to turn in. Conversation has ceased. I look round, and all eyes are gazing fixedly in the glowing embers. Each of us sees something there. I am back in my old seat in the choir. I can hear the beautiful words of the 23rd Psalm, to the grand old tune, "Wiltshire" – "Yea, tho' I walk in death's dark vale, yet will I fear none ill." Again, I see the loch. It is full tide, "but such a tide as moving seems asleep." And all is still. I can see the summer sun just sinking over the hill above Clendrie. Again, it is bright moonlight, and I am in Finnarts Glen, spellbound by its beauty and its majesty. Many a time, in the happy days of peace, have I gazed on Lochryan in all her various moods, and just as often have I been forced to exclaim, "Lochryan, in calm or in storm, there is none like thee." Bill's thoughts must have been similar to mine, for he turns over on his elbow and in a clear, low baritone begins "The Lord's my Shepherd." I join on with the bass. Our thoughts are all one now. I look across at Joe, for it is time to be moving. Joe jumps up, and with a hasty "goodnight, boys" walks slowly away. The rest of us follow his*

example. Hearts are too full for words. We are thinking of our comrades who are no more, and of those at home who sorrow for them, and we are thinking of dear ones who wait and watch for us. "But there's a wideness in God's mercy, like the wideness of the sea," and we shall put our trust in Him, and He will lead us through the shadows of this dark'ning night into the Paths of Peace.

Both of Bill Peebles' brothers are on Kirkmaiden War Memorial. Four men, all with the name John Smith were killed from Portpatrick, perhaps one of them was the man referred to above as Jock. James was gassed at Ypres in 1917 and was sent to Wigan Military Hospital to recover. Bill, Joe and James survived the war.

18th March 1915

Though the author of the following letter is not named, it was sent home to his parents in Stranraer by a private in a Highland territorial regiment who had been fighting at Neuve Chapelle:-

Thanks for your letter dated 13th inst. The delay in writing was caused by my being in the trenches for a week at a stretch. I expect that ere this you will have received my letter, commenced on the 7th and finished on the 16th. In explanation I am on the mortar gun...When we did come out I had little heart to write, the thought of seeing one's comrades stretched out, or carried off in the field, is bound to make one think. It is not for me to say what the Battalion's casualties were, but I can say that very few of my friends are left in my company. Our Major was killed, and the Colonel and some other officers wounded. The mortar gunners follow the advance. The German trenches were well made "dug outs" with blankets in them, and I noticed a few spring beds for the officers. The Germans did themselves very well, left cigars, cigarettes and all sort of things behind them. Quite a number surrendered. They looked well fed. The prisoners were mainly men about 40-45 years of age, and boys of 15-16. You will notice by the papers that we are close up against a wood, and I think it will be pretty difficult to take. One is always having near "shaves," but I think the biggest fright I got was while I was on guard over the guns about 12 midnight. After the advance, the Indians were out scouting for snipers left behind in the houses. Our guns happened to be among these houses, and as the scouts were told that no troops occupied them, you may guess that I was taken for a sniper. When they came along, I will not say what happened, but I am alive to tell the tale.

Indian and Scottish soldiers from the 1st/5th Cameronians at Neuve Chapelle.

May 1915

James McCormack again writes to his friend in the Free Press:

Dear Old Blue, The undernoted distinguished representatives of the Stranraer and District Junior League met somewhere in France this afternoon. (Sunday May 30th). The merits of players, referees, and committees of past seasons were under discussion and there were several very forcible arguments. After the individual players, referees, and members of committees had been duly slandered, the critics came up for their coffee. Your fate, Old Blue, was for a time in the balance, and it is just possible that, with a bit of luck, you might have been given the benefit of the doubt. Unfortunately (for you), Ballantyne and McCandlish appeared on the scene and Ballantyne clinched the matter, in spite of McCandlish's effort on your behalf.

Ballantyne has not yet forgiven your sarcastic notes concerning the Harp, which he maintains had in its ranks the cream of the Stranraer athletic world, not to speak of the shining lights among its many distinguished supporters – Matthew Cook etc. The meeting came to an abrupt conclusion when Joe asked Ballantyne if he recalled the occasion when he (Joe) jumped on his chest and left him in the corner of the net. That settled it. Lance-Corporal McCandlish glanced at the stripe on his arm, and muttering something about having to call the roll, sped off to his billet. Cracky went to look for his tea; Peebles bolted, shouting that Stoneykirk had to play referee and all every match; McNaught loaded his rifle and stood at the ready, until Ballantyne and Joe cooled down, and I got my notes completed.

After tea, the company again assembled and were joined by Private Spence, of Kirkcolm, the famous bomb-thrower. At the time of writing, Private Kilpatrick, late Kirkbryde, Kirkcolm, had not yet put in an appearance, by was expected every minute.

The other Rhins men have not yet inscribed their names on our membership roll, but no doubt there will be a big addition of well-known names when next we write.

Cracky is looking well. He says if the Germans catch him, he's going to plead that it was only in fun. I'm lying back till I see how Cracky's plan works. If Cracky tries his hand at refereeing this game, he'll have a few fouls to register against the other side. Yours etc.

D. Spence (three times wounded and once gassed)
R. McCracken, 'Cracky'. (Stranraer Memorial)
Joe Irons
S. McCandlish (Stranraer Memorial)
S. Ballantyne
W. Peebles (Wounded, both brothers on Kirkmaiden Memorial)
W. McNaught
D. Kilpatrick (Kirkcolm Memorial)
J. McCormack (gassed)

Matthew Cook mentioned within the letter is also on Stranraer War Memorial.

5th Battalion R.S.F. Champions of the South Scottish Brigade.

Officers right to left: Capt. Farquhar, Lieut.Col. Pollok-McCall, Lieut G. Murray. Players right to left from the back: Semple, Rae, Reid.

Centre: Hunter, Hill, Howie, Capperauld, Brown, Hastie and the trainer.

Front: Hendrie and Wilson.

July 1915

Again addressed to his friend in the Free Press, James McCormack writes home:

> *Saturday July 10th. The Stranraer contingent have had several meetings since last I wrote you, but the heat and lack of energy, due to recent hard spells in the trenches and subsequent long marches, have prevented me sending you copies of the minutes, as I had intended to do. We had a visit last Sunday from Corporal McCandlish and Pte. Ballantyne of the R.S.F. They had been in an attack since last I saw them , and were indeed fortunate to come through unscathed, I am pleased to say that the courage of Corporal McCandlish has been recognised by the General, but I have no doubt you have information of this already. All I can say is that Stranraer should be proud of him. Ballantyne has been appointed policeman, and his appearance should be sufficient to strike terror into the heart of the most hardened evil-doer. He was telling us on Sunday that he had been reprimanded for being on the 'force' for three days and never had a 'case'. He was determined however, that he wasn't going to lose his good job on that account, and on leaving us, he (to use his own words), 'went off to make a capture.' Just to show that he meant business: - I was coming along the road last night, when I caught up on a huge wagon drawn by a pair of horses. I thought it was wounded men for hospital until I heard sounds of revelry from within, and observed my friend, Ballantyne, standing on the back step, armed to the teeth. He jumped down on seeing me, and quite casually remarked, "I've got eight 'cases' inside. They just lay down and kicked up their heels at me, so I had to commandeer this wagon to bring them in." Any doubts I had of Ballantyne's fitness to be a "polis" were thee and then instantly dispelled. "Cracky" is having a rest in hospital, but I hear he is all right again. All the other Stranraer boys are well except for a general complaint of corns and blistered feet. There are a good few additions to the crowd now – some Kirkcowan and Portwilliam chaps. Our comrades in the Dardanelles seem to be having it hard, and we are all very sorry to see we have had losses there. Will write again soon.*

Samuel McCandlish wrote home the same month to Mr J. Johnson, Seapark, Stranraer, that he had seen James McCormack, Peebles, and Smith, but had not had much time to spend as he had not realised their billets were as far away from him as they turned out to be. He mentioned that Joe Irons and 'Cracky' McCracken were not there. The men had talked about football, and after a short while he left with two scones and a piece of Wigtownshire butter which had arrived in a food parcel addressed to James McCormack 'somewhere in France' from 'somewhere in Scotland'. He hoped he would be present when the next food parcel arrived.

In July there was very fierce fighting at the Dardanelles and Private Claude Forsyth of the 1st/5th Royal Scots Fusiliers, had been injured in the back wrote home to his parents in Stranraer about the fighting:-

> *Achi Baba...suddenly became like a volcano. The scene was a thrilling one, and filled us with a fierce delight...we breakfasted well ...and moved quickly up the trench...To our great surprise we soon found ourselves in the first line of the Turkish trenches. What a terrible scene of carnage! It was one long open grave and paid a grim tribute to the manner in which our artillery had done its work. As we went forward we had to trample over the dead Turks as the trench was so narrow. Turks were lying in every conceivable corner, and some who had died perhaps weeks previously, were falling off the parapets into the trenches. It is little wonder those captured were eager to get away from the trenches...Shells came in from all directions, sweeping away the parapets and burying the men in clouds of dust and earth... These shells also made great holes in the trenches into which the Turks poured a hail of lead from rifles and machine guns. There was very little cover, and we had to double along with our heads down, men falling all the time. The call for reinforcements was still very urgent. In passing one of these gaps in the trench, a splinter of a shell went right through my pack, and knocked me to the ground. I thought my number was up; I soon got up and found my neck scorched and a bleeding cut at the back of my left ear. Shortly afterwards the Lieutenant shouted, "Come on, boys; I could take the hill myself with a shot gun and a dog." In an instant we were all over the parapet, and made straight over open ground for the trenches 100 yards in front...the Lieutenant fell as did many others... on reaching the other side we found a few men from another regiment... We made another attack on what appeared to be a trench, but it was a dummy and we had little cover from the fire directed at us.*

At that point Claude was shot in the chest through the identity disc, the bullet came out under his arm-pit. A comrade put on a field dressing and Claude made his way back to a dressing station. After passing through two or three stations he was taken to a hospital ship. He was returned to England and put on a train for hospital in Aberdeen. Claud is mentioned in a letter home from Hugh Small and mentioned again under the entry for Alex Rennie.

September 1915

A letter from Lance Corporal J. Agnew was printed alongside his photograph when he home to his parents at High Auchneil:-

> *I got wounded at Vermelles on Monday 27th September, but must thank God for my life being spared, as I don't know how any of us came through it. I was hit with shrapnel in the elbow, but went through an operation last Wednesday and had it taken out, and am now getting on all right. I came here on Saturday morning, 25th September, we went over the parapet about 6.30, and it was nothing but hell after that. We took three lines of trenches from them in less than an hour, and advanced all Saturday. They came up against us in thousands, but they were only mowed down. It was awful and I never wish to see the same again. I was in a bayonet charge on the Sunday morning, and one on Monday afternoon, but they can't stand the cold steel. Whenever you get within twenty yards of them, up go the hands to plead for mercy and they get it too! On the Monday we lost very heavily, but nothing like the Huns, some of their trenches being full up of dead; it was an awful sight. You might send me on a box of tobacco and a pipe, as I have lost everything, my watch also being torn off my wrist.*

Pte. Thomas McMeikan, wrote home to his mother at Whitepark, Castle-Kennedy mentioning his brother Alexander:-

> *You will be surprised when this letter reaches you, as I got a knock-out blow from one of the Turks last Tuesday morning, but it is not serious – a bullet below my shoulder – and I am getting it taken out tomorrow. It will be a simple matter. We came here on the hospital ship, and then through Alexandria to this hospital which is a fine place, and we are getting the best of treatment. We are on the beach, and it is nice and cool in our light clothes...You will see all our casualties in the papers. There are a good few belonging to Stranraer Wounded, and three or four killed...I have not seen Alexander this while...he is still in the sick list... also Thomas Hyslop...I don't know whether Horace Lock was hit or not; he was all right when I came away; and W. Colman,... My officer, who I look after (Mr Brotherston) got shot through the neck, he is pretty bad, but keeping all right and he is luckier than I am, as he is away home to England.*

October 1915

Stranraer officer Lieut. John Kyle, Trench Battery, 2nd Scots Guards, wrote home to his mother:

> *As I have already informed you, I am now in a different part of the line. I am opposite a large German redoubt, which you will likely have read about in the papers. We captured most of it the other day. It was a glorious charge, and the men did very well. I picked up a German rifle in the redoubt, which I will bring home when on leave. I was introduced to the Prince of Wales the other day. I had to go and see the General about this last attack, and he asked me to stay for dinner. I sat next to the Prince of Wales during dinner. Sorry I was unable to write sooner, but I have been in the trenches and very busy with my guns.*

James McCormack writes again to the Free Press:

> *I wish you could get me struck off as war correspondent for the "Free Press," for I could write volumes on the past three weeks, pages of history that would make the future generations of Scotland – I say Scotland – thrill with pride as they read what their regiments have done out here. I daresay you have heard of Loos and Hill 70, but have you heard how the 3rd Brigade of Guards marched up that hill in front of Loos to the aid of the 2nd Brigade, hard pressed on that never-to-be forgotten hill. I shall tell you about my own regiment. We left billets at 7am on the Sunday morning. For ten days previous the whole earth had quaked under the terrific bombardment that never ceased day or night. All day we marched in a drizzling rain, and late in the afternoon we reached the zone of horror – long streams of ambulances that held us up for hours, those of the wounded that could be seen, covered with mud and wearing respirators, showing that they had been among that inhuman gas. Late at night we reached reserve trenches. Guns in front, guns behind, guns as far as the eye could see, and every one flashing death. Here we lay till the following afternoon, when we were told we had to complete the attack on Hill 70. We formed up and marched off. To reach Hill 70 we had to climb a slight incline behind which was a valley and the town of Loos. When we reached the town of Vermeilles, we broke into artillery formation, that is, each platoon took its own route, and spread out as much as possible to give the enemy as small a target as possible. We had to lie right beside the big guns till the preceding battalions of the Brigade had reached the summit of the rise and secured the communication trench. My platoon halted in front of a battery of 8 inch guns. The concussion was terrific. Every time a gun fired, the whole platoon (every man was flat on his stomach) rose six inches into the air. By this time the Grenadiers and Welsh were in full view of the enemy on the summit of the rise overlooking Loos. We could see the shells bursting in hundreds over and apparently amongst them. We knew it would be worse for us, for by the time we*

reached the summit the enemy would have secured the accurate range. At last we moved off. Behind us were the bombers. I turned round and shouted to Joe Irons, Bill Peebles, D. Spence, and W. McNaught, who are all bombers, and we were the first or second section of fours. They all gave me a cheery wave. The shells were shrieking through the air, and the noise was terrifying, yet I can remember observing how every platoon was marching in perfect formation, every man in step, and marching by his right. Just as we reached the summit, a shell burst on our immediate right. The communication trench was seventy yards in front, so we got the order to double for cover. I looked back and saw Joe, but he didn't notice me. By this time splinters of shell were falling like rain, and I regard it as nothing short of a miracle that the whole battalion was not wiped out. To me it was the hand of Providence. Down in the valley nothing could be seen for smoke and the flame of bursting shells. Up on Hill 70 our 1st Battalion was pressing the enemy back, but was suffering heavily. Through Loos we rushed to their aid, and just in time. Night came and with it rain, and with the rain and the darkness came a lull in the din. Three days and nights we lay in the open trenches without shelter, the rain pelting down relentlessly, every man numbed with cold. Just before we were relieved on the third night, the rain ceased and the moon broke through the clouds. I shall never forget the march back across what is certainly the greatest battlefield in the war. Here and there, dotted as far as the eye could see, lay the poor broken bodies of comrades who had fallen in the charge. I noticed the Seaforths had been in the thick of it. Further on, an ammunition column, galloping up to the guns had met swift destruction. Part of a gun-limber here, part of a horse there, told that a German gun had been as usual well laid. What a scene of horror spread before us and around us! Glad were we when we staggered into the ruins of a house to throw our weary limbs on the floor, and let our minds sink into sweet oblivion. Up on Hill 70 we left a good comrade and a brave man, my old schoolmate, W.McNaught. One of his last acts was to leave the shelter of the trench and go out with a drink of water to a sorely-wounded comrade, in the open, remarking to Davie Spence, - "Well, that's one good turn I've been able to do." W.Peebles, Lyburn and Caven were all wounded in the attack we made on the Hohenzollern Redoubt. If spared, I shall tell you all about it next week, and you shall hear the story of the heroism of three Stranraer Bomb-throwers, a story of bravery that has not been excelled in this war.

Mr and Mrs Peebles received word that week that their son William (Bill) had been wounded on the head and left hand, but that he had been taken to hospital and was progressing favourably.

November 1915

James McCormack follows on from his previous letter, to tell about the Hohenzollem Redoubt.

We reached the trenches that night, and took up position in the front line. The British had attacked at this spot the previous day, so that we were occupying the first and second line of German trenches. We soon realised that we were in a hot corner, to say the least of it. Night had scarcely fallen when the Germans attacked us with bombs. At several points the distance separating us from the enemy did not exceed thirty yards. At these points our bomb-throwers were stationed, and they bore the brunt of the fighting. My thoughts were often with Joe, Spence, Lyburn and Bill Peebles. You can imagine their duty was one to try the strongest nerve. Standing or rather crouching, in a shallow sap, hour after hour, grenade in hand, ready for the first movement in front, yet wondering whether "Fritz" or they would score first...but our bomb throwers held their ground, while the rest of us put round after round through our rifles till they were almost too hot to hold. Sunday morning was to be our turn. I shall never forget it. The bomb-throwers were to go first, and I thought of my dear old comrades then. Quietly we prepared to go across. Orders were whispered, men spoke below their breath. It would be an hour yet till dawn. I remember wondering what Stranraer would be like at that moment, and pictured the loch calm and placid. A few moments of perfect stillness, then – crash- the first bomb had been thrown. In an instant our brave bombers were the centre of an inferno of flames and shrieking missiles. Fritz had been ready. Words could not describe the horror of the next few hours. I looked across once, and when I saw what it was like, I never expected to see my chums again. Step by step, however we drove the enemy back, until it was impossible to advance further. So we made secure the trench gained. Things had just got a little quieter, and I had just sat down for a rest, fearing the worst for Joe and the others, when Davie Spence came along the trench, his head bandaged. He had been wounded early in the attack, but stuck to his post like a hero. His first words were, "Ha'e ye heard onything aboot Joe or Bill? Poor Lyburn is wounded." I replied that i had not seen either. Davie, too must have feared the worst, for with the strain and the thought of his mates, he almost broke down. I told him to get away out of it, but he had not gone far when an aerial torpedo burst in the trench in front of him, the shock knocking him down, but, fortunately, inflicting no injury. One safe; what about the others! I could get no news of them whatever. It was well on in the afternoon when a squad mate of Joe's, who is in my platoon, remarked to me that he had been away for water, and had stood up to hear Joe kicking up a devil of a row about not getting enough to eat. Good old Joe! I knew Jock Smith was safe, for he was in the next traverse to me, smiling all the time, as usual. Kevan had passed along the trench, wounded earlier in the day. I was amused at him. He sat down and had a chat with his acquaintances as he passed along the trench. Lyburn came in later, and although he was sorely wounded, and must have been suffering great pain, yet he refused to be carried. It was two days before I heard that Bill Peebles was safe in hospital in Rouen.

We have been back from the line for a fortnight now. We arrived here on Tuesday, and almost the first person I saw when we marched in was Pt. McDavitt. Danny Lewis, of the Welsh Guards, is also stationed here. Both looking well. I am looking forward to having a few days in Stranraer Soon, so will give you all the news when I come.

Christmas 1915

A photo sent to the Free Press of Stranraer Pals taken the day before they went back to the trenches. Lance-Corporal D. Spence could not be with the group as he had to parade to give an exhibition of bomb-throwing, but another picture of him was inserted beside the pals when the photo was reproduced in the Free Press.

In the group at the back from the left: Pte. Herbert Smith, 4th Grenadier Guards, Pte. Joe Irons, bomb-thrower, 2nd Scots Guards, Pte. J. Smith, 2nd Scots Guards, Pte. Dan Lewis, 1st Welsh Guards. Second row: Pte. James Cathcart, 2nd Scots Guards (son of Mr A Cathcart, mason, Ardwell), Pte. P McDavitt, R.S.F., Pte. John Arnott, 2nd Scots Guards. Pte. James McCormack, signaller, 2nd Scots Guards, clad in sheepskin and seated on the ground. He is displaying a board which reads "Christmas greetings from Stranraer pals somewhere in France."

Mrs Galloway, Agnew Terrace, Stranraer received a letter from her brother Pte. James Bell, 2nd Battalion, Argyll and Sutherland Highlanders.

> *I hope you had a good New Year, for I won't forget this one for a long time. We went into the trenches on the 28th of last month, so we spent the New Year in front of the Germans. I was on outpost duty as the New Year came in. We were standing to the waist in water, and the Huns fired everything possible at us, but we held our own. Sunday, the 2nd, I will never forget. It was an awful experience, as I saw certain death. The Germans mined our trenches and blew us up. It was something I don't want to see again – men buried alive. I thought my end had come, but I was pulled out of my grave. Shells were sent at what of us were left. I lost my senses for some time, and then rushed into it. There were only a few left, but we held the bunch till we got reinforced. I lost some good old pals in this. It was the worst I had ever seen. I was sent to hospital, and the idea of it makes me feel to think of being buried alive. It must be a terrible death. I lost all my belongings; the only thing I had was a pair of short drawers. I had the kilt off to dry, but it was buried. I could not get writing paper; I could not get a smoke; one was as bad as the other. It will rest in my memory as long as I live....I am attending the doctor for I am all bruised.*

James Bell's experience in the trenches was nothing like he had ever seen before; and he had served throughout the South African War. As a professional soldier he was one of the first to be draughted to France. At the time of writing the letter to his sister, James had already served 23years in the army, but this particular experience stayed with him for the rest of his life.

BRIEF TIMELINE OF THE WAR

1914

28th June –	Assassination of Archduke Franz Ferdinand
23rd July –	Ultimatum sent from Austria to Serbia
1st August –	Germany declares war on Russia and France
4th August –	Britain declares war on Germany
10th August –	France declares war on Austria
12th August –	Britain declares war on Austria and Hungary
22nd/23rd August –	Mons Battle
23rd August -	Japan declares war on Germany
6th-9th September -	Germans defeated in the Battle of Marne
October -	British men start to enlist in their thousands
11th-14th October -	Allies occupy Ypres
1st November -	Pacific battle
5th November -	Britain declares war on Turkey
8th December-	Naval Battle off the Falklands
Christmas -	Short Christmas Truce in some areas of the trenches. Princess Mary organises gifts tins for the forces.

1915

24th January -	Naval battle off Dogger Bank, Dutch coast.
2nd February -	Germany announces intention to blockade Britain
10th March -	Battle at Neuve Chapelle
18th March -	British ships sunk at the Dardanelles
22nd April -	Poison gas used at Ypres
25th April -	Allies land at the Dardanelles
7th May -	Lusitania torpedoed
25th September-	Battle of Loos
12th October-	Nurse Edith Cavell shot at dawn
11th November-	Winston Churchill sacked because of Gallipoli disaster
20th December-	Allies begin to retreat at Gallipoli

1916

January -	Conscription begins
February -	Long battle at Verdun begins
24th April -	Irish protest about British rule at Dublin Post Office

31st May - Naval Battle of Jutland
5th June - Kitchener killed with 650 men when Hampshire hits a mine
1st July - Battle of the Somme
19th July- Battle of Fromelles
15th September- Tanks used on the Somme
14th November - The end of the battle of the Somme
6th December – Germans occupy Bucharest

1917

1st February - Unrestricted U-boat blockade
13th March - Tsar of Russia abdicates
5th April - America enters the war
8th April - Canadians take Vimy Ridge
9th April - Battle of Arras
August - Heavy rainstorms cause flooding in the trenches
26th October- Another Battle at Passchendaele begins
9th December - British take Jerusalem
30th December - Battle at Cambrai

1918

10th February- Russia deserts the Allies
21st March - Launch of the Great German Offensive, Allies retreat
1st April - Formation of the Royal Air Force
3rd April - Germans break through lines at Neuve Chapelle
17th July - Russian Royal Family executed
18th July - French counter attack at Marne. Allies stop retreating
8th August - Allies win a battle at Albert. German retreat begins
30th September - Bulgaria surrenders
October - Many cities retaken by the Allies
German fleet ordered to attack the British fleet.
30th October - Turkey surrenders
8th November - Austria surrenders
9th November - Abdication of Kaiser Wilhelm II
11th November - Capture of Mons, Germany surrenders, Armistice signed

Index of names

Graham	Glenluce, Kirkcolm, Stoneykirk
Govan	Kirkcolm, Stranraer
Gurney	Glenluce
Hainey	Stoneykirk
Hall	Stranraer
Halliday	Stranraer
Hannah	Stoneykirk, Stranraer, Glenluce
Hamilton	Inch, Stranraer
Hart	Inch
Harvey	Drummore, Glenluce, Leswalt Stranraer
Hawthorn	Kirkcolm
Herdsman	Leswalt, See Alexander, Stranraer
Heron	Glenluce, Stranraer
Hewitson	New Luce
Higgins	Stranraer
Hill	Inch
Hollis	Stranraer
Holmes	Stoneykirk
Hood	Stranraer
Houston	Stranraer
Hounam	Stoneykirk
Hughan	Stranraer
Hunter	Glenluce, Stoneykirk
Ion	Cairnryan
Jardine	Glenluce
Jenkins	Leswalt
Jess	Inch
Johnson, Johnston, Johnstone	Inch, Drummore, Stoneykirk, Stranraer
Keatings	New Luce
Keenan	Stranraer
Kelly	Portpatrick, Stoneykirk, Stranraer
Kennedy	Glenluce, Inch, Stoneykirk
Kerr	Glenluce, Inch, Portpatrick, Leswalt
Kilgalan/ Kilgallen	Inch, Stoneykirk
Kilpatrick	Kirkcolm, Stranraer
King	Stranraer
Kirkland	Cairnryan
Kirkwood	Stranraer
Kyle	Kirkcolm, Stranraer
Lafferty	Stranraer
Laidlaw	Glenluce, Stranraer
Laurie	Stranraer
Lavery	Glenluce
Leckie	Drummore
Lees	Inch, Stoneykirk, Leswalt, Stranraer
Lightbody	Kirkcolm
Little	Drummore, Leswalt, Stranraer
Living	Stranraer
Lock	Stranraer
Logan	Stoneykirk
Logie	Stranraer
Lynch	Glenluce
Lyon	Glenluce
MacKie	Glenluce
Mann	Stranraer
Marchbanks	Inch
Marsh	Drummore
Marshall	Inch, Stranraer
Martin	Inch, Stoneykirk
McCabe	Stranraer
McCaig	Glenluce, Stoneykirk
McCandlish	Stranraer
McCarlie	Inch, Stoneykirk, Leswalt Stranraer
McCash	Stranraer
McClelland	Stoneykirk
McClumpha	Drummore Stranraer
McCluskie	Stranraer
McClymont	Glenluce, Inch Stoneykirk, Stranraer

McColm	Drummore, see Cobbledick
McConnell	Stranraer
McCracken	Glenluce Stranraer
McCrae	Inch, Stranraer
McCreadie, McCredie	Glenluce, Kirkcolm, New Luce, Stranraer
McCrorie	Glenluce
McCubbin	Leswalt
McCulloch	Drummore, Glenluce, Portpatrick, Stoneykirk
McDonald	Stoneykirk, Kirkcolm.
McDowall	Drummore, Kirkcolm, Stranraer
McGarrie	Inch
McGarva	Glenluce
McGaw	Drummore
McGeoch	Stranraer
McGibney	Kirkcolm
McGill	Glenluce
McGivern	Stranraer
McGregor	Portpatrick
McHarrie	Cairnryan, Glenluce, Inch Stranraer
McIntyre	Kirkcolm, Stoneykirk, Stranraer
McKay	Stranraer
McKeand	Drummore
McKenzie	Portpatrick Stranraer
McKerrow	Stoneykirk
McKie	Drummore, Glenluce, Inch, Stranraer
McKillops	Leswalt Stranraer
McLagan	Inch
McLean	Stoneykirk, New Luce
McLellan	Glenluce
McLennan	Stranraer
McLelland	Inch
McMillan	Stranraer
McMeekin, McMeckan,	
McMeeking, McMeckan	Drummore, Inch, New Luce
McNaught	Leswalt
McNeillie	Leswalt
McRobert	Portpatrick
McWhinnie	Stranraer
McWhirter	Leswalt, Stranraer
McWilliam	Stranraer
Miller	Portpatrick
Milroy	Cairnryan, Glenluce, Inch, Stoneykirk, Leswalt, New Luce
Mitchell	Inch
Moir	Cairnryan
Monteith	Inch, Stoneykirk, Leswalt, Stranraer
Montgomery	Drummore
Morgan	Stranraer
Morland,	
Morlan	Drummore, Glenluce
Morrison	Stranraer
Morrow	Kirkcolm
Muir	Leswalt
Murchie	Stranraer
Murdoch	Stranraer
Murray	Drummore, Glenluce, Leswalt, New Luce, Stoneykirk, Stranraer
Myall	Portpatrick
Neil	Cairnryan, Stranraer
Nelson	Stranraer
Neville	Inch
Nish	New Luce, Stranraer
O'Brien	Portpatrick
O'Keefe	Stranraer
Ormiston	Stranraer
Palmer	Kirkcolm, Stranraer
Parker	Glenluce
Paterson	Kirkcolm, Leswalt, Stranraer
Paton	Stoneykirk

Paxton	Drummore	Slaven	Inch
Patrick	Stranraer	Small	Leswalt Stranraer
Peebles	Drummore	Smellie	Stranraer
Pirrie	Stranraer	Smith	Inch, Portpatrick
Pizzey	Stranraer	Snodgrass	Stranraer
Porteous	Stranraer	Stewart	Kirkcolm, Stranraer
Preston	Cairnryan	Stevenson	Drummore
Quarrell	Stranraer	Wallace	Drummore, Kirkcolm
Ralph	Cairnryan	Templeton	Glenluce
Ralston	Glenluce	Thom	Stranraer
Rankin	Stoneykirk	Thomson, Thompson	
Reid	Glenluce, Inch,		Portpatrick, Stranraer
	Leswalt	Thorburn	Stranraer
Rennie	Leswalt, Stranraer	Todd	Stoneykirk
Richardson	Drummore, Leswalt,	Torrance	Inch, Leswalt, Stranraer
	Stranraer	Trueman	Cairnryan, Leswalt
Riley	Stoneykirk	Tunnock	Stranraer
Robbins	Stoneykirk	Tully	Portpatrick Stranraer
Robertson	Stoneykirk, Stranraer	Wallace	Stranraer
Robinson	Stranraer	Watson	Glenluce, Leswalt
Ross	Cairnryan, Kirkcolm,	Whyte	Stranraer
	Stranraer	Williamson	Stranraer
Rowden	Stranraer	Wilson	Drummore, Glenluce,
Russell	Stranraer		Inch, Stranraer
Saul	Stranraer	Wither	Stoneykirk, Leswalt
Scott	Inch	Wood	Stranraer
Shaw	Portpatrick	Wright	Stranraer
Simpson	Drummore, Kirkcolm	Wyllie	Stranraer

Thanks

To the families of the men who contacted me with information and so much more. Earl of Stair, Frances Alexander, Betty Allen, Jayne Baldwin, Elaine & Alan Barton, Edward Beck, Davie & Hilda Brown, Marybelle Buchanan, John Cameron, Beverley Chadband, Isobel Duffy, Kevin Erskine, Paul Goodwin, Jack Hyslop Heron, Jean Heron, Davie Hunter, Mary & Malcolm Milligan, Lily McClymont, Hugh McCormick, Jay McDowall, Colin Monteith, Renee Murdoch, Donnie Nelson, Rena & Alex Peebles, Sandy Rankin, Bob Simpson, John Small, Gina Young, and many more including the staff of Stranraer Library, the staff of Stranraer Museum, Scottish War Memorials Project.

Photographs

Auckland Weekly News : 43

Australian War Memorial: 73

Frances Alexander: 115 top

Elaine Barton: 83, 84, 85, 103, 104, 121, 197, 230, 291, 310

David Brown: 290 right

Marybelle Buchanan: 220

John Cameron: 11, 212 right

Paul Goodwin: 299

Jack Hyslop Heron: 294

Jean Heron: 107, 113, 282

Julia MacDonald: 8, 9, 21, 22, 24, 27, 47, 57, 85, 122, 144, 153, 168, 194, 208, 221, 328.

Colin Monteith: 132

Mary & Malcolm Milligan: 187 top

Donnie Nelson: 205 top

Bob Simpson: 45

University of Glasgow: 58

Wigtown Free Press: 18, 19, 20, 28, 29, 30, 33, 36-41,44, 51-56, 59-61, 67, 69-76, 79, 81, 87, 88, 90, 91, 92, 94, 96, 97, 101, 106, 110, 111, 115-120, 125-131, 134, 135, 139, 141, 143, 147-149, 152, 157-159, 164, 166, 173, 176-178, 180, 181, 183, 184-187 bottom, 189-190, 199, 200-203, 206-208 bottom, 210, 211 left, 213-215, 218-220, 223, 225, 227, 231-241, 245-248, 250, 251, 252, 255 bottom, 258, 260, 264-267, 270, 271, 274-280, 284, 287-290 left, 298, 311, 318,

Bibliography

Ashworth, T. (1980) Trench Warfare, 1914 – 1918. Pan Books. London.

Brown, M. (2001) The Imperial War Museum Book of the Western Front. Pan Books. London.

Dalrymple, M. (1962) Memory's Voyage. Simpson Bell & Co. Edinburgh.

Deary, T. (1998) The Frightful First World War. Scholastic. Reading.

Devlin, I. (2005) We Will Remember Them. Kirkcudbright's Sons 1914-1918. Kirkcudbright History Society. Dumfries.

Evans, M.M. (2008) Battles of WW1. Arcturus. London

Galloway Advertiser and Wigtownshire Free Press Microfiche Archives. (1914-1922)

Hamilton, R. (2004) The History of World War 1 in Photographs. Parragon. Bath.

McCormack, B. (2004) Every Beach A Port: The Story of William McCormack & Sons Ltd. Stranraer and District Local History Trust.

www.cwgc.org

www.snwm.org

www.uboat.net

www.collectionscanada.gc.ca

www.awm.gov.au

www.abmc.gov

www.cast.org.uk/dagwargraves.htm

www.scotlandspeople.gov.uk

www.aucklandmuseum.com/130/cenotaph-database

An old postcard of 1st Gn.Batt. Royal Scots Fusiliers, Sergeants. Included here because it was the local regiment and there are undoubtedly local men in the picture.